IMAGES
of America

THE GREAT PASSION PLAY

On the Cover: *The Great Passion Play* featured Robert Hyde as Christ when it opened in 1968. Since its inception, the play has been viewed by more than seven million people. (Courtesy Elna M. Smith Foundation.)

IMAGES
of America

THE GREAT PASSION PLAY

Dr. Timothy M. Kovalcik

ARCADIA
PUBLISHING

ISBN 978-0-7385-5324-5

Published by Arcadia Publishing
Charleston, South Carolina

Printed in the United States of America

Library of Congress Catalog Card Number: 2007934721

For all general information contact Arcadia Publishing at:
Telephone 843-853-2070
Fax 843-853-0044
E-mail sales@arcadiapublishing.com
For customer service and orders:
Toll-Free 1-888-313-2665

Visit us on the Internet at www.arcadiapublishing.com

This volume is dedicated to all of the anonymous employees who have made this Passion Play the "Great" Passion Play.

CONTENTS

ACKNOWLEDGMENTS

The Elna M. Smith Foundation provided the majority of the photographs for this album. The foundation also gave unlimited access to the archives and detailed information about the history of the organization. Their generosity is greatly appreciated.

I especially wish to acknowledge Marvin Smith, who enthusiastically approved and supported this project. Mary Murray, a long-time cast member, provided many photographs and memories. My mother and father, John and Anne Kovalcik, also provided important materials. I am extremely grateful to all of you for your enthusiasm.

Millikin University has provided academic resources and support for my individual research at all levels. In particular, I appreciate my colleagues Kevin Murphy, Dan Monroe, and Bill Keagle. They provide encouragement tempered with appropriate criticism. I could imagine no greater friends.

Kate Crawford and Katie Stephens, my editors at Arcadia, receive special thanks. This was a unique project for Arcadia, and I am grateful they have been patient and encouraging.

My wife, Helene, has given me time and space. With four small children at home, her sacrifice is the greatest of all, and without her, this project would not be possible.

INTRODUCTION

The Elna M. Smith Foundation was the product of Gerald L. K. Smith and Elna M. Smith. The two retired to Eureka Springs, Arkansas, in 1964. In a matter of years, their vision and leadership transformed the small, remote, Ozark town into a thriving city built on tourism and religious devotion. Their work is only 40 years old, but it has touched millions.

Gerald L. K. Smith was a controversial politician of the 1930s and 1940s. He was associated with Huey Long in Louisiana and with an anti–United Nations position in post–World War II America. He was an outspoken critic and brilliant organizer. However, upon his retirement, Smith vowed to leave politics behind and devote his attention strictly to projects that would provide a more substantial legacy.

Smith initially believed his legacy would be in the collection of items related to Americana. As a devoted patriot, Smith collected his personal correspondence with important figures such as Henry Ford and Gen. Douglas MacArthur. He also purchased several historic homes. He hoped that such items and antique homes would be used to illustrate the American spirit. These pursuits eventually brought the Smiths to Eureka Springs.

Eureka Springs was the town that time forgot. At the turn of the 20th century, it was a bustling resort city, popular with socialites from Kansas City and St. Louis, Missouri, and Chicago, Illinois. However, travel to Eureka Springs was difficult. Most visitors traveled by train or horseback. As the automobile became more popular in the United States, the out-of-the-way resort town was left behind. What remained was a unique collection of Victorian homes and hotels. Along the famous Spring Street were colossal stone buildings and mansions that dated to the late 19th century. Furthermore, Eureka Springs had an abundance of oddities. By the 1960s, the city claimed that no street crossed another (due to the fact that streets were always renamed at four-way stops), and that the town had the oldest neon sign west of the Mississippi. Ripley's Believe It or Not had twice featured the region and its geography. A modest tourist industry was built around these attractions.

The Smiths found Eureka Springs while researching historical homes. One of their agents mentioned that a popular Victorian location in the city, known as Penn Castle, was being sold at a reduced price. As part of their legacy building, the Smiths aggressively pursued the home, purchasing it in 1964. Penn Castle was built in the 1880s. When the Smiths bought it in 1964, it was intended to be a summer home, as well as a type of museum. The Smiths fell in love with the quaint little village of Eureka Springs, and their attention slowly turned toward developing the region. In 1965, partially based on a dream, the Smiths proposed a giant statue that would stand tall over the town and its surrounding mountains.

In order to support this project, the Elna M. Smith Foundation was announced as a separate organization sponsored by beneficiaries from across the United States. Charles F. Robertson, a long-time associate of the Smiths, was identified as the chief coordinator. But this was only the beginning. Within a decade, under the leadership of the Smiths and Robertson, the Elna M. Smith Foundation built the statue, created the largest outdoor drama in the United States, collected one of the greatest repositories of rare Bibles in the world, established a gallery of world-class religious art, and constructed a replica Holy Land. They are five Sacred Projects, the substantial legacy of the Smiths.

The images in this volume are designed to help tell the story of the five Sacred Projects. This is not a complete record, in fact the emphasis is on the first 30 years. Forty years of photographs are not possible, but there is a story to tell. More than 7 million people have set foot on the grounds of the Elna M. Smith Foundation. They are attracted to sites that are truly amazing. These sites have grown, changed, and developed. Plans were made, and plans were changed. Such decisions changed Eureka Springs and the surrounding area forever.

One

A Statue for the Ozarks

On June 11, 1965, the Elna M. Smith Foundation broke ground on Magnetic Mountain. The project was the result of a dream by Gerald L. K. Smith. He envisioned a large statue hovering over the mountains as a solemn symbol of faith. In keeping with his promise to remain apolitical, Smith did not speak at the ceremony. Instead he trusted the project to his associate Charles F. Robertson. Robertson immediately began a campaign that organized resources and guided the project to completion by June of the next year.

The Elna M. Smith Foundation wanted the statue to be a reminder of God's providence. It was also to be an inspiration; therefore, the foundation aggressively promoted and advertised the project. By the day of the *Christ of the Ozarks* statue's dedication, newspapers from around the country were mentioning the new monument in Eureka Springs.

Prior to its completion, perhaps the most important decision surrounding the sculpture was the choice of the architect and craftsman, Emmet Sullivan. Sullivan was an apprentice to the sculptor of Mount Rushmore, Gutzon Borglum. He was also the designer of several landmarks in South Dakota, including a life-size dinosaur park. His credentials were more than adequate, but it was his passion for the project that endeared him to both the Smiths and Robertson.

His creation became an inspiration to the Smiths and to millions of visitors. Today the graves of both Elna M. Smith and Gerald L. K. Smith are close to the statue. It was their chosen place of beauty.

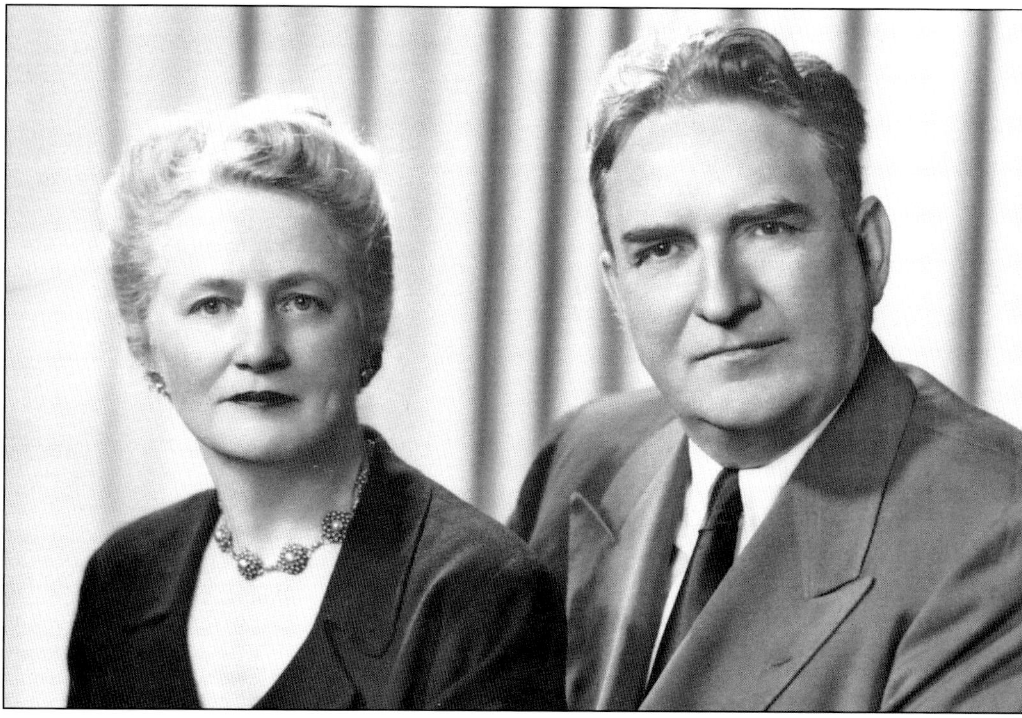

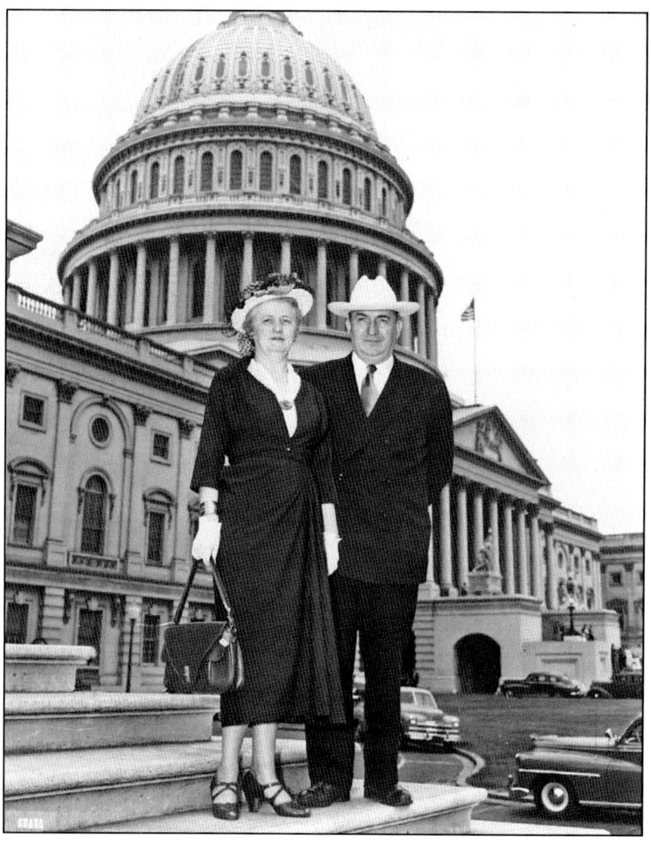

Gerald L. K. Smith and Elna M. Smith were fond of Eureka Springs long before their arrival in 1964. Their extensive and sometimes controversial careers as political activists took them all over America. They were familiar with many powerful figures inside and outside of Washington, D.C. They claimed many home states, including Michigan and California, yet it was Eureka Springs that eventually claimed them in retirement. Together they found Eureka Springs the ideal venue for their shared dreams of a lasting legacy, one that was more sacred in nature.

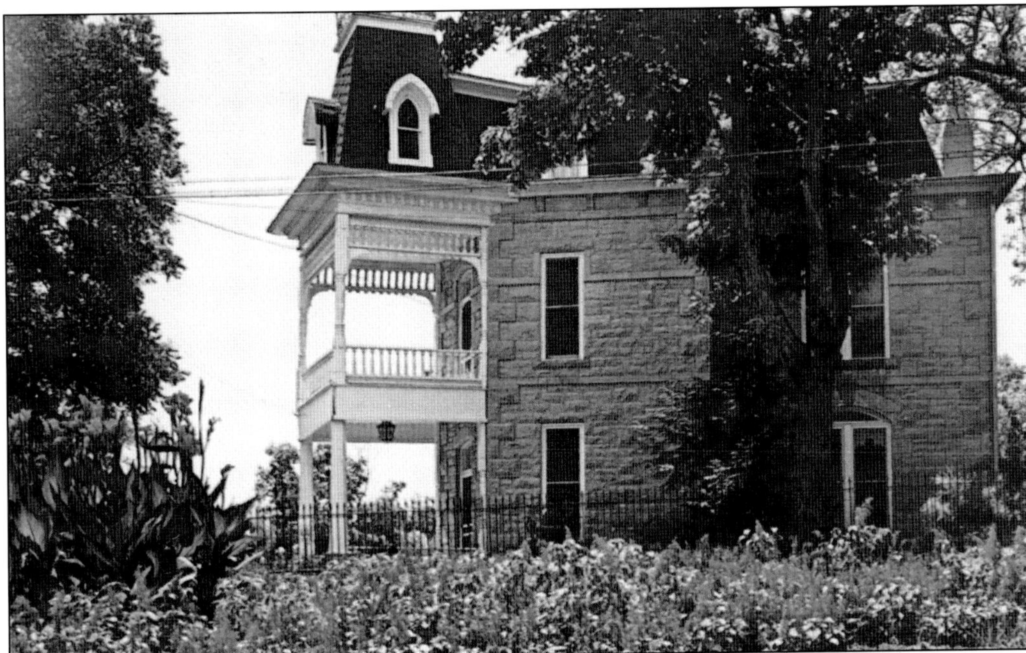

Penn Castle, purchased by Gerald L. K. and Elna M. Smith in 1964, was itself a project. The Smiths transformed the 1888 mansion into a virtual museum of American memorabilia. On display were numerous pieces of Christian artwork, a Navajo jewelry collection, and personal letters from Henry Ford and Gen. Douglas MacArthur. Long before the Sacred Projects, it was the Smiths' hope that their wealth and experiences would be a patriotic reminder of the American spirit.

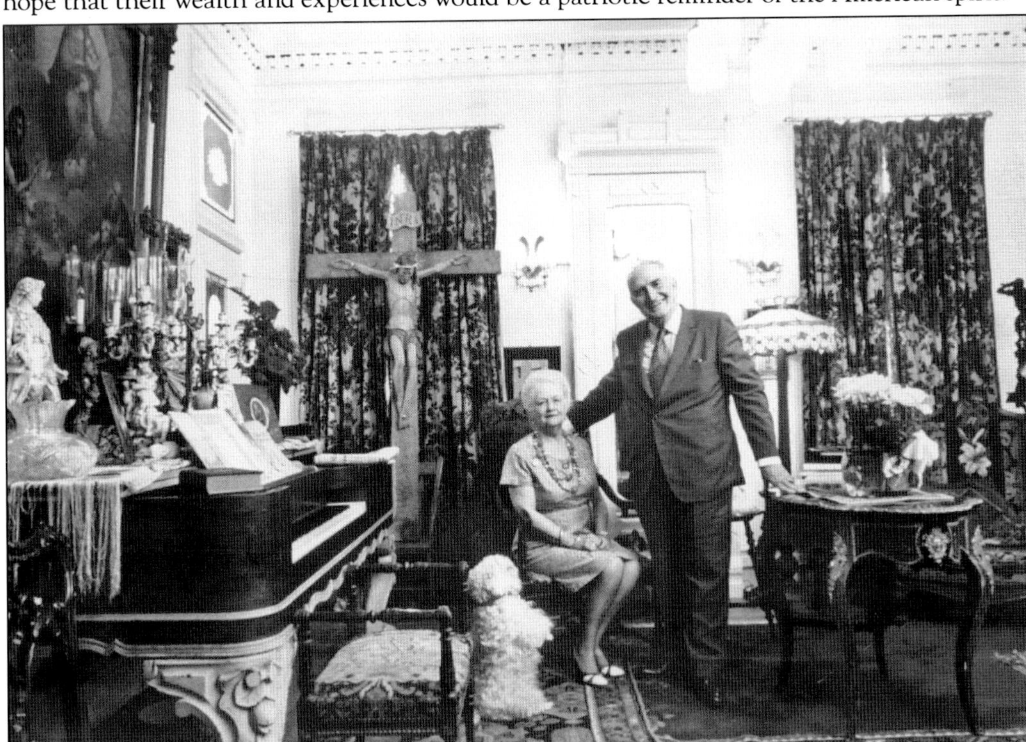

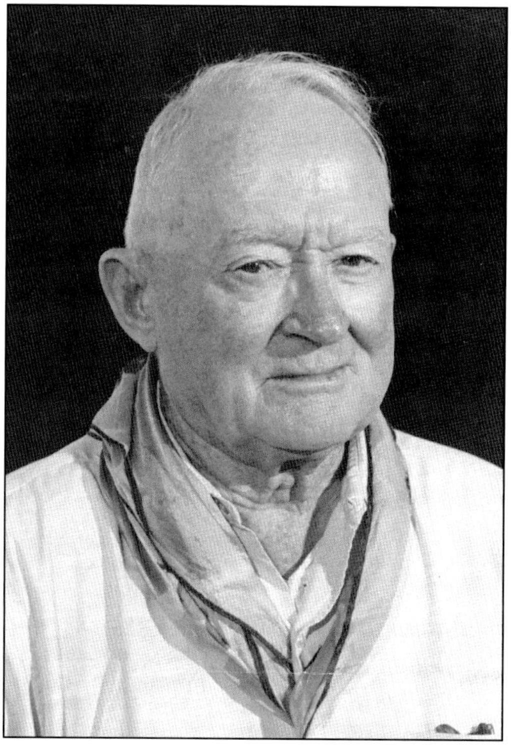

The first step toward completion of the statue was the choice of Emmet Sullivan as its sculptor and designer. Sullivan's credentials were impressive, especially his work as an apprentice to the Mount Rushmore sculptor, Gutzon Borglum. However, it was also Sullivan's patriotic and Christian spirit that attracted the commission of the Elna M. Smith Foundation.

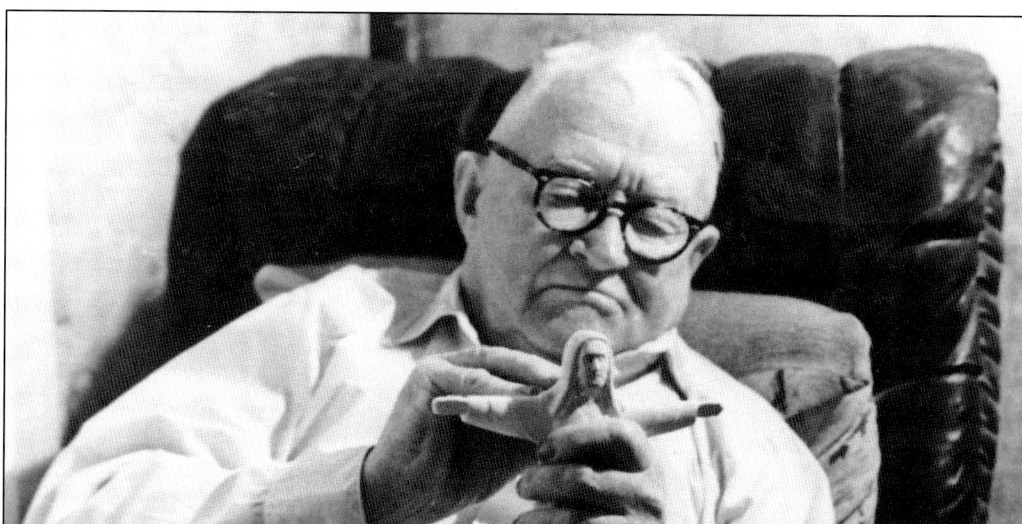

Emmet Sullivan designed statues by first carving them from wood. He made several designs, including a number with large pedestals. The final statue had no pedestal, but when Sullivan later designed souvenir miniatures, the weight and design required a base in order for it to remain standing.

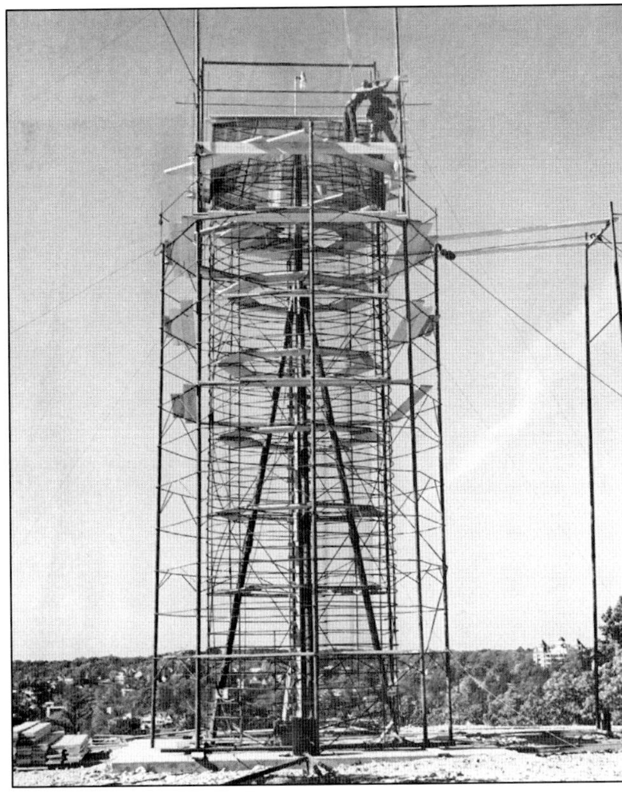

The body of the statue was constructed separately from its features. Whereas the face and hands were sculpted in a studio, the body was cast from a frame of steel wire and concrete. Features to the robe of Christ had to be added later.

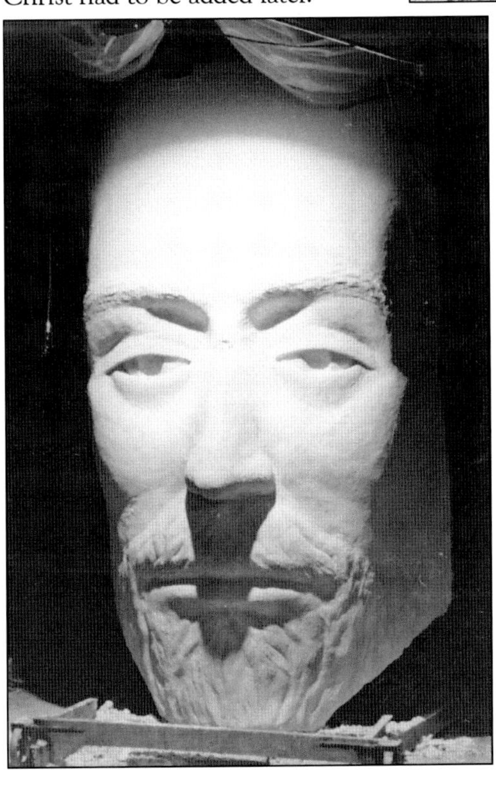

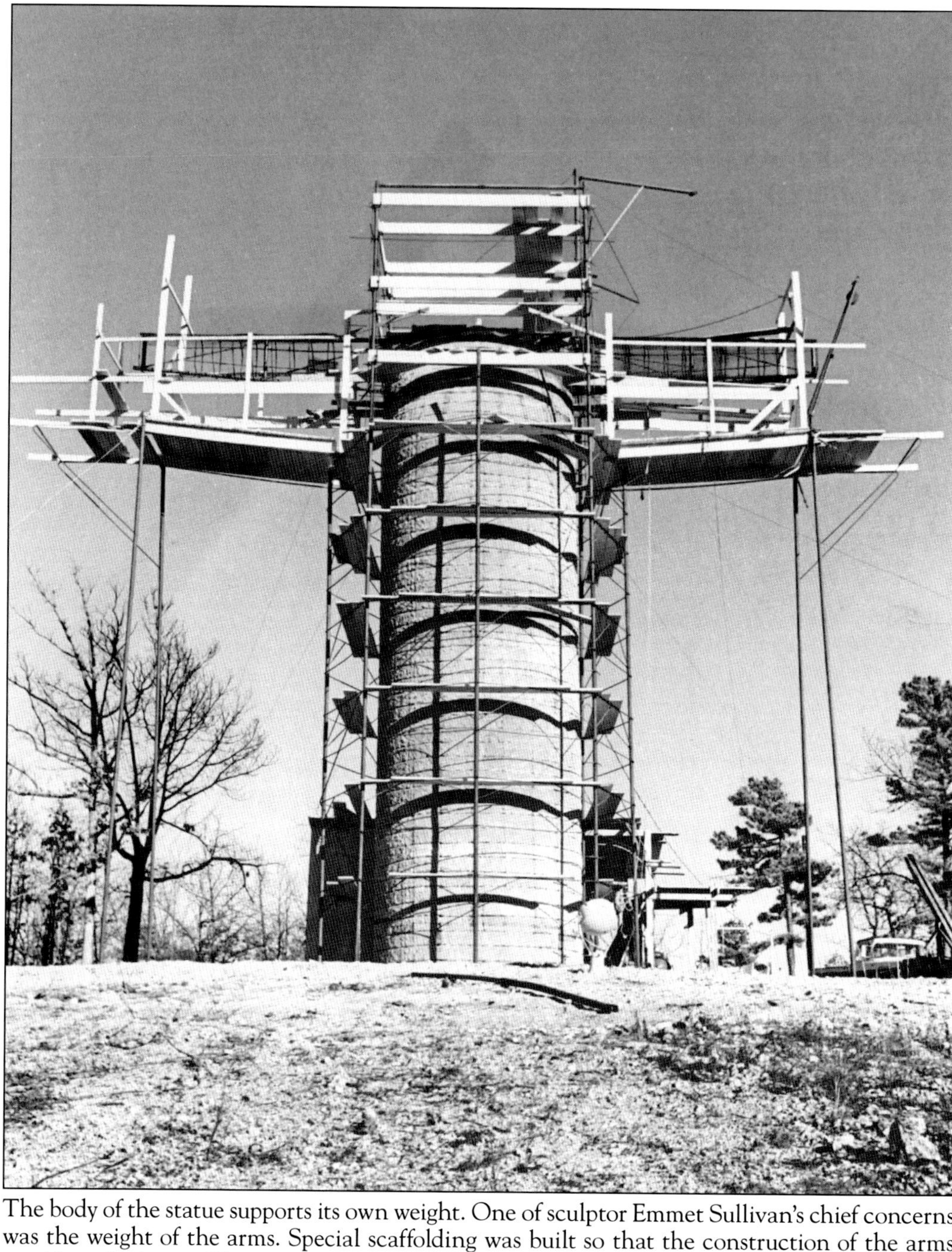

The body of the statue supports its own weight. One of sculptor Emmet Sullivan's chief concerns was the weight of the arms. Special scaffolding was built so that the construction of the arms would not be hasty. Close examination of the statue also reveals the fact that the arms are not proportional. This was a matter of necessity in order to the keep the structure sound.

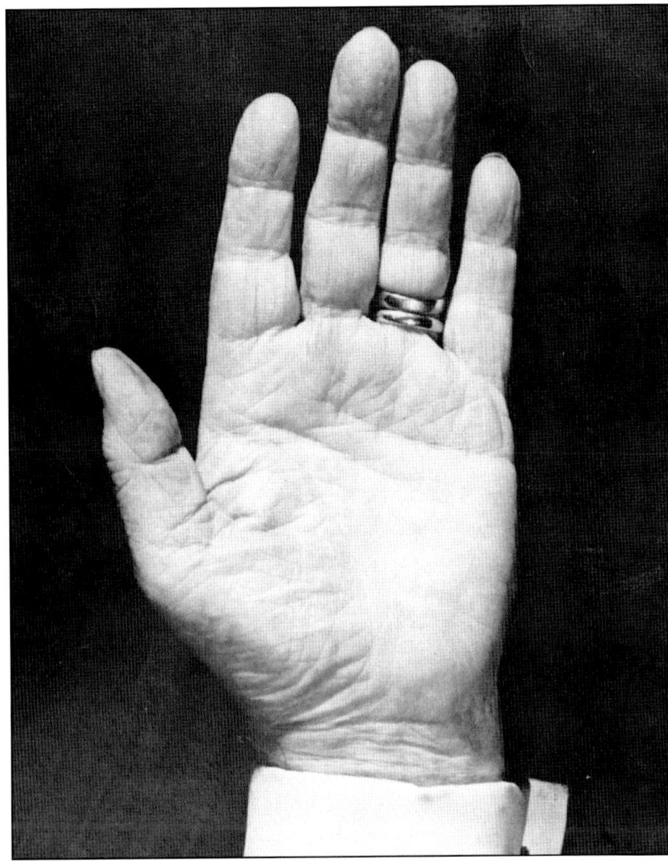

The most intricate pieces of the statue were the hands. Not only were the artistic details important, but so were the elements of mathematical design. Working from pictures of outstretched hands, several computations were made before a final version of the hands was acceptable.

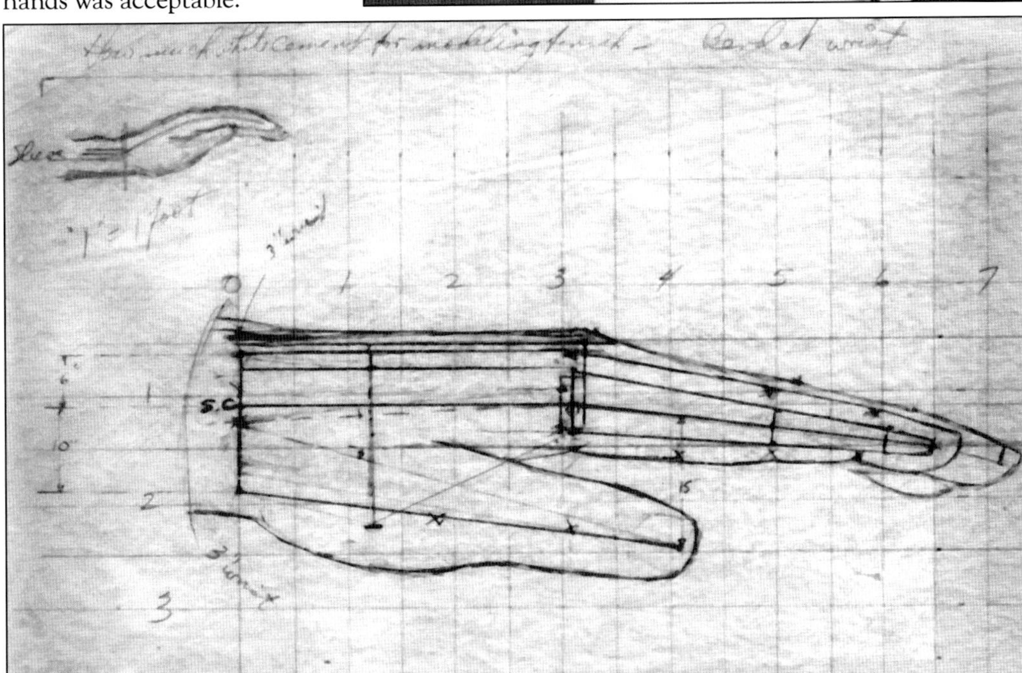

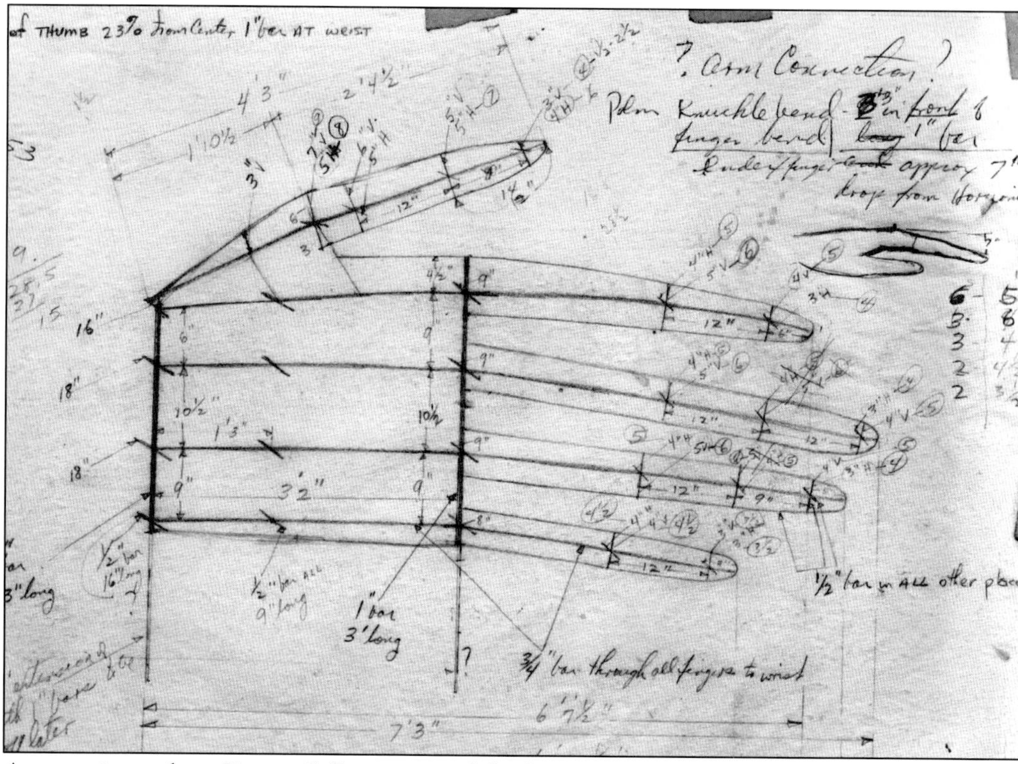

As an artist, sculptor Emmet Sullivan wanted the features of the statue to appear lifelike. However, as an engineer, he worked to ensure the mathematical integrity of the structure. Sullivan made several sketches and worked methodically on different models before choosing the final design.

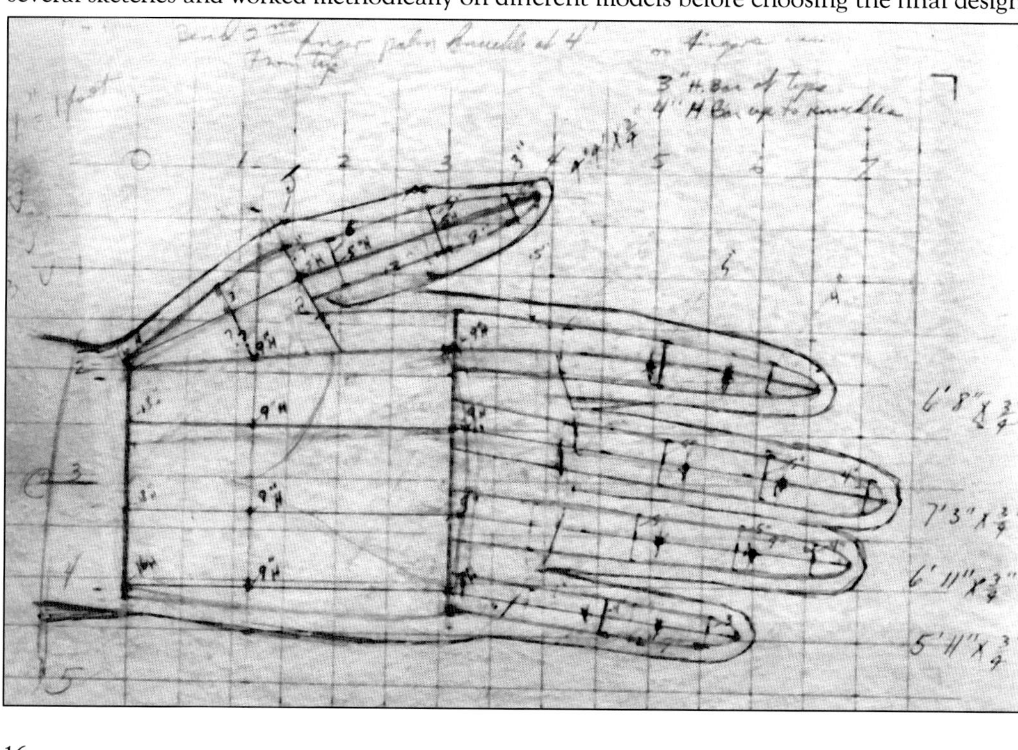

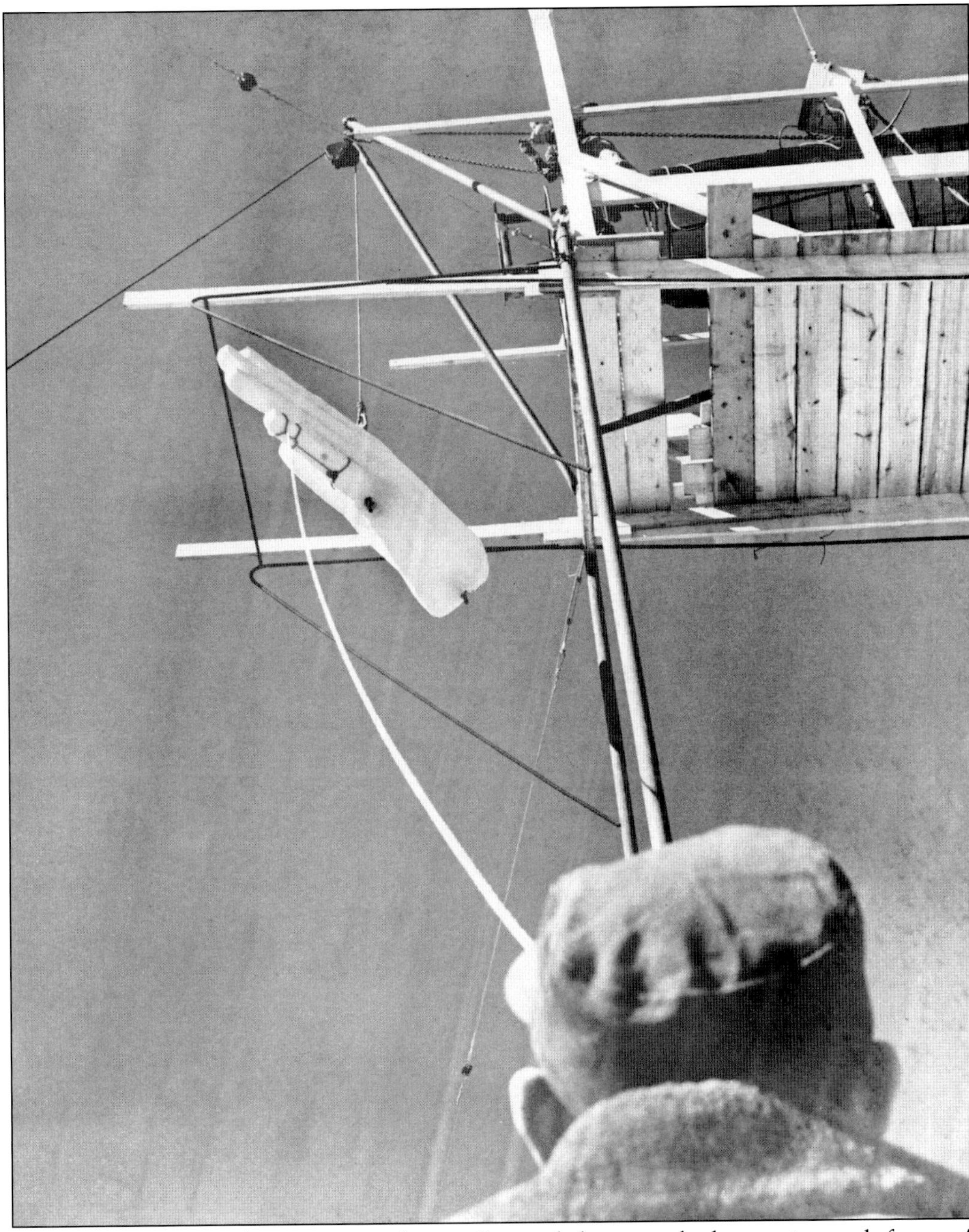

The hands were raised into position by a pulley and then attached to a wire-mesh frame. A workman watches from below as a hand swings into place.

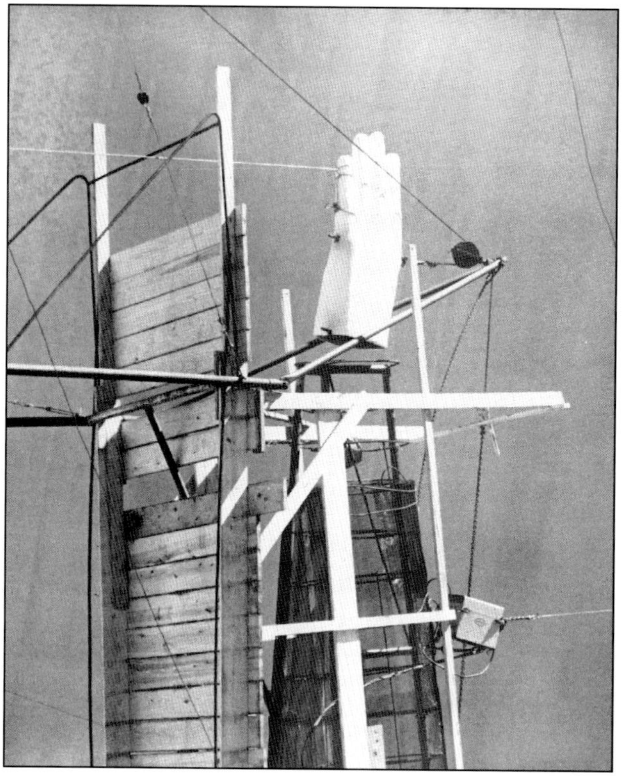

The *Christ of the Ozarks* statue came together like a large puzzle. The weight of the body, with little artistic detail, supported the forthcoming features, including the face and hands.

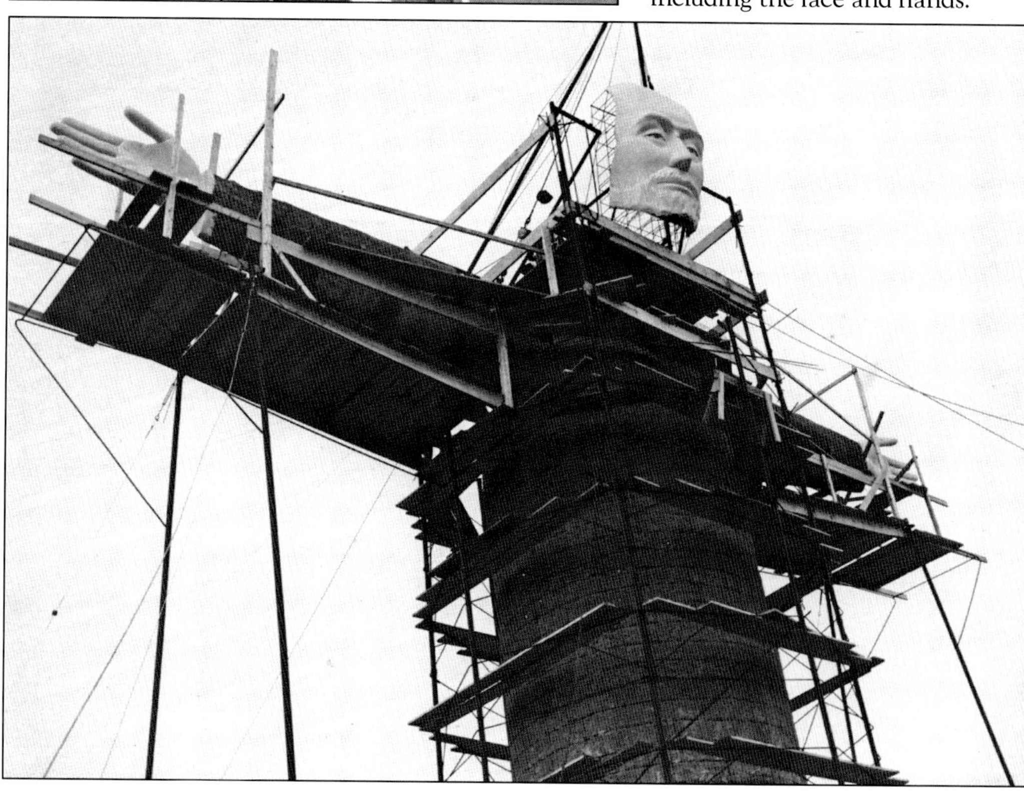

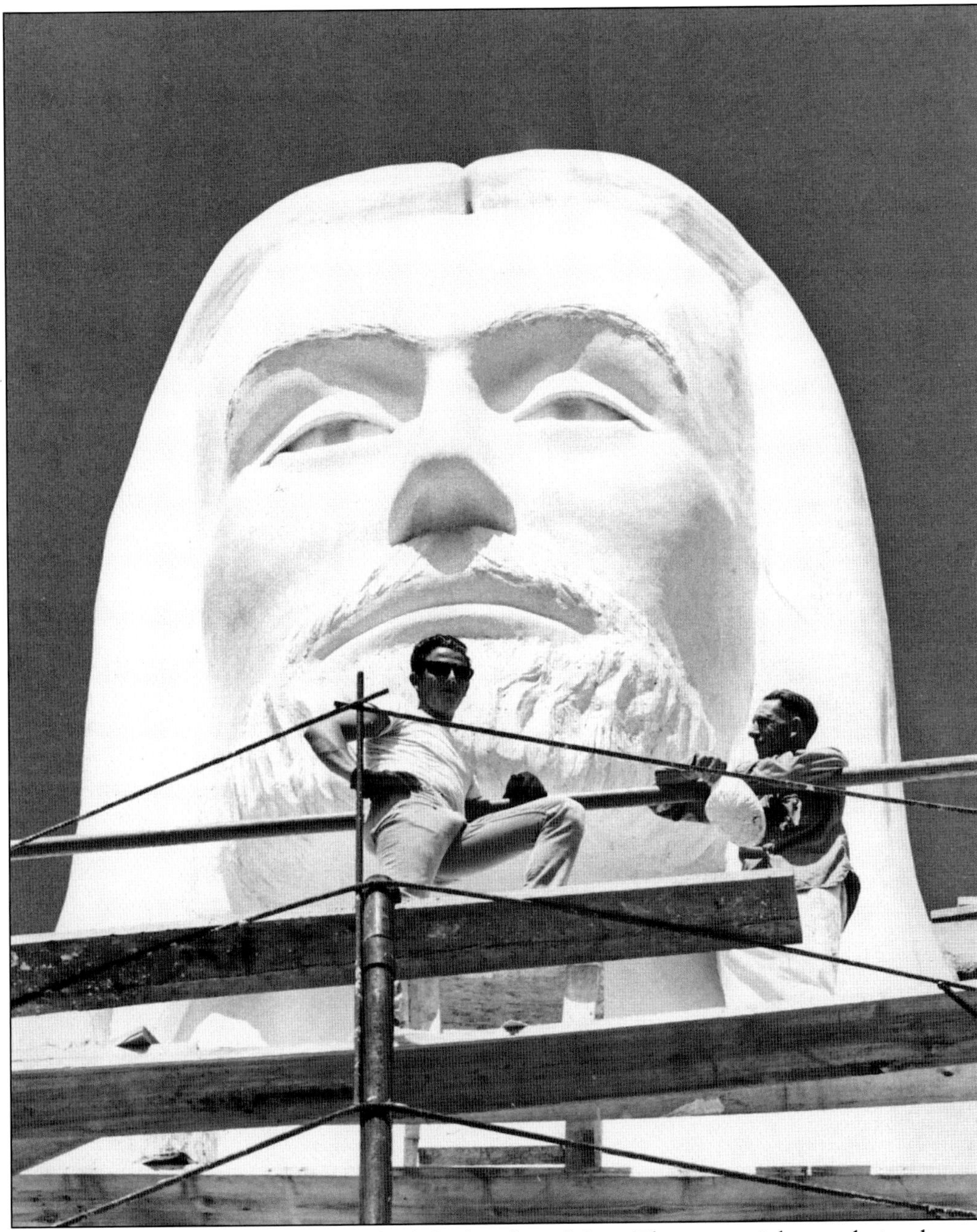

Teams of workers semamlessly attached the hands and face. Their materials were hoisted seven stories and carried across scaffolding that was only a few feet wide. While the final product revealed a smooth surface, the real construction was the delicate yet sturdy frame.

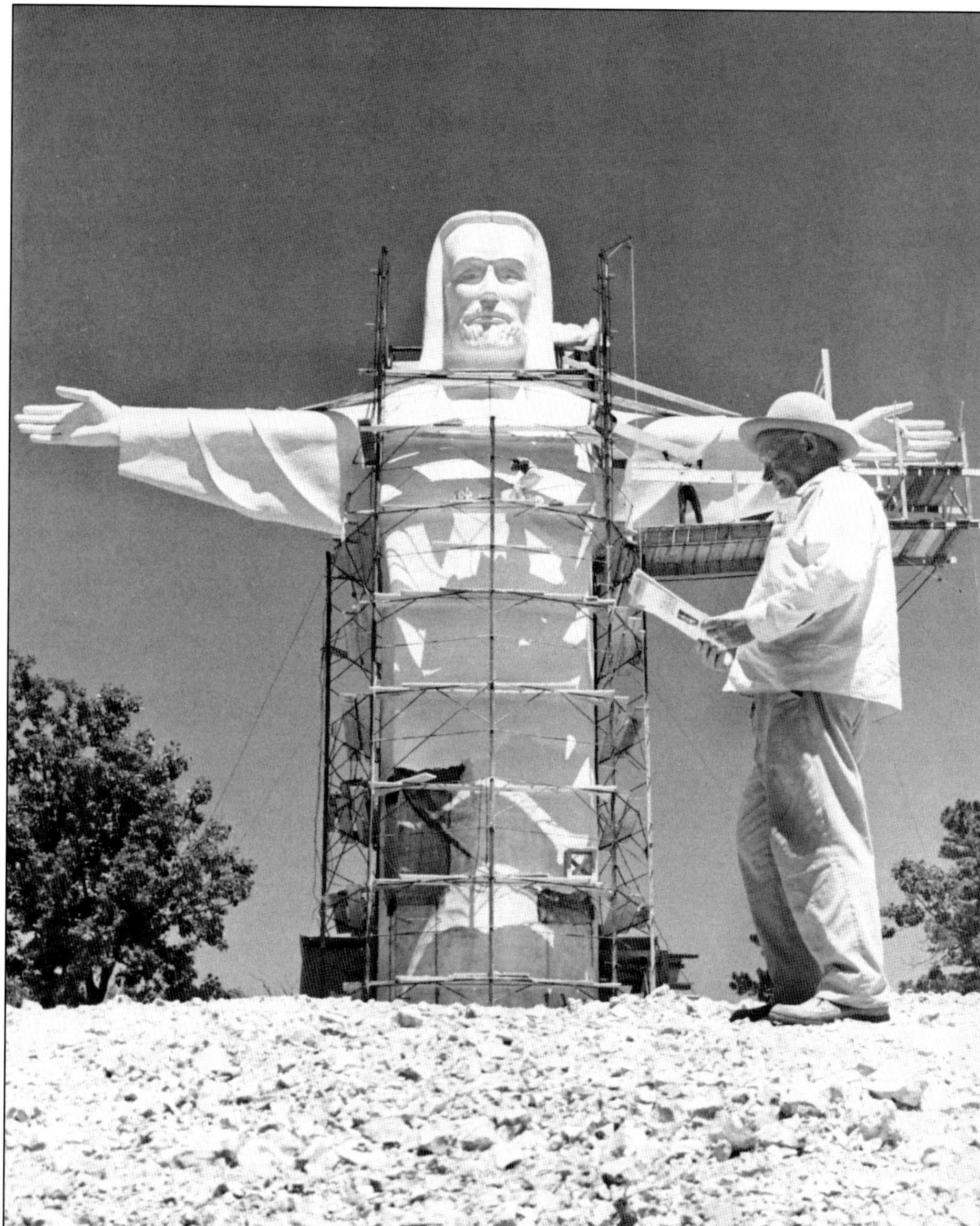

As the statue took its final form, sculptor Emmet Sullivan could stand tall with pride. His statue was immense and stood tall above the rocky Ozark Mountains of Eureka Springs.

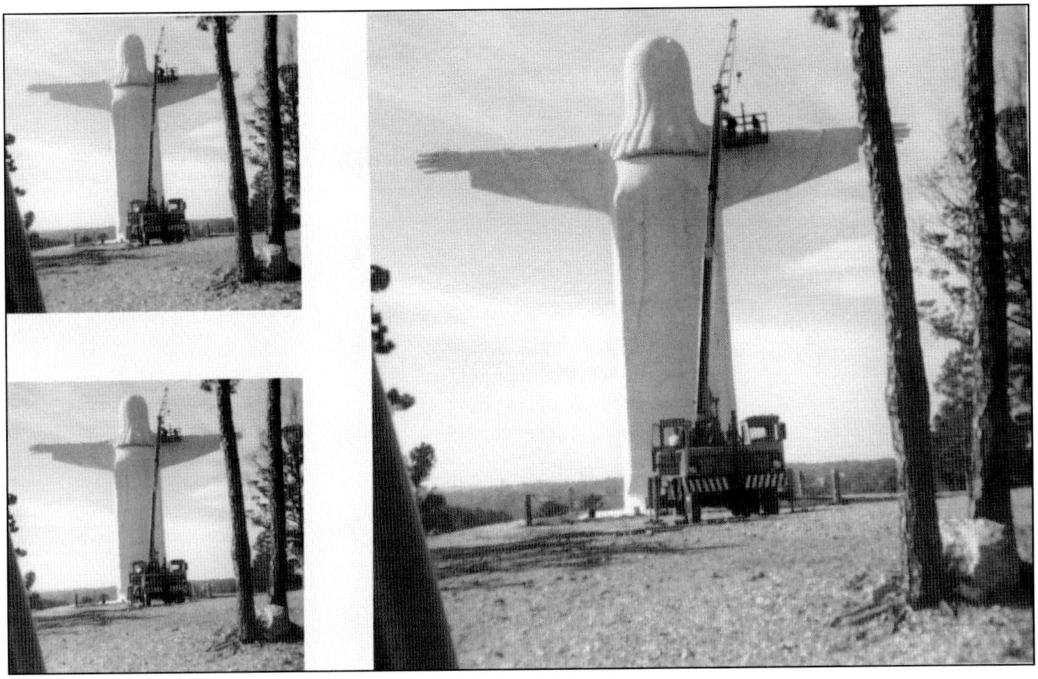

The final details to the statue were added by crane. Workers were forced to carefully carve some of the folds in Christ's robe. It was delicate work, and it was feared that the impact of the machinery could crack the entire facade. After 40 years, such concerns have been vanquished.

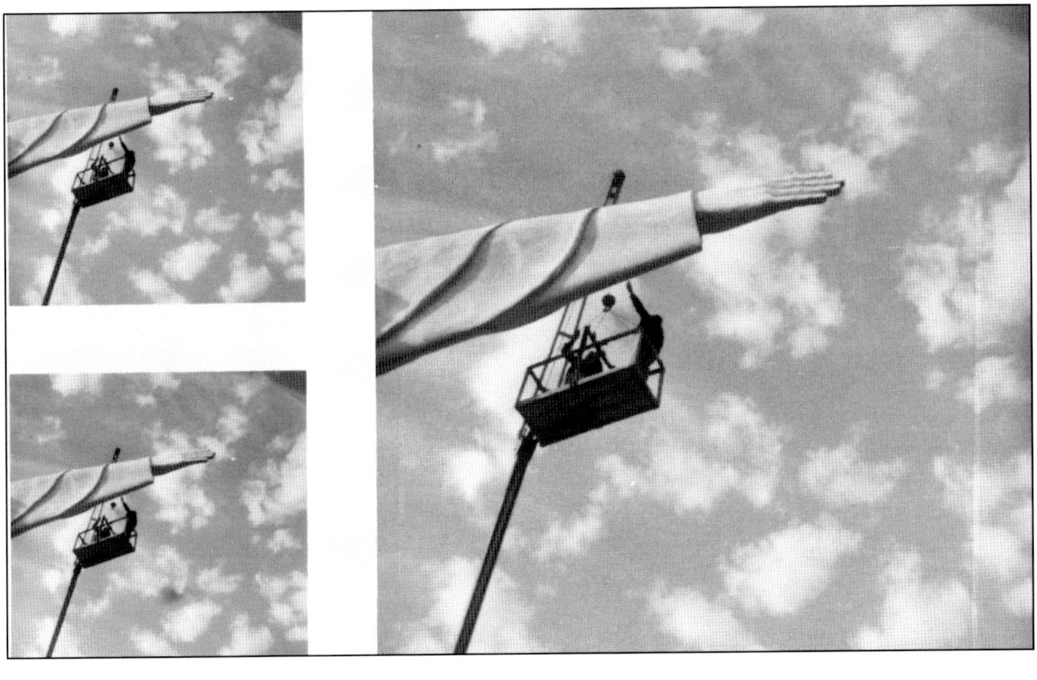

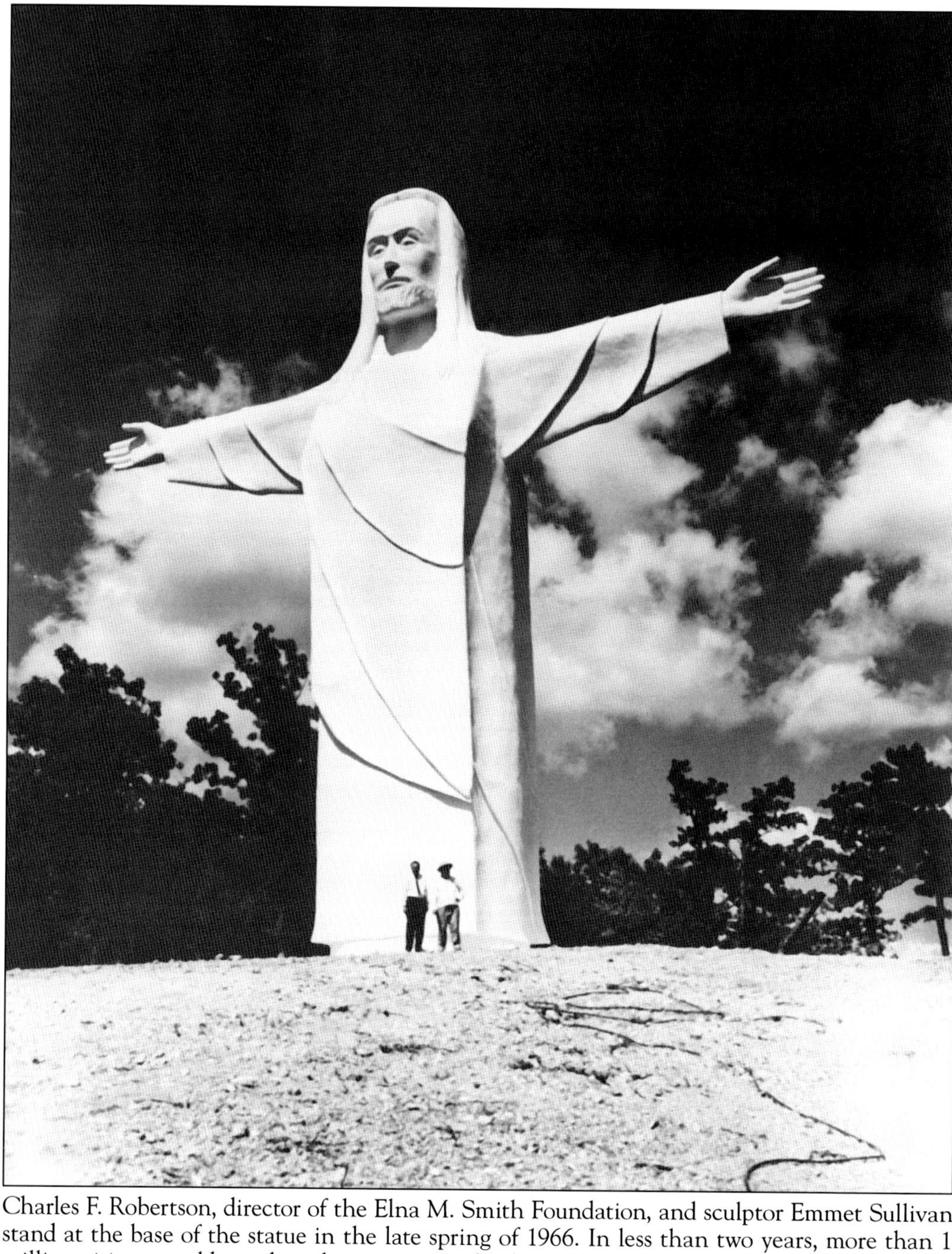

Charles F. Robertson, director of the Elna M. Smith Foundation, and sculptor Emmet Sullivan stand at the base of the statue in the late spring of 1966. In less than two years, more than 1 million visitors would stand on the same ground, admiring such an immense achievement.

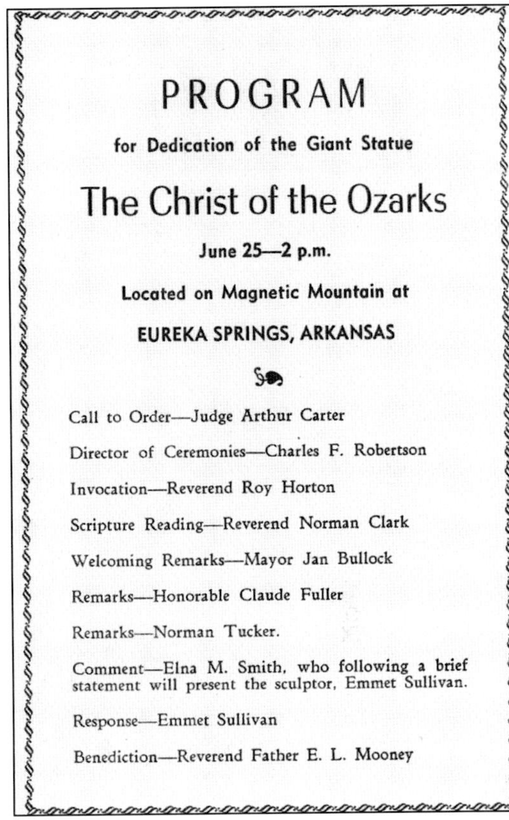

PROGRAM

for Dedication of the Giant Statue

The Christ of the Ozarks

June 25—2 p.m.

Located on Magnetic Mountain at

EUREKA SPRINGS, ARKANSAS

Call to Order—Judge Arthur Carter

Director of Ceremonies—Charles F. Robertson

Invocation—Reverend Roy Horton

Scripture Reading—Reverend Norman Clark

Welcoming Remarks—Mayor Jan Bullock

Remarks—Honorable Claude Fuller

Remarks—Norman Tucker.

Comment—Elna M. Smith, who following a brief statement will present the sculptor, Emmet Sullivan.

Response—Emmet Sullivan

Benediction—Reverend Father E. L. Mooney

Charles F. Robertson was director of ceremonies for the June 25, 1966, dedication. The honored guests included Gerald L. K. and Elna M. Smith, and local dignitaries. However, the role that Robertson played in the entire project was critical. While the Smiths were visionaries and Emmet Sullivan was the artist, the organization and clerical skill that helped make the statue a reality came from Robertson.

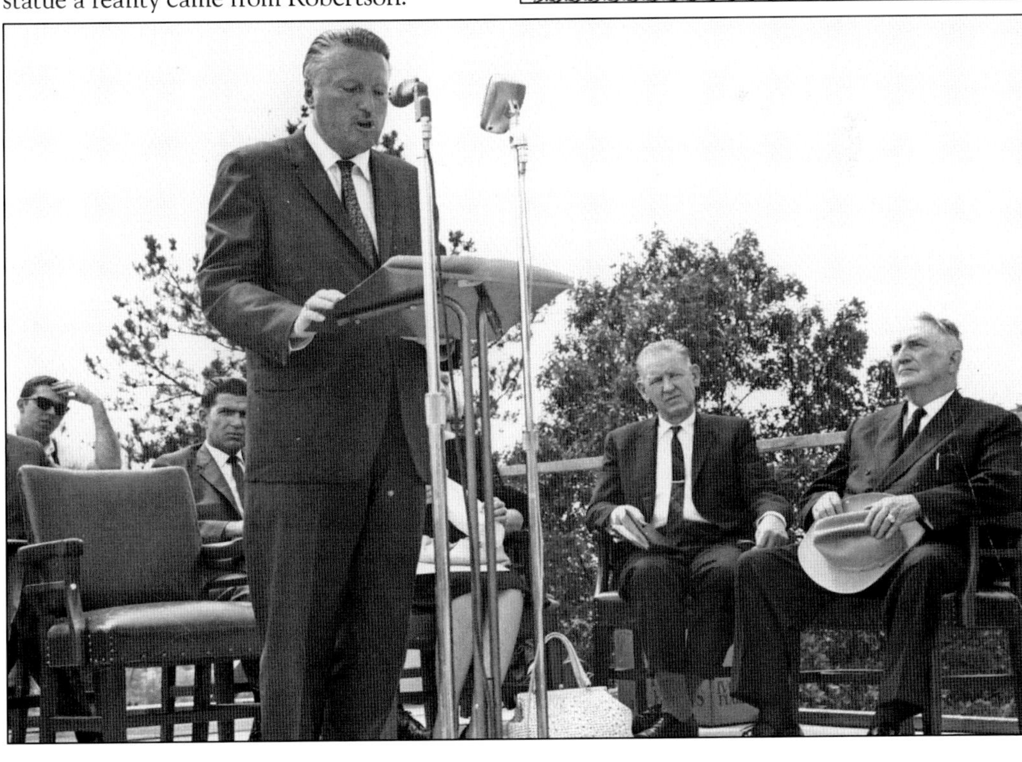

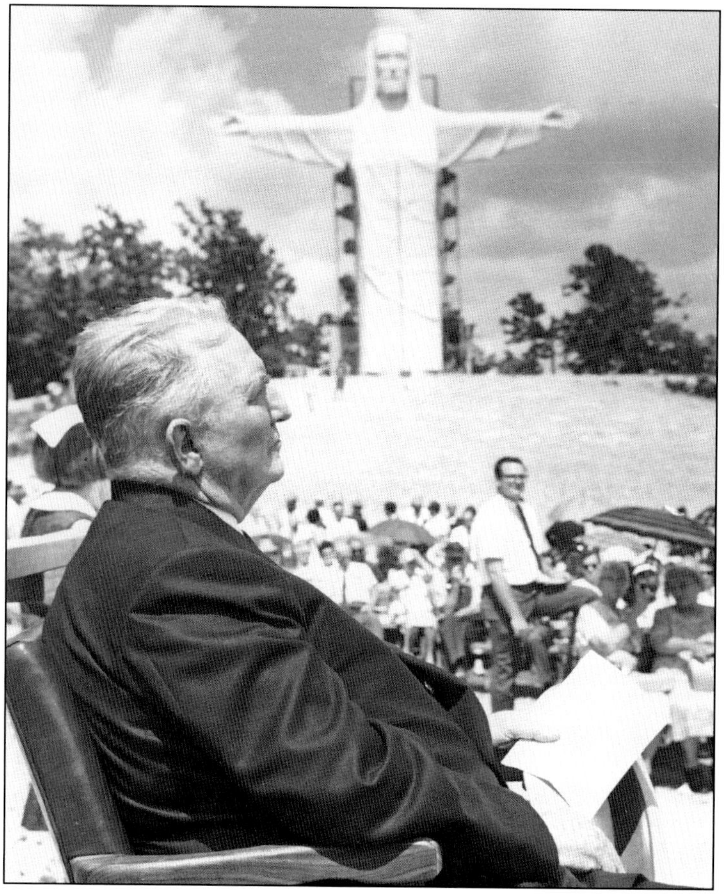

The *Christ of the Ozarks* project required enormous cooperation. Gerald L. K. Smith provided inspiration, Emmet Sullivan brought artistic and logistical expertise, and Claude Fuller, owner of the local bank, represented the cooperation of local business and town leaders. Together the project was completed in less than a year and quickly revitalized the tourist industry of Eureka Springs.

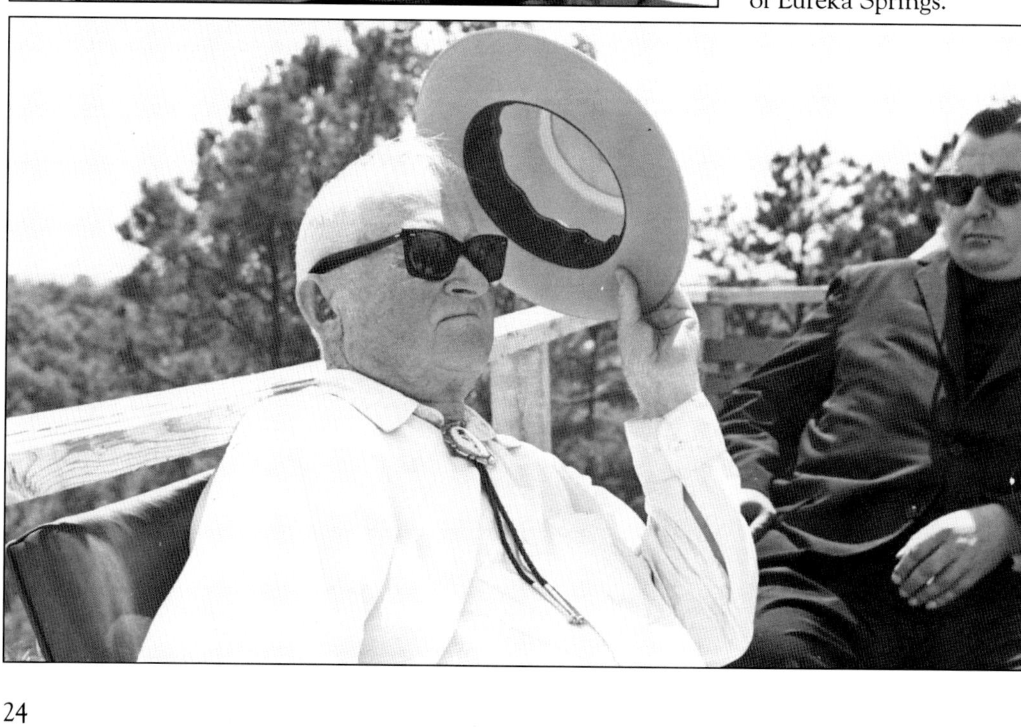

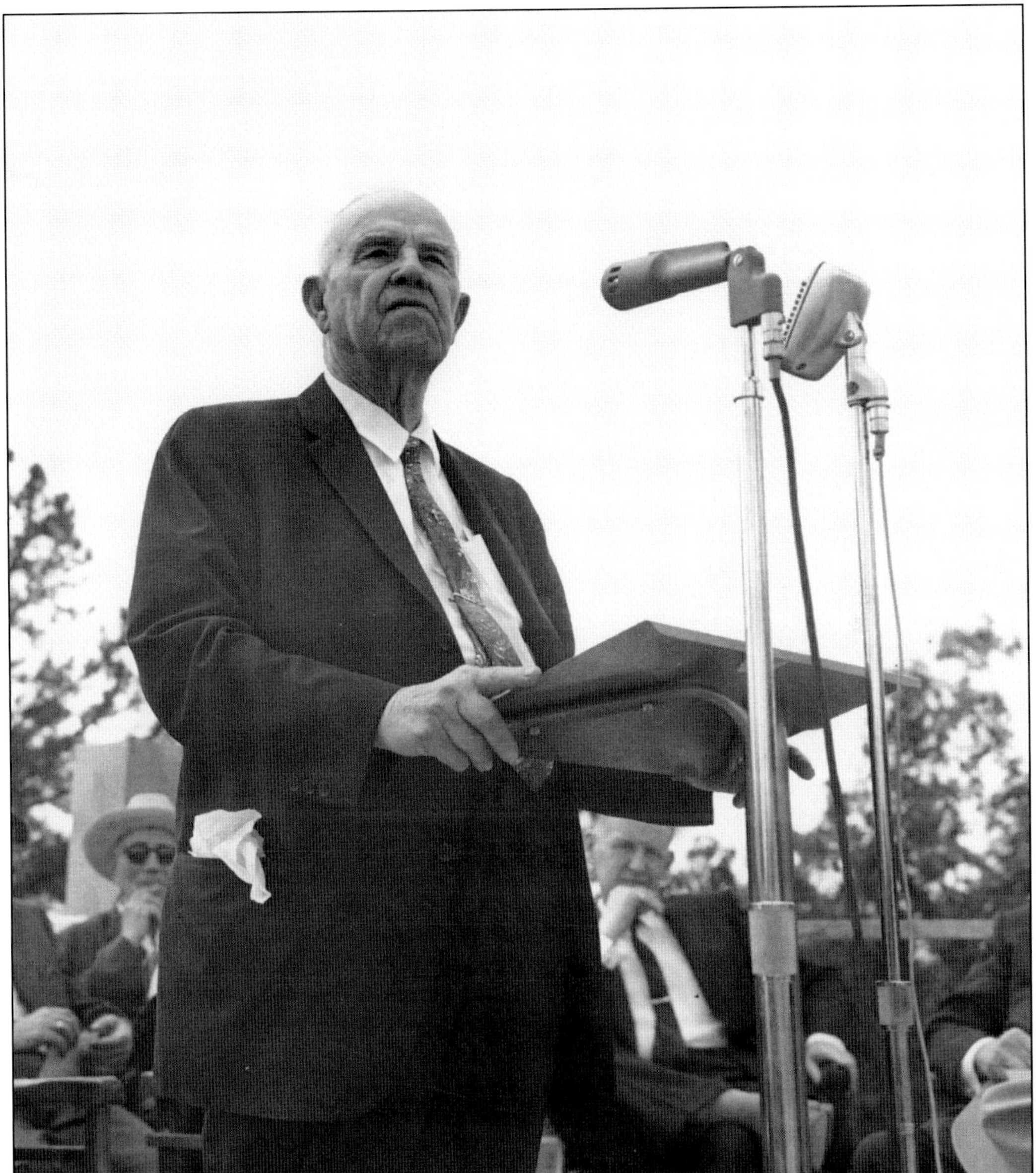

Claude Fuller also spoke at the statue's dedication. Fuller was a long-time resident of Eureka Springs, a former U.S. Congressman, and the owner of the Bank of Eureka Springs. His presence signified the gratitude and blessing of the community.

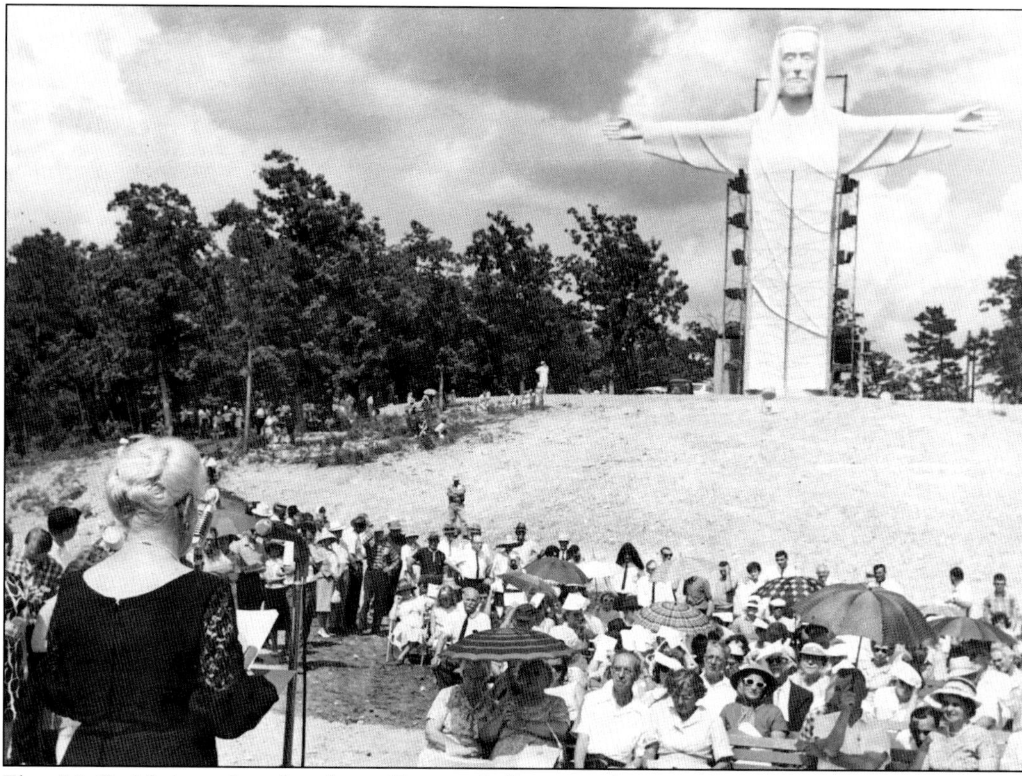

Elna M. Smith introduced sculptor Emmet Sullivan to the assembled crowd. It was a hot June afternoon, and some chose to stand in the tree line, as opposed to sitting in the sun. Regardless, Smith delivered a four-page introduction entitled "Artist, Genius, Patriot, Scholar." The text was later published by Gerald L. K. Smith as a posthumous tribute to the sculptor.

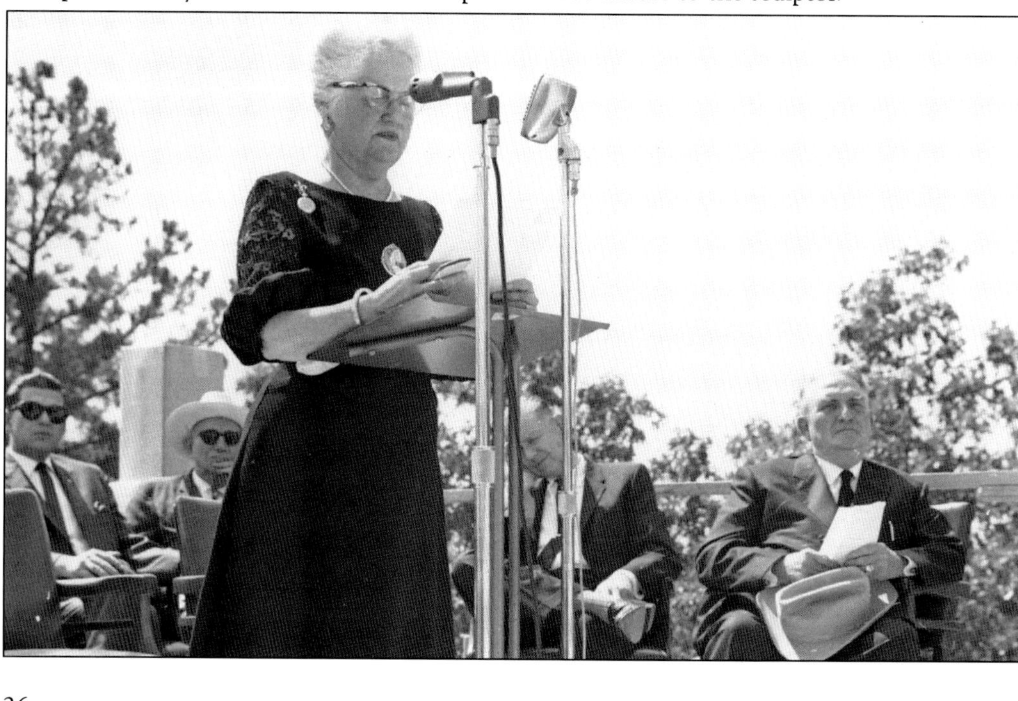

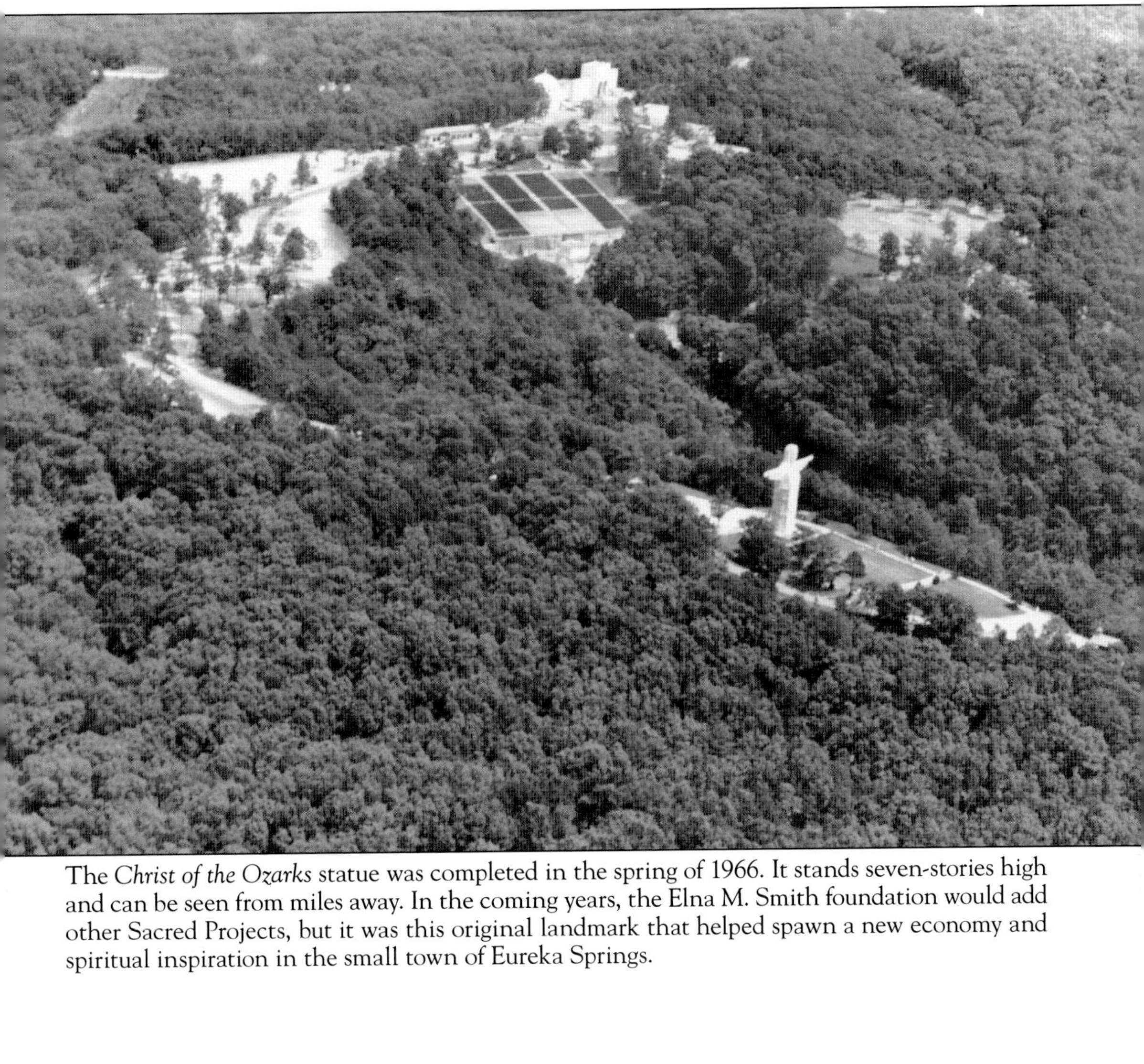

The *Christ of the Ozarks* statue was completed in the spring of 1966. It stands seven-stories high and can be seen from miles away. In the coming years, the Elna M. Smith foundation would add other Sacred Projects, but it was this original landmark that helped spawn a new economy and spiritual inspiration in the small town of Eureka Springs.

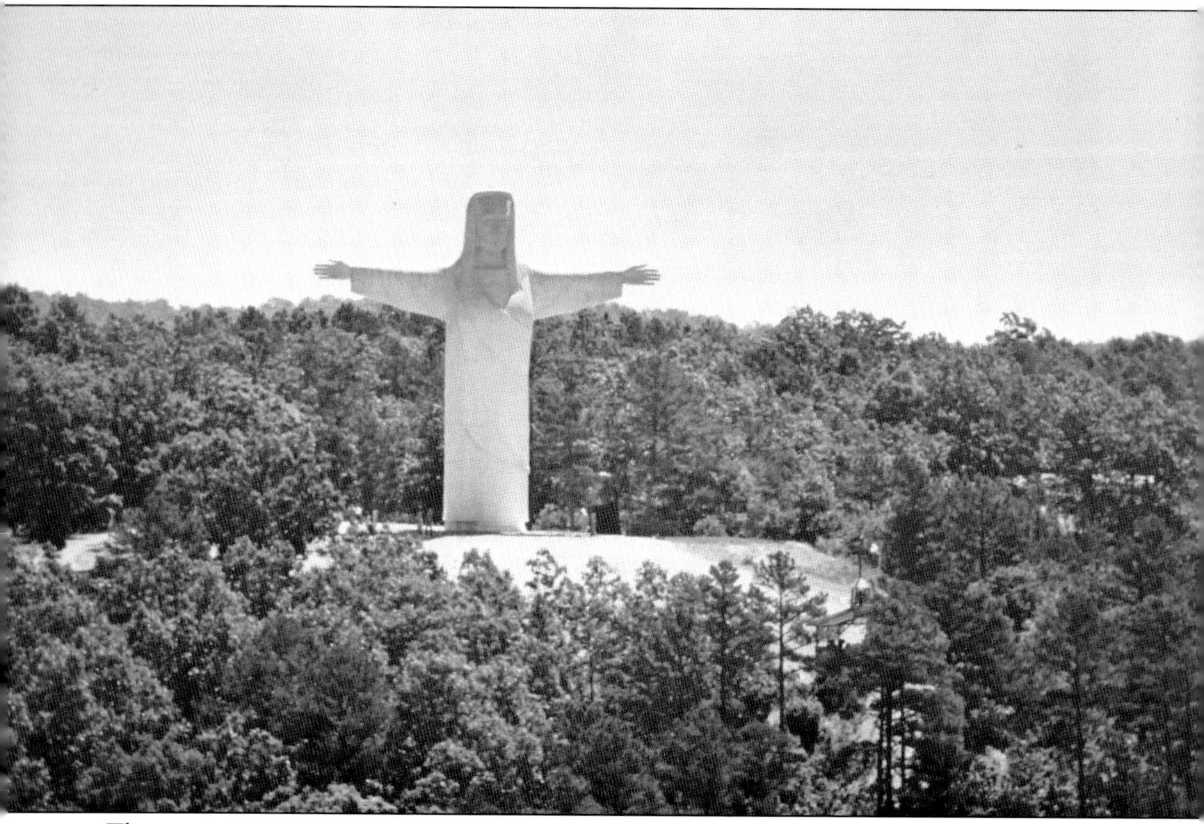

The statue is seven-stories tall and dominates the local scenery. It has been visited by millions from all over the world. Sculptor Emmet Sullivan was immensely proud of this work, and after 40 years, his statue remains an inspiration.

Two

The Greatest Story Ever Told

Gerald L. K. Smith explained that divine intervention made *The Great Passion Play* possible. While watching the construction of the *Christ of the Ozarks* statue, Smith began to dream even greater dreams. He suggested to one of sculptor Emmet Sullivan's key assistants, Adrian Forrette, that a play not unlike the Passion play of Oberramagau, Germany, could easily be staged in the natural amphitheater of Magnetic Mountain close to the statue. Unbeknownst to Smith, Forrette was good friends with a producer, director, and actor named Robert Hyde. Hyde had experience in outdoor dramas and was looking for such a project. With Forrette as the go-between, Hyde and Smith were introduced.

Smith was overcome by Hyde's enthusiasm and ingenuity. Hyde supervised the writing of a script, designed the original set, ordered costumes, made props, and recorded the first sound track. Furthermore, he was able to manage costs by creating a cast from members of the local community. It was an enormous undertaking, but within two years of Smith's off-hand remark about a play in the Ozarks, it was a reality. On July 14, 1968, *The Great Passion Play* opened to a small crowd of mostly invited press. For the next 10 years, its audience grew at a rate of 25,000 per year. By 1976, *The Great Passion Play* welcomed its millionth visitor. By 1989, it welcomed its 4 millionth visitor. The play is now the largest outdoor drama in the United States.

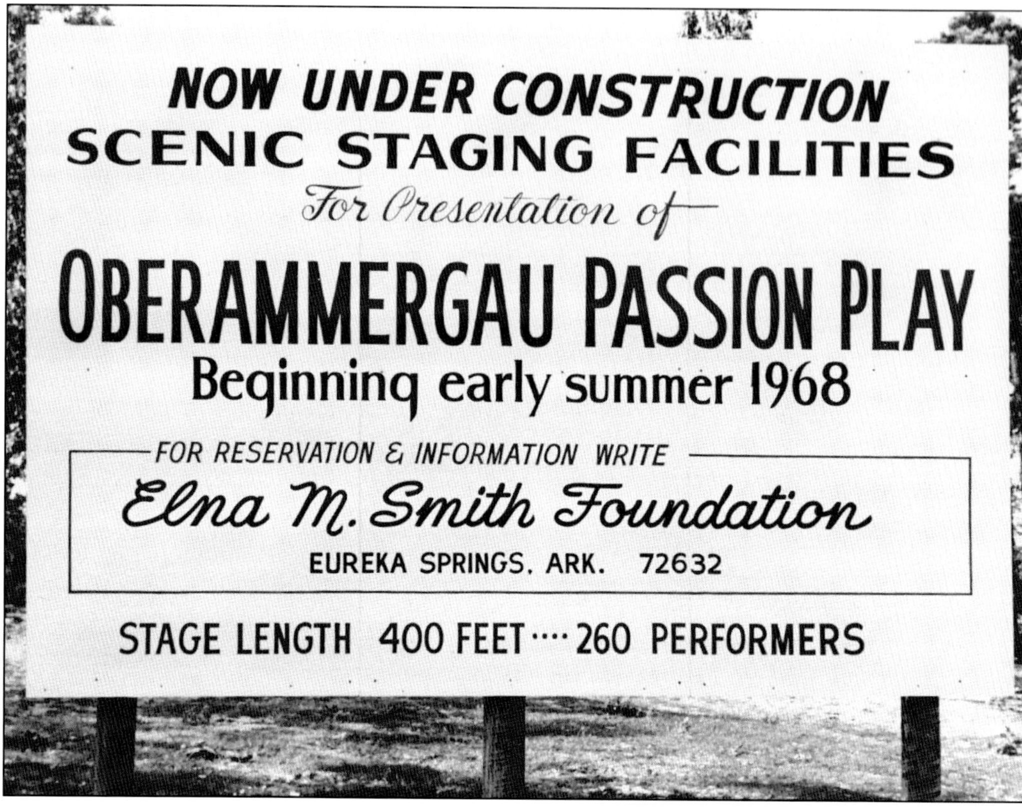

Construction of the Passion play stage and set began in the summer of 1967. A rough sketch was publicized in local and regional newspapers, along with a description of the play. In honor of the original Passion play staged in Oberramagau, Germany, the mountain was renamed Mount Oberramagau.

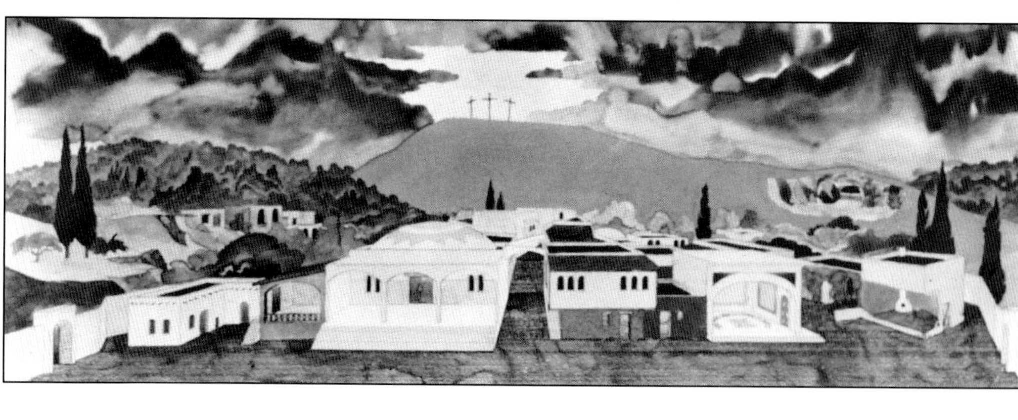

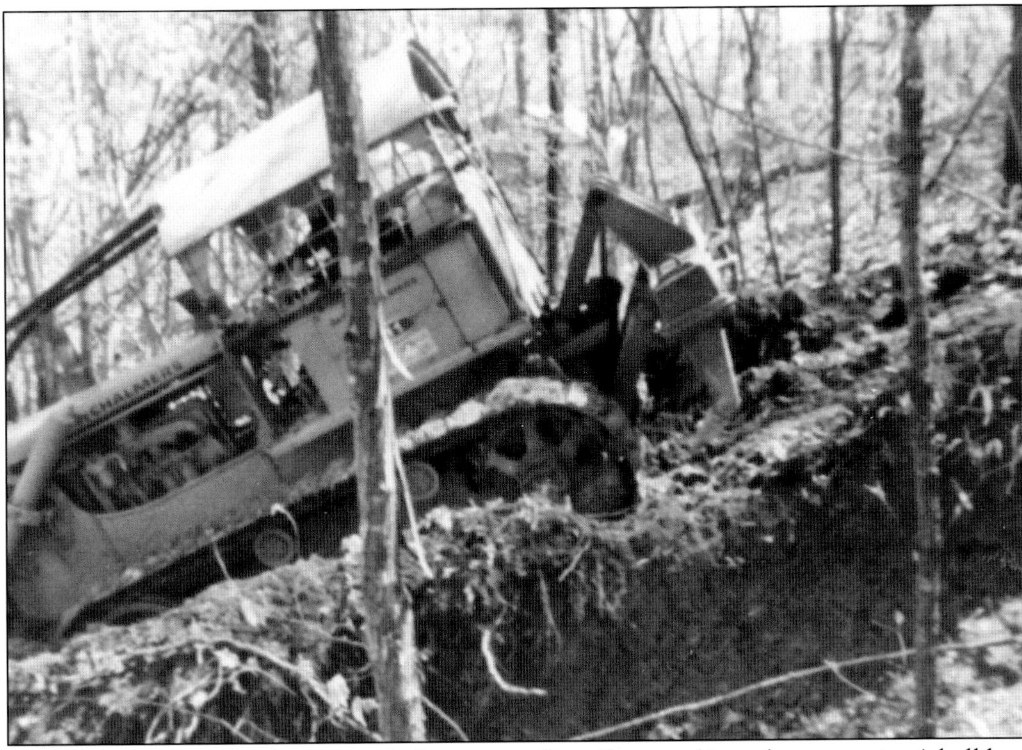

The staging and seating for the amphitheater were literally carved into the mountain. A bulldozer cut away at the trees and rock, attempting to provide a level ground. Ironically stones were required to keep the rocky Ozark earth in place.

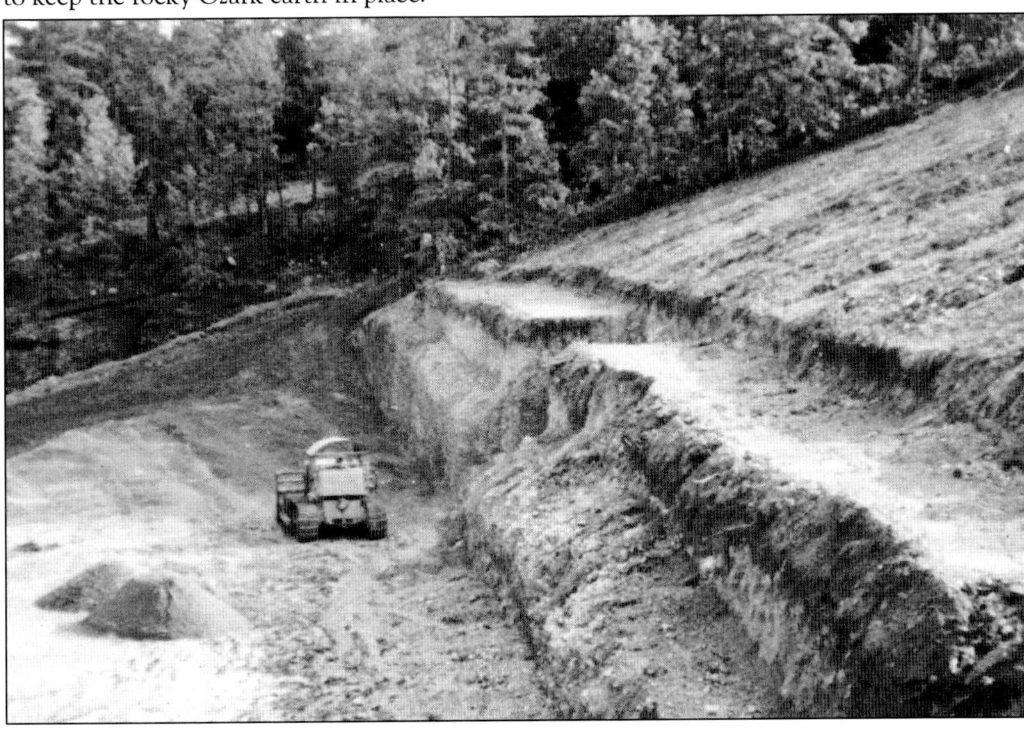

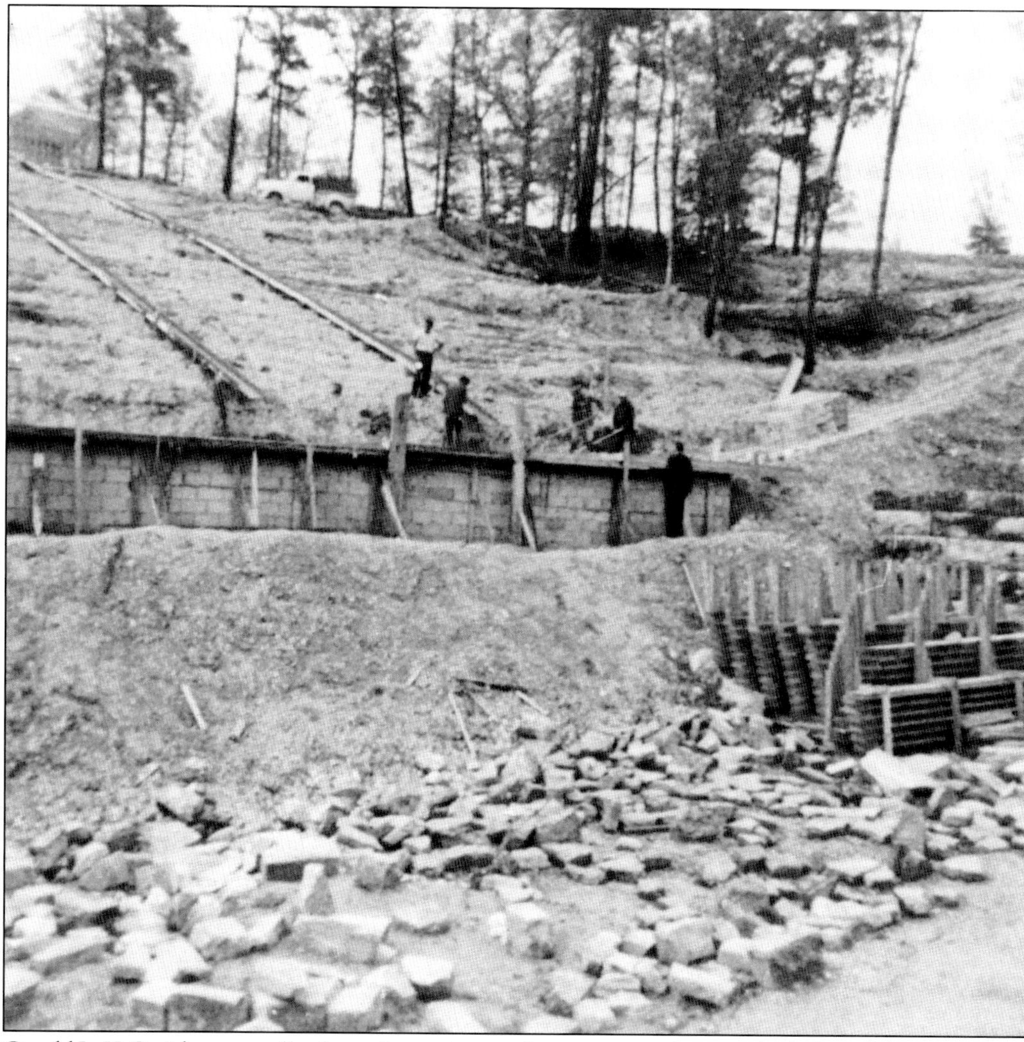

Gerald L. K. Smith personally chose the staging and seating areas because he believed the mountains formed a natural amphitheater. As the bulldozers carved their way through the landscape, they proved his predictions correct.

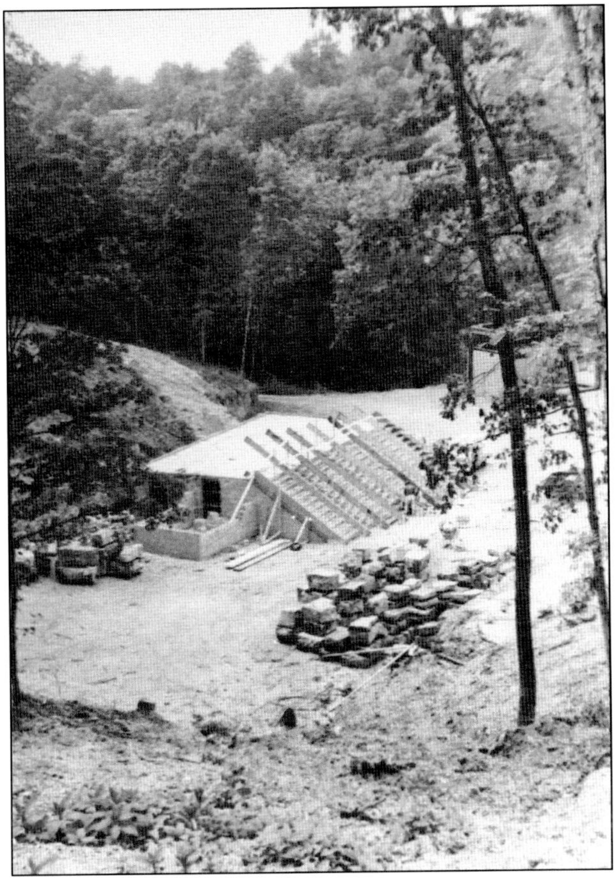

The set was designed with multiple structures and stages. The center of the stage was the temple and its massive steps. Robert Hyde intended for most of the action to occur on or around the steps; therefore, builders worked from the center outward. They framed the steps, and a network of smaller stages and buildings slowly developed.

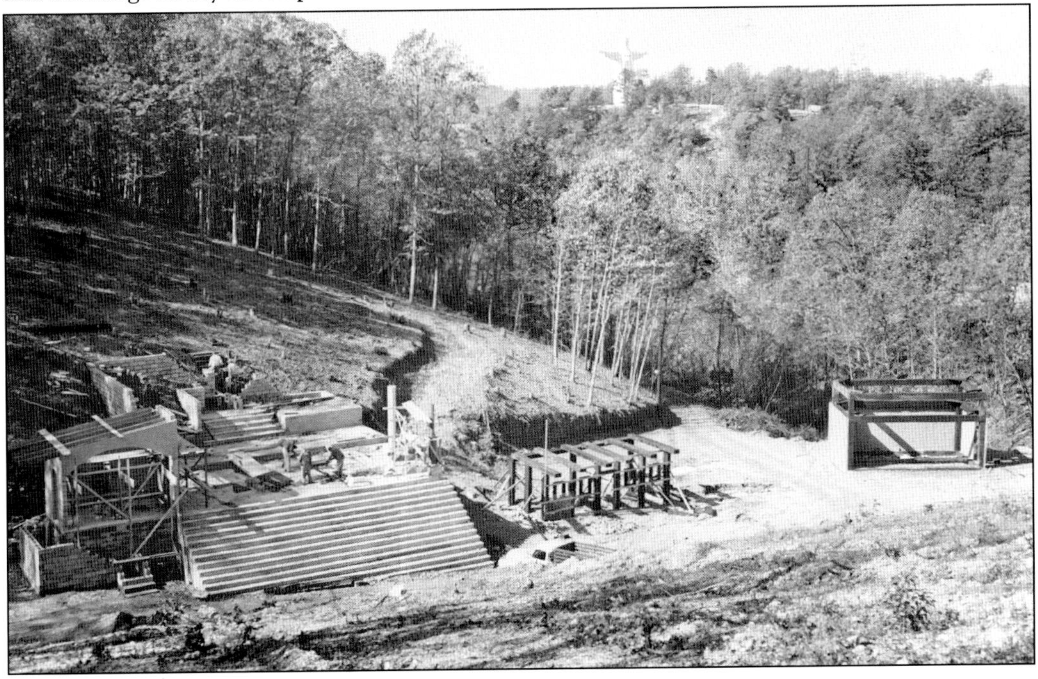

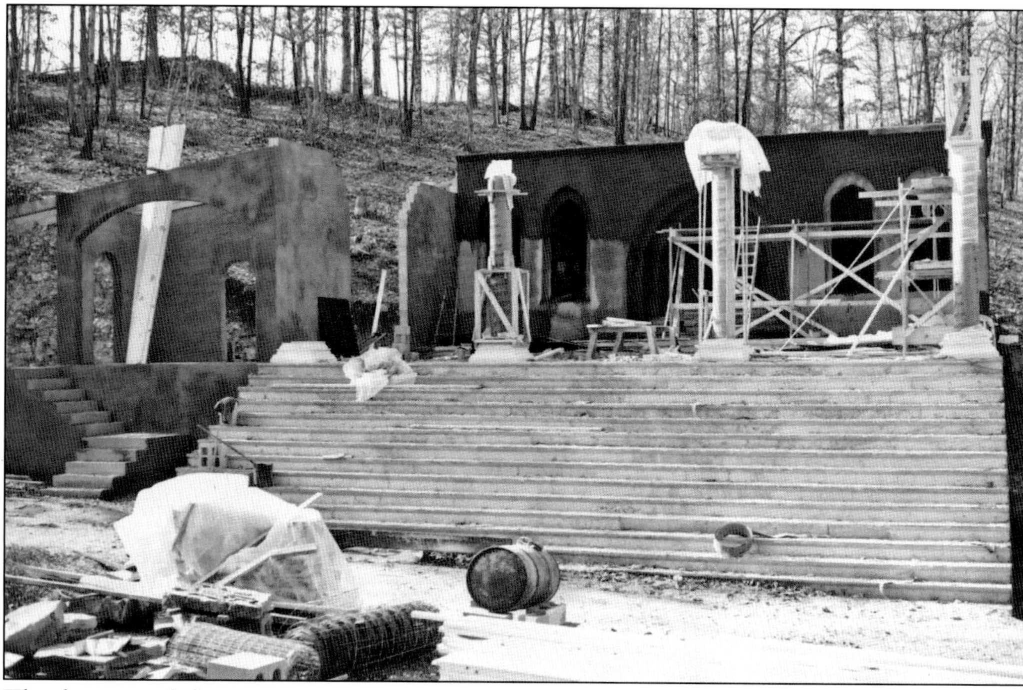

The features of the set emerged slowly. For example, the pillars of the temple served a dual purpose: they had to be strong enough to hold the temple canopy and be artistic enough to look authentic.

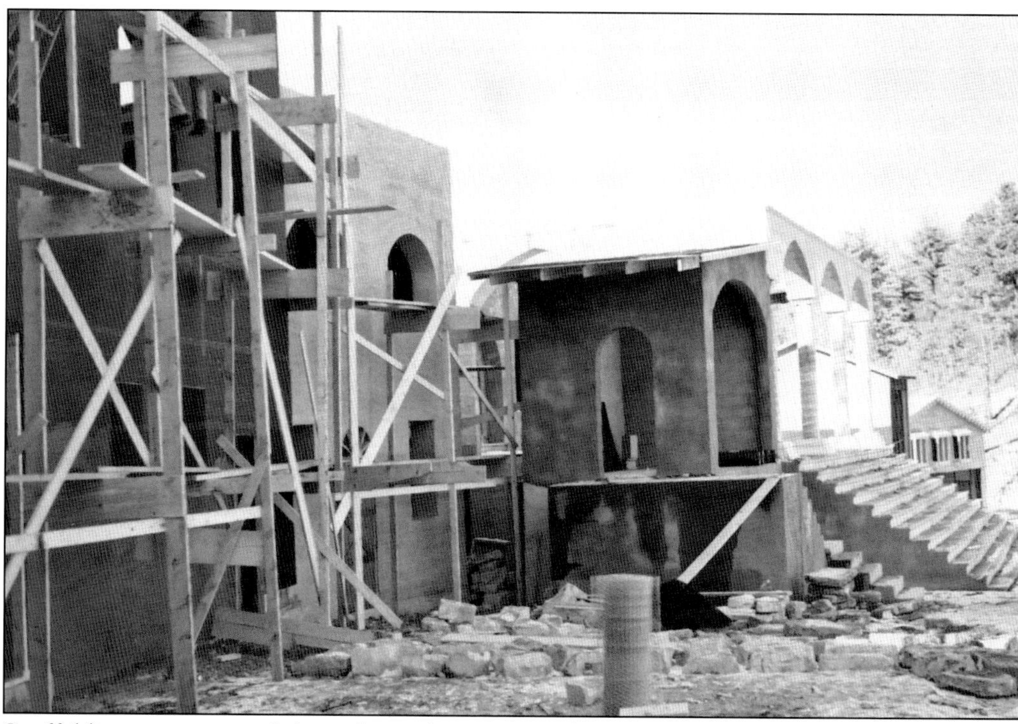

Scaffolding was required throughout the winter. The stage had multiple levels and designs, including wood, stone, and cement facades.

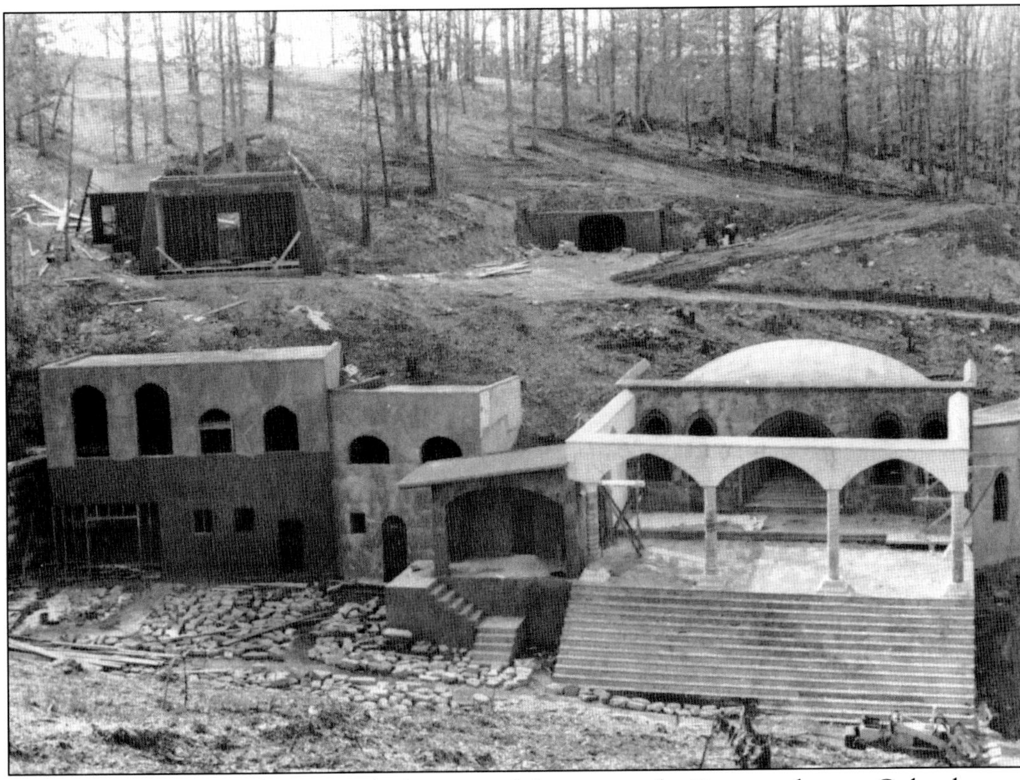

As the lower level of the set took shape, work began on the Emmaus house, Golgotha, and the tomb.

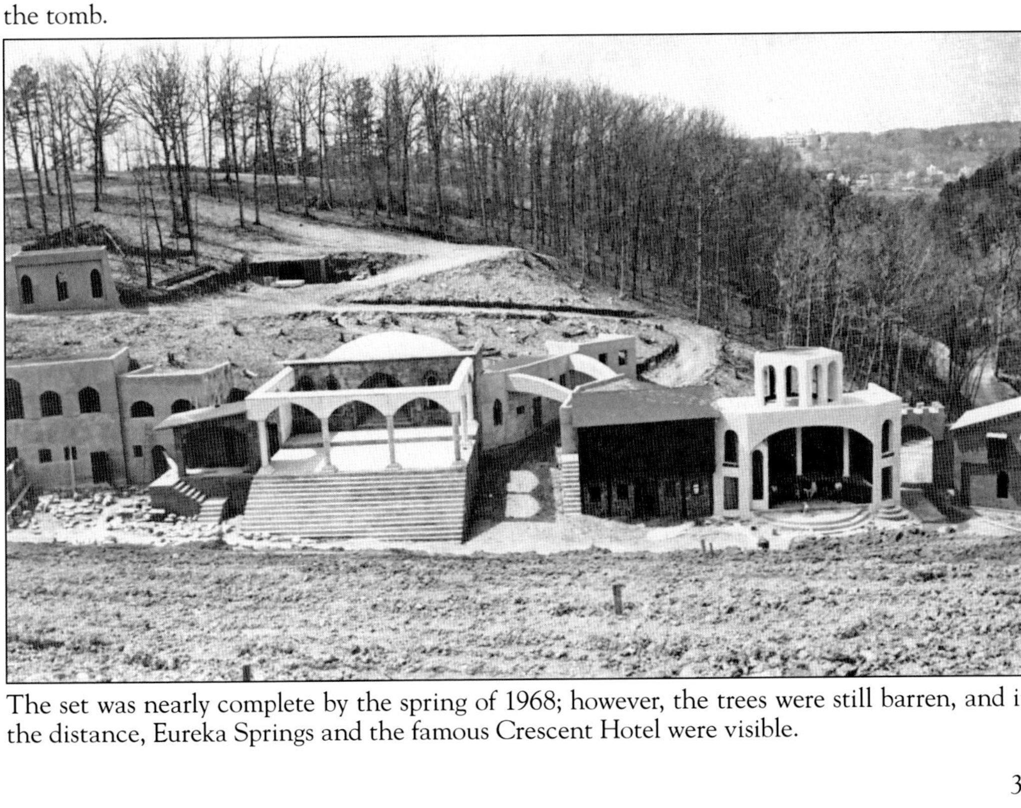

The set was nearly complete by the spring of 1968; however, the trees were still barren, and in the distance, Eureka Springs and the famous Crescent Hotel were visible.

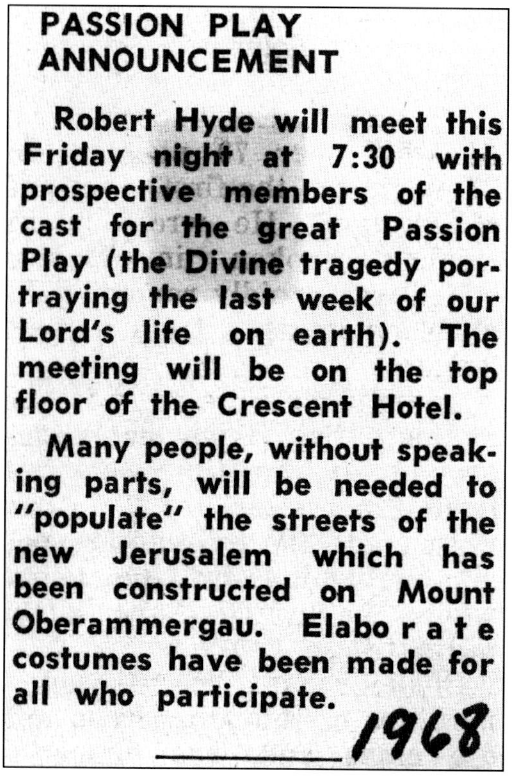
PASSION PLAY ANNOUNCEMENT

Robert Hyde will meet this Friday night at 7:30 with prospective members of the cast for the great Passion Play (the Divine tragedy portraying the last week of our Lord's life on earth). The meeting will be on the top floor of the Crescent Hotel.

Many people, without speaking parts, will be needed to "populate" the streets of the new Jerusalem which has been constructed on Mount Oberammergau. Elabo r a t e costumes have been made for all who participate.

1968

In May 1968, details of the production were shared with the community. A casting call was required, and a costume ceremony was held at the Crescent Hotel. Pictured below was Charles F. Robertson, the chief coordinator of the Elna M. Smith Foundation.

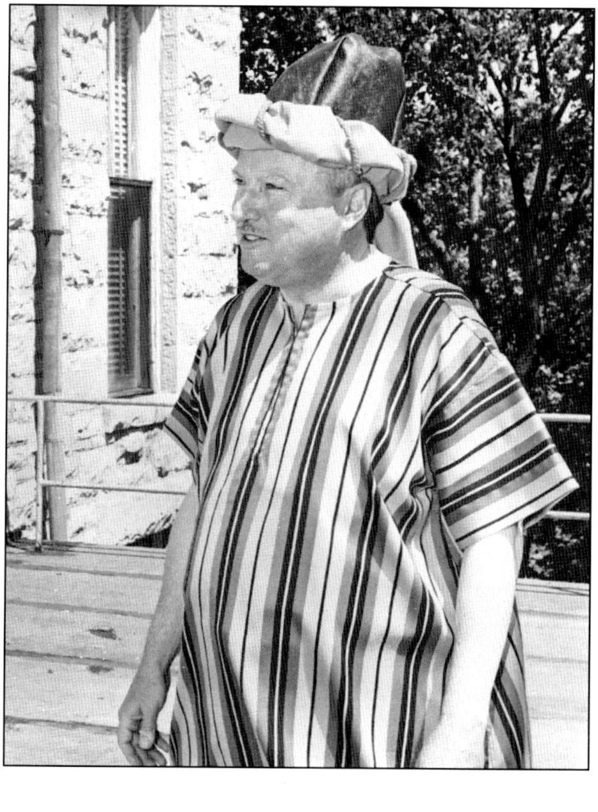

Locals were cast in supporting roles. Most of the costumes were sown and handcrafted locally, but the Roman outfits and their equipment required a special order from California.

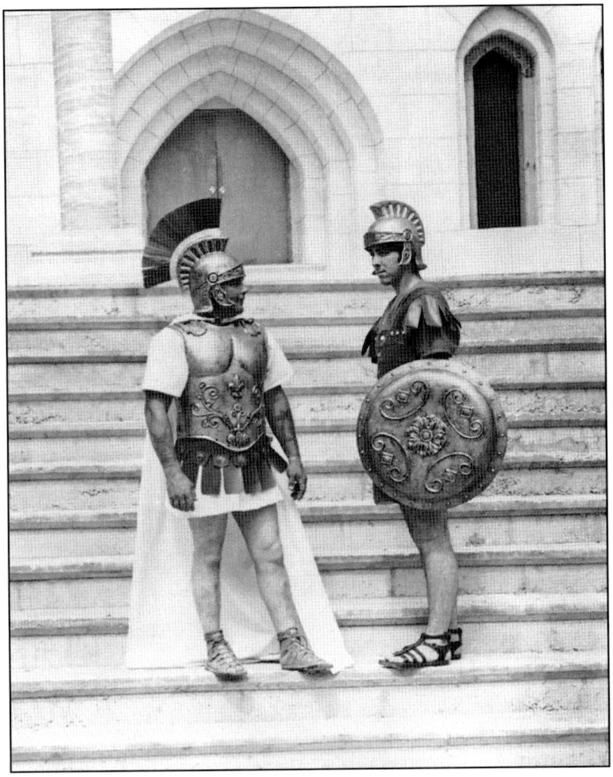

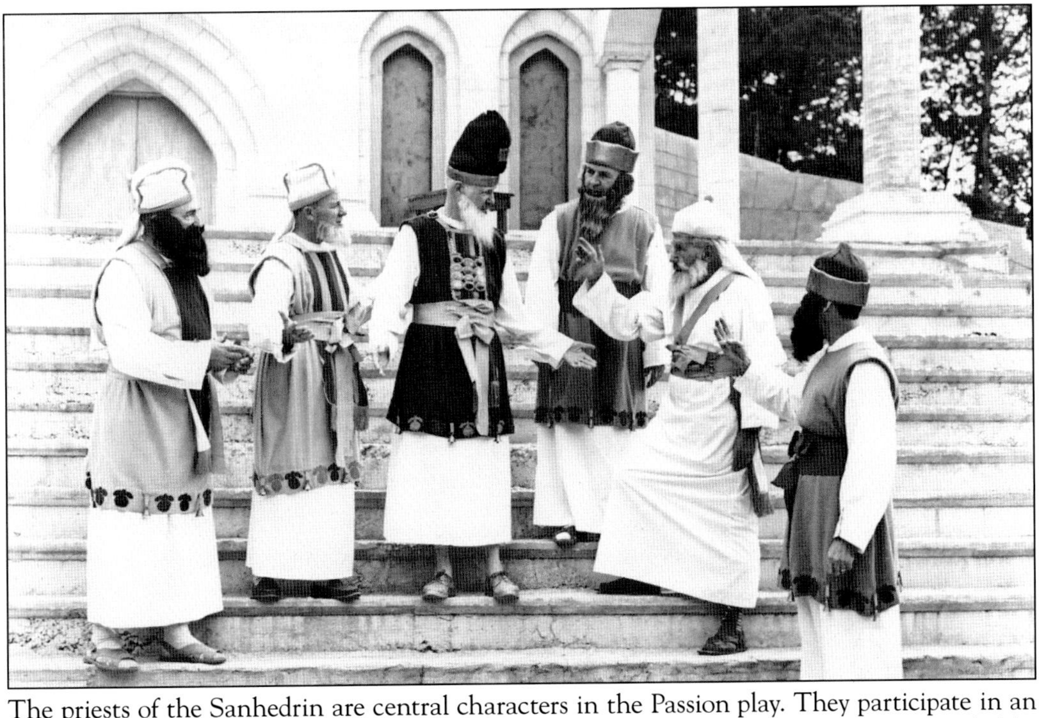

The priests of the Sanhedrin are central characters in the Passion play. They participate in an enormous amount of dialogue and action. In order to make the key characters distinguishable, they were outfitted with a variety of colorful costumes.

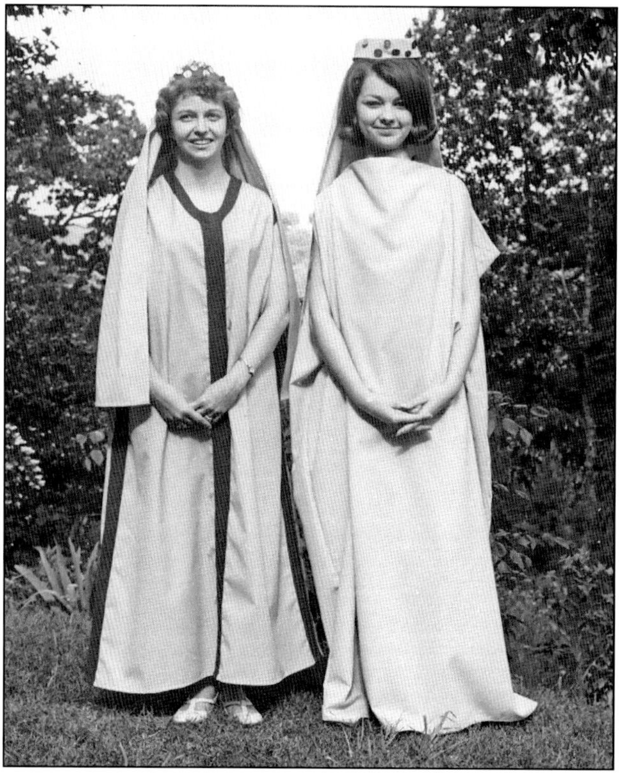

The first costumes were remarkably simple but also quite diverse. Among the 200 non-speaking parts were extras that represented the Biblical streets of Jerusalem.

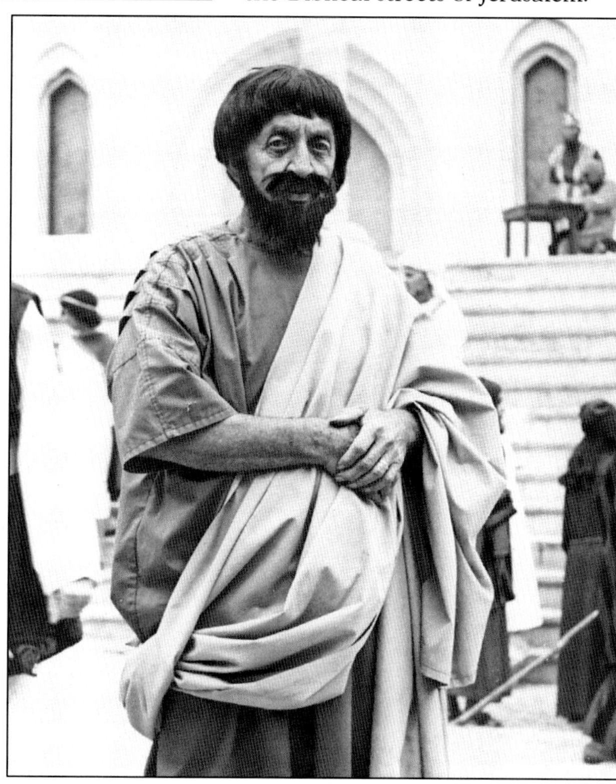

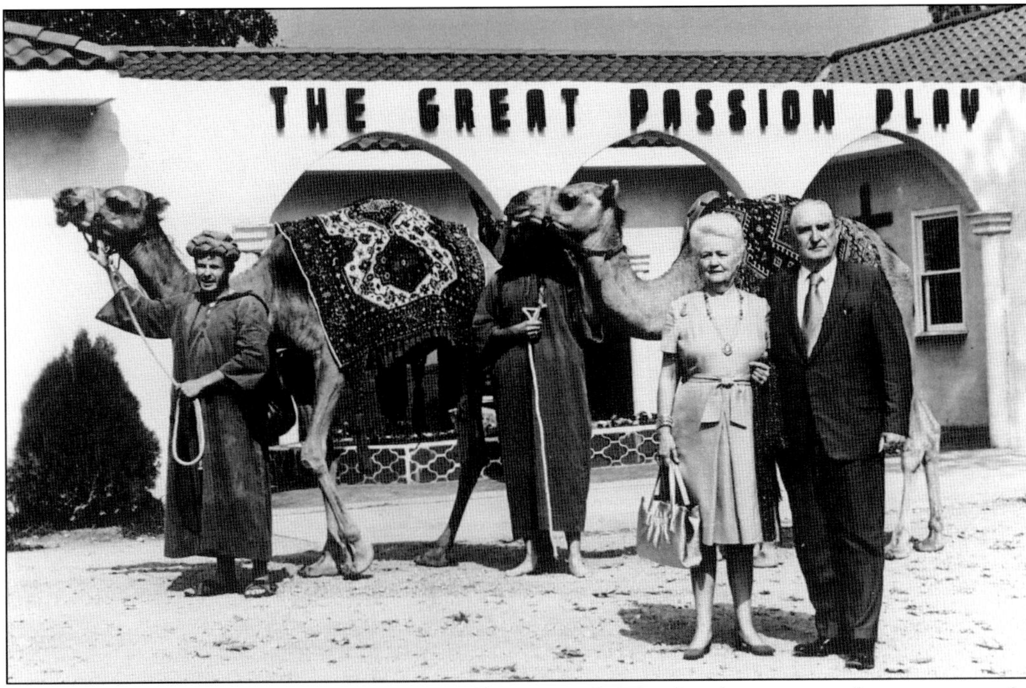

The set was designed to incorporate the use of live animals. The Smiths were proud to announce the purchase of two camels and a set of highly trained horses. The animals were fine, but participants had to learn how to handle exotic animals, as well as how to ride bareback.

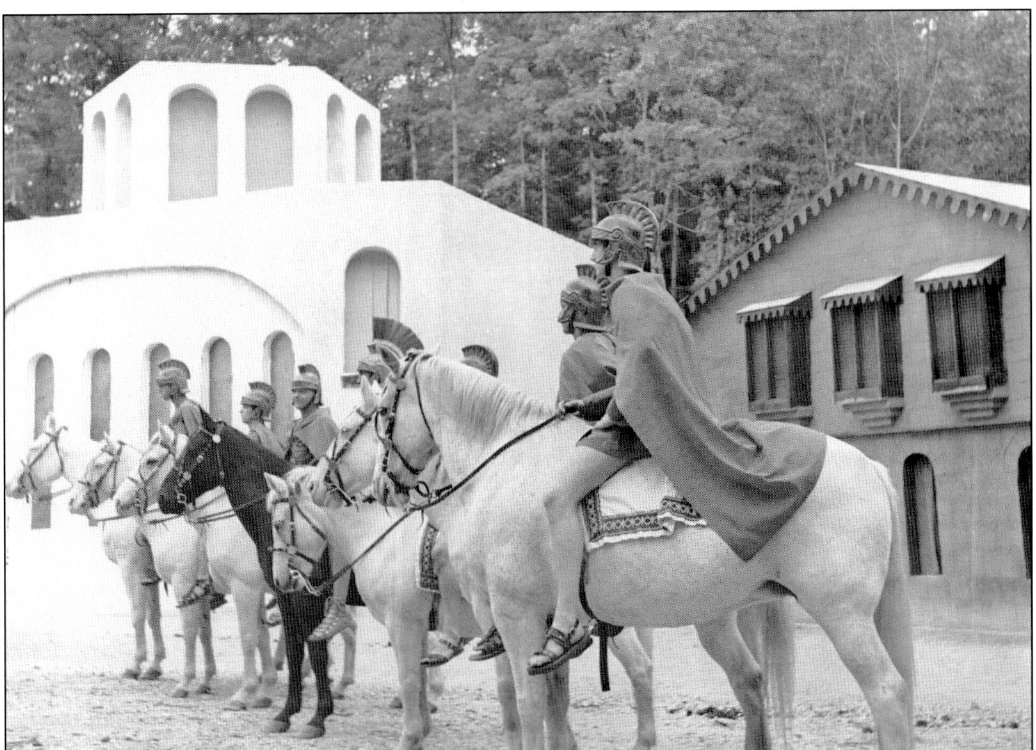

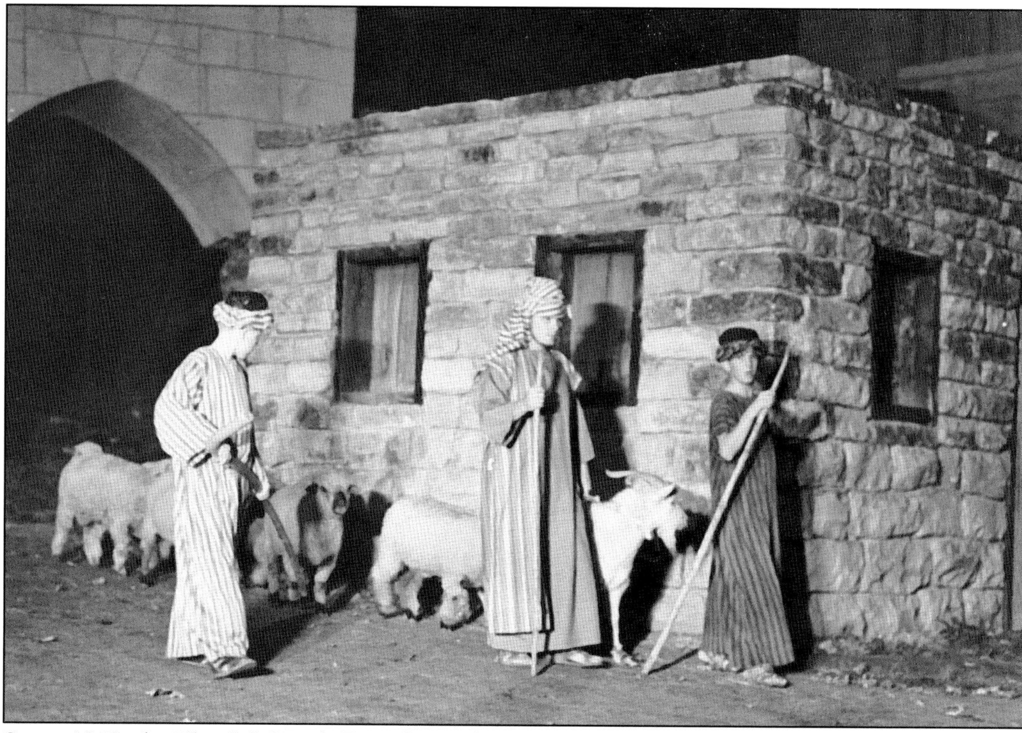

Since 1968, the Elna M. Smith Foundation has kept its own flock of sheep. While professionals are responsible for their care, the flock is guided on and off the set by child shepherds, another common sight in Jesus' Jerusalem.

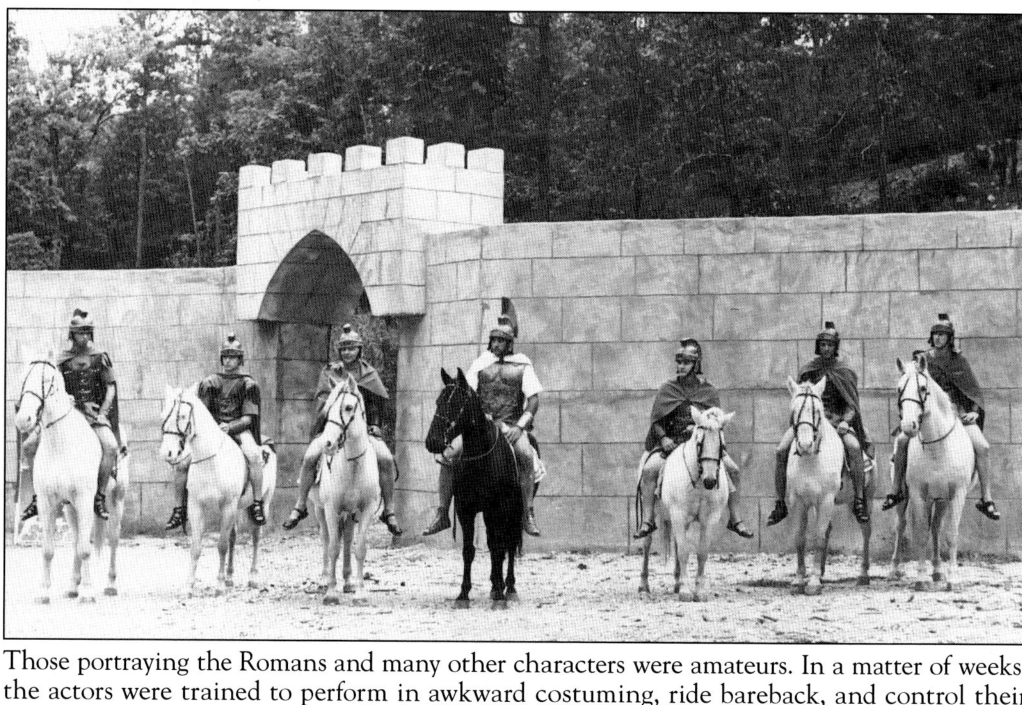

Those portraying the Romans and many other characters were amateurs. In a matter of weeks, the actors were trained to perform in awkward costuming, ride bareback, and control their animals on set.

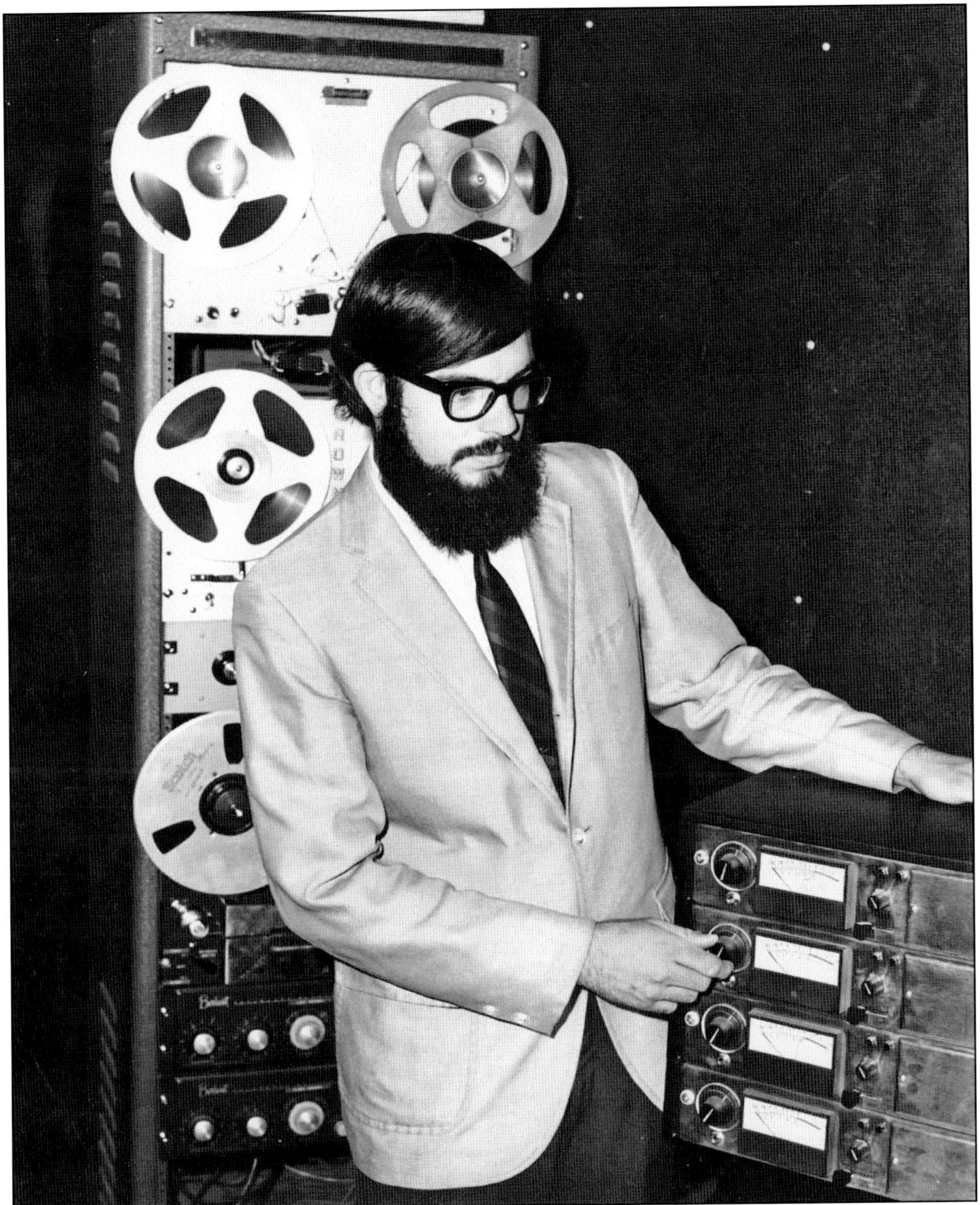

Robert Hyde's vision of a 400-foot amphitheater required an enormous sound system. Grant Hofley was the first soundman, engineering a state-of-the-art stereophonic system.

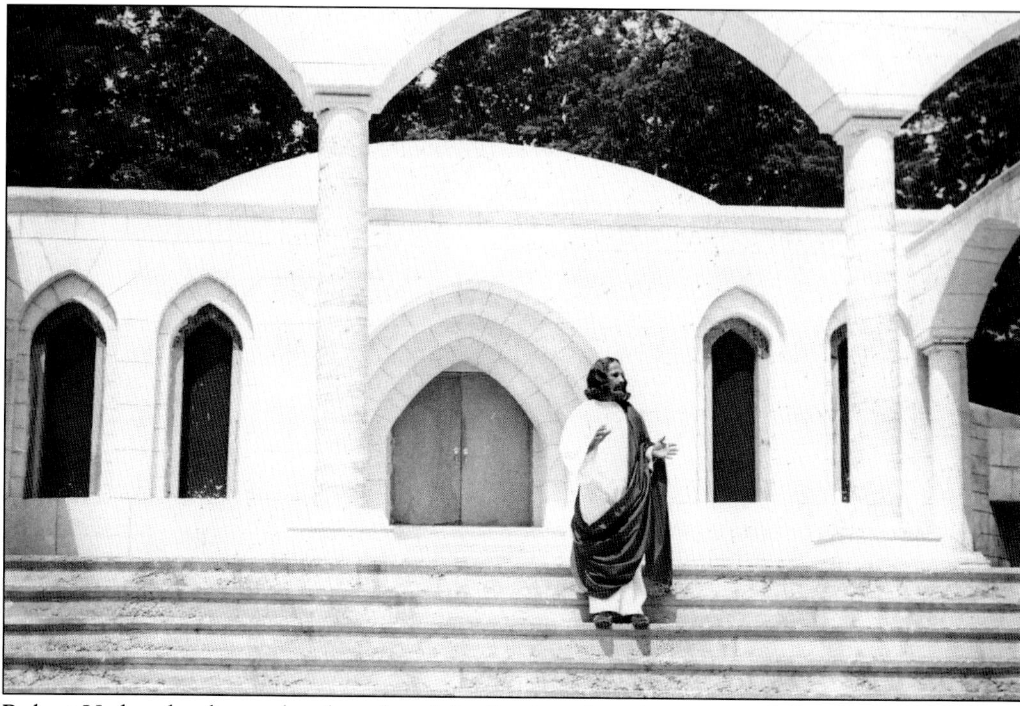

Robert Hyde, who directed and produced the Passion play, also portrayed the character of Christ from 1968 to 1979. He originally had no plans to play the role; however, at the costume unveiling, he donned the robes of Christ in the absence of actors. The Smiths were convinced he was the perfect picture of Christ. Eventually, they compelled him to play the part.

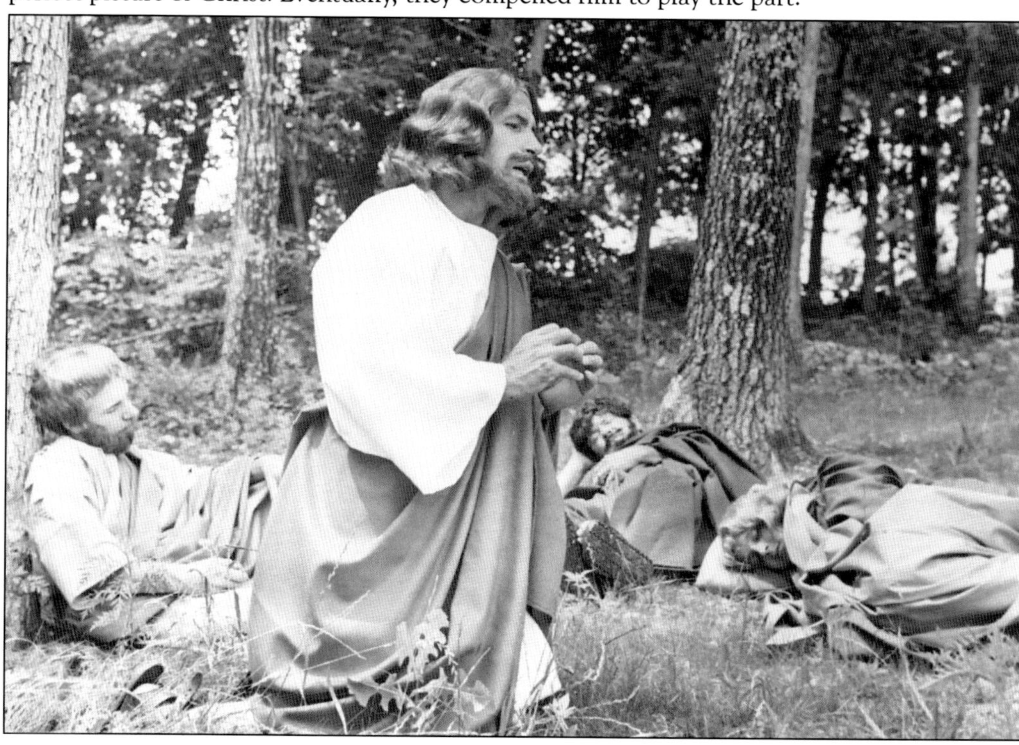

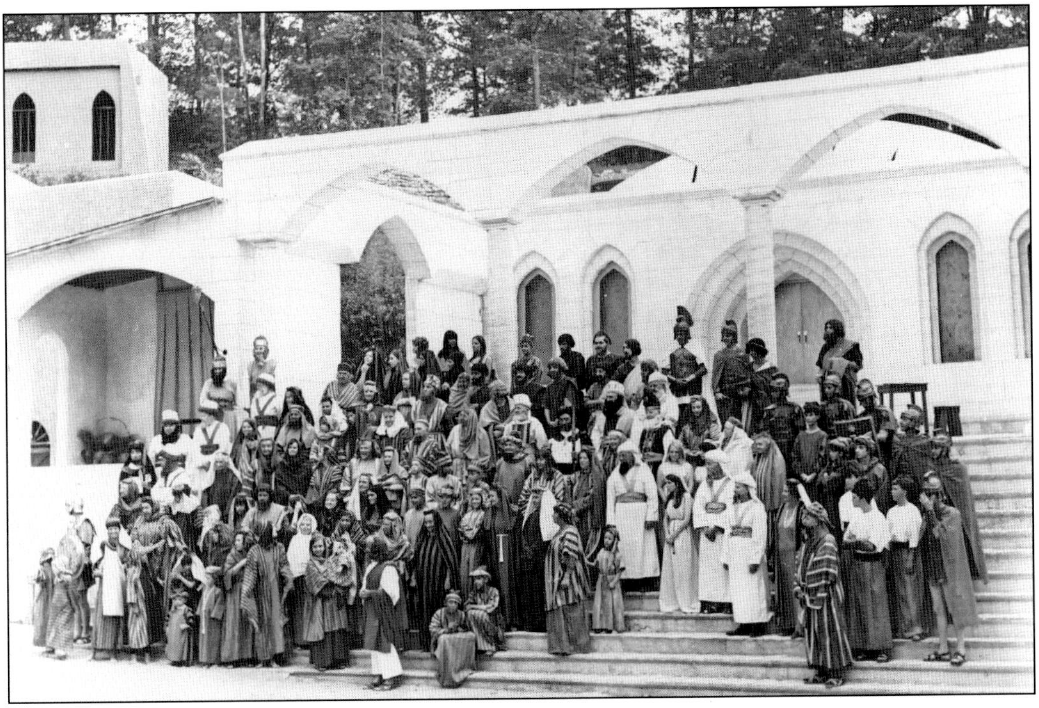

The first cast represented a logistical triumph. Within in a year, a stage and set were carved out of the mountain, costumes were created from scratch, amateur actors were chosen and trained, animals were purchased and housed, sound equipment was installed, and a soundtrack was recorded. The Elna M. Smith Foundation was extremely proud of these accomplishments and heralded the play's opening on July 14, 1968.

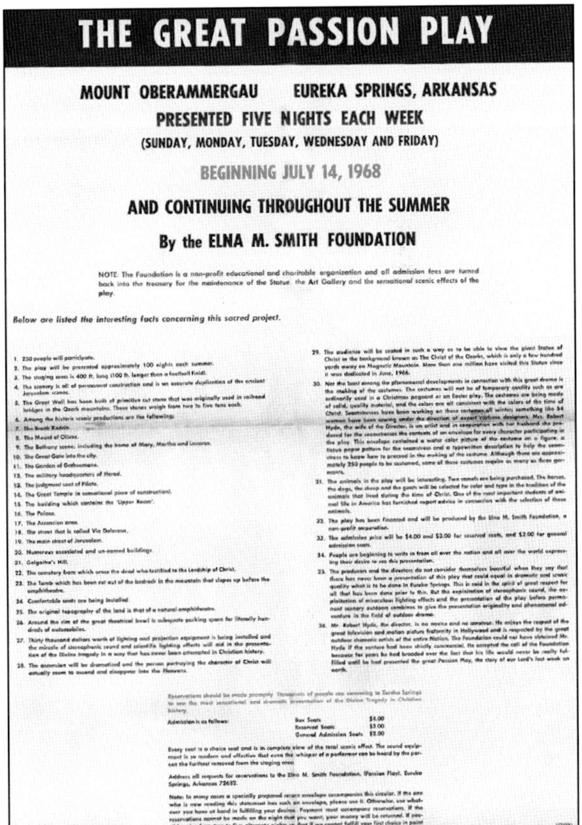

THE GREAT PASSION PLAY

MOUNT OBERAMMERGAU EUREKA SPRINGS, ARKANSAS

PRESENTED FIVE NIGHTS EACH WEEK

(SUNDAY, MONDAY, TUESDAY, WEDNESDAY AND FRIDAY)

BEGINNING JULY 14, 1968

AND CONTINUING THROUGHOUT THE SUMMER

By the ELNA M. SMITH FOUNDATION

NOTE: The Foundation is a non-profit educational and charitable organization and all admission fees are turned back into the treasury for the maintenance of the Statue, the Art Gallery and the sensational scenic effects of the play.

Below are listed the interesting facts concerning this sacred project.

1. 250 people will participate.
2. The play will be presented approximately 100 nights each summer.
3. The staging area is 400 ft. long (100 ft. longer than a football field).
4. The scenery is all of permanent construction and is an accurate duplication of the ancient Jerusalem scenes.
5. The Great Wall has been built of primitive cut stone that was originally used in railroad bridges in the Ozark mountains. These stones weigh from two to five tons each.
6. Among the historic scenic productions are the following:
7. The Brook Kedron.
8. The Mount of Olives.
9. The Bethany scene; including the home of Mary, Martha and Lazarus.
10. The Great Gate into the city.
11. The Garden of Gethsemane.
12. The military headquarters of Herod.
13. The judgment seat of Pilate.
14. The Great Temple (a sensational piece of construction).
15. The building which contains the 'Upper Room'.
16. The Palace.
17. The Ascension area.
18. The street that is called Via Dolorosa.
19. The main street of Jerusalem.
20. Numerous associated and un-named buildings.
21. Golgotha's Hill.
22. The cemetery from which arose the dead who testified to the Lordship of Christ.
23. The Tomb which has been cut out of the bedrock in the mountain that slopes up before the amphitheatre.
24. Comfortable seats are being installed.
25. The original topography of the land is that of a natural amphitheatre.
26. Around the rim of the great theatrical bowl is adequate parking space for literally hundreds of automobiles.
27. Thirty thousand dollars worth of lighting and projection equipment is being installed and the miracle of stereophonic sound and scientific lighting effects will aid in the presentation of the Divine tragedy in a way that has never been attempted in Christian history.
28. The ascension will be dramatized and the person portraying the character of Christ will actually seem to ascend and disappear into the Heavens.
29. The audience will be seated in such a way as to be able to view the giant Statue of Christ in the background known as The Christ of the Ozarks, which is only a few hundred yards away on Magnetic Mountain. More than one million have visited this Statue since it was dedicated in June, 1966.
30. Not the least among the phenomenal developments in connection with this great drama is the making of the costumes. The costumes will not be of temporary quality such as are ordinarily used in a Christmas pageant or an Easter play. The costumes are being made of solid, quality material, and the colors are all consistent with the colors of the time of Christ. Seamstresses have been working on these costumes all winter; something like 54 women have been sewing under the direction of expert costume designers. Mrs. Robert Hyde, the wife of the Director, is an artist and in cooperation with her husband she produced for the seamstresses the contents of an envelope for every character participating in the play. This envelope contained a water color picture of the costume on a figure, a tissue paper pattern for the seamstress and a typewritten description to help the seamstress to know how to proceed in the making of the costume. Although there are approximately 250 people to be costumed, some of these costumes require as many as three garments.
31. The animals in the play will be interesting. Two camels are being purchased. The horses, the dogs, the sheep and the goats will be selected for color and type in the tradition of the animals that lived during the time of Christ. One of the most important students of animal life in America has furnished expert advice in connection with the selection of these animals.
32. The play has been financed and will be produced by the Elna M. Smith Foundation, a non-profit corporation.
33. The admission price will be $4.00 and $3.00 for reserved seats, and $2.00 for general admission seats.
34. People are beginning to write in from all over the nation and all over the world expressing their desire to see this presentation.
35. The producers and the directors do not consider themselves boastful when they say that there has never been a presentation of this play that could equal in dramatic and scenic quality what is to be done in Eureka Springs. This is said in the spirit of great respect for all that has been done prior to this. But the exploitation of stereophonic sound, the exploitation of miraculous lighting effects and the presentation of the play before permanent scenery outdoors combines to give the presentation originality and phenomenal adventure in the field of outdoor drama.
36. Mr. Robert Hyde, the director, is no novice and no amateur. He enjoys the respect of the great television and motion picture fraternity in Hollywood and is respected by the great outdoor dramatic artists of the entire Nation. The Foundation could not have obtained Mr. Hyde if the venture had been strictly commercial. He accepted the call of the Foundation because for years he had brooded over the fact that his life would never be really fulfilled until he had presented the great Passion Play, the story of our Lord's last week on earth.

Reservations should be made promptly. Thousands of people are streaming to Eureka Springs to see the most sensational and dramatic presentation of the Divine Tragedy in Christian history.

Admission is as follows:

Box Seats	$4.00
Reserved Seats	$3.00
General Admission Seats	$2.00

Every seat is a choice seat and is in complete view of the total scenic effect. The sound equipment is so modern and effective that even the whisper of a performer can be heard by the person the furthest removed from the staging area.

Address all requests for reservations to the Elna M. Smith Foundation, (Passion Play), Eureka Springs, Arkansas 72632.

Note: In many cases a specially prepared return envelope accompanies this circular. If the one who is now reading this statement has such an envelope, please use it. Otherwise, use whatever you have at hand in fulfilling your desires. Payment must accompany reservations. If the reservations cannot be made on the night that you want, your money will be returned. If possible, give from two to five alternate nights so that if we cannot fulfill your first choice in point of time we can send you reservations for one of the alternate dates.

(OVER)

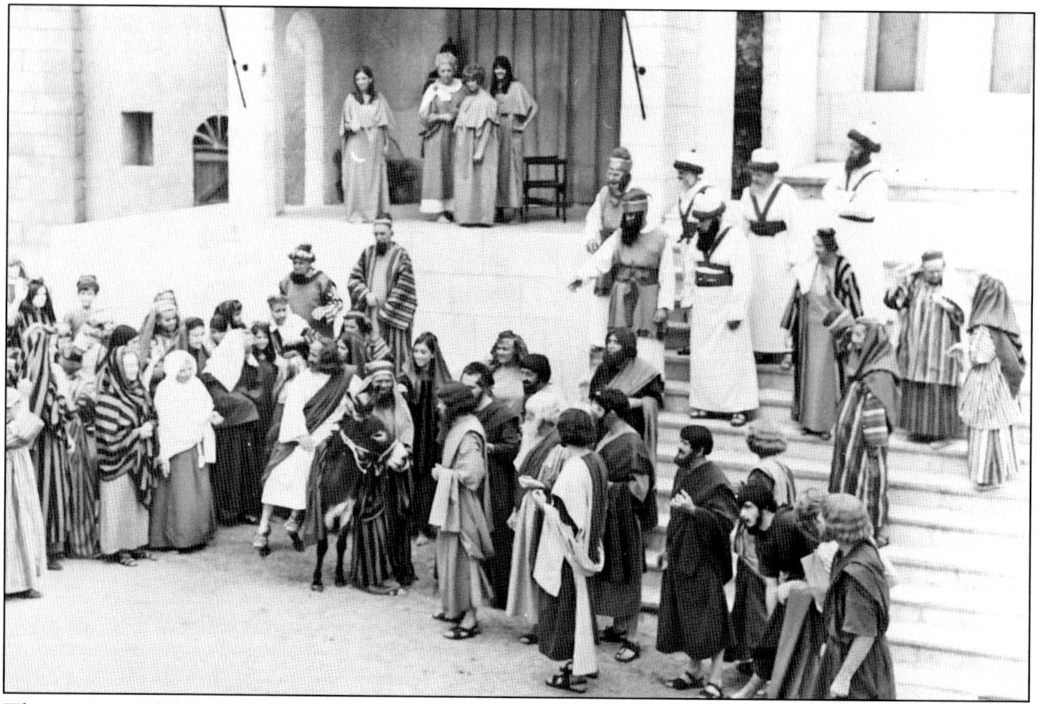

The staging of the Passion play requires enormous coordination, especially for the street scenes. Years after the original vision, various special effects were added, including ascension wires. However, the original challenge was simply organizing the various elements. Even moving from one part of the set to the next required special attention.

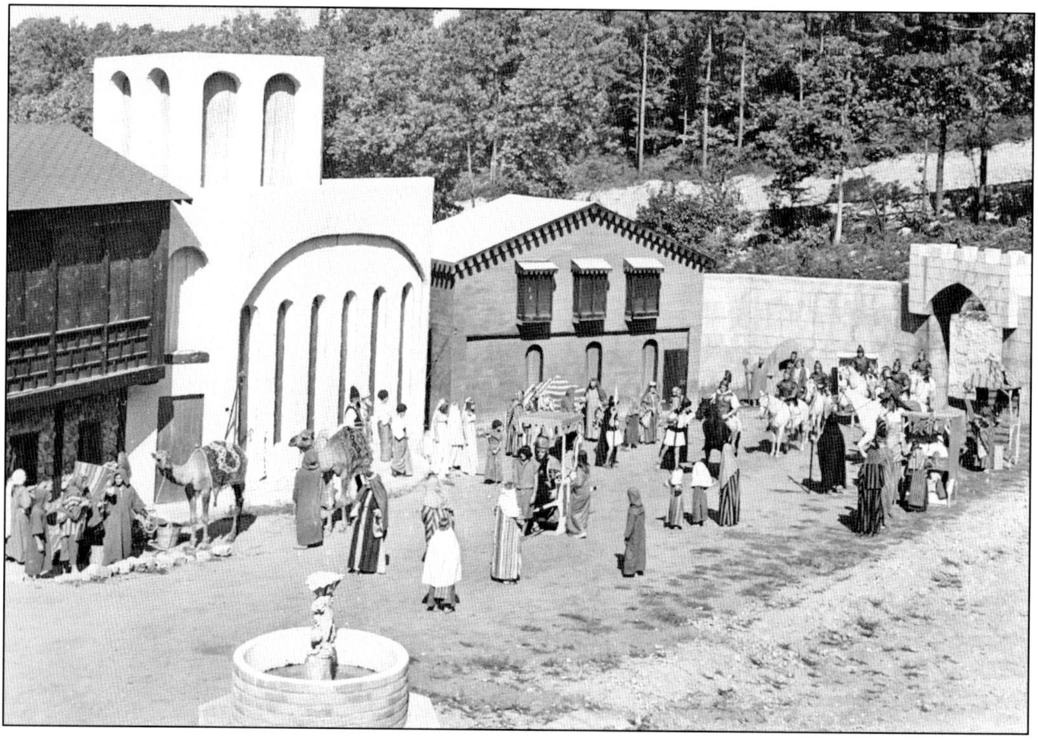

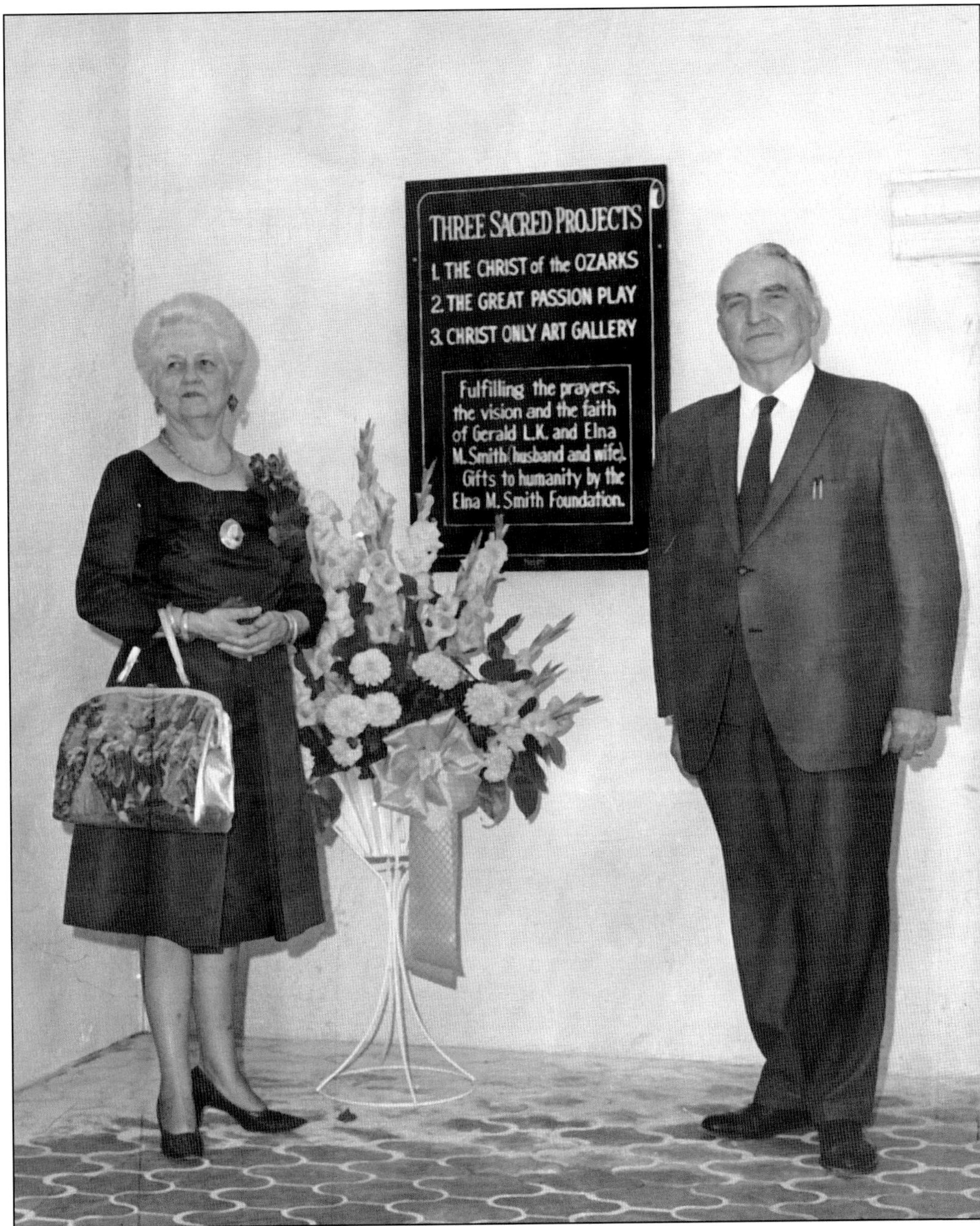

Opening night was a proud moment for the Smiths. Their vision and sponsorship were fulfilled. At the time of this picture, it was pouring rain, but by the time of the performance, the skies had cleared.

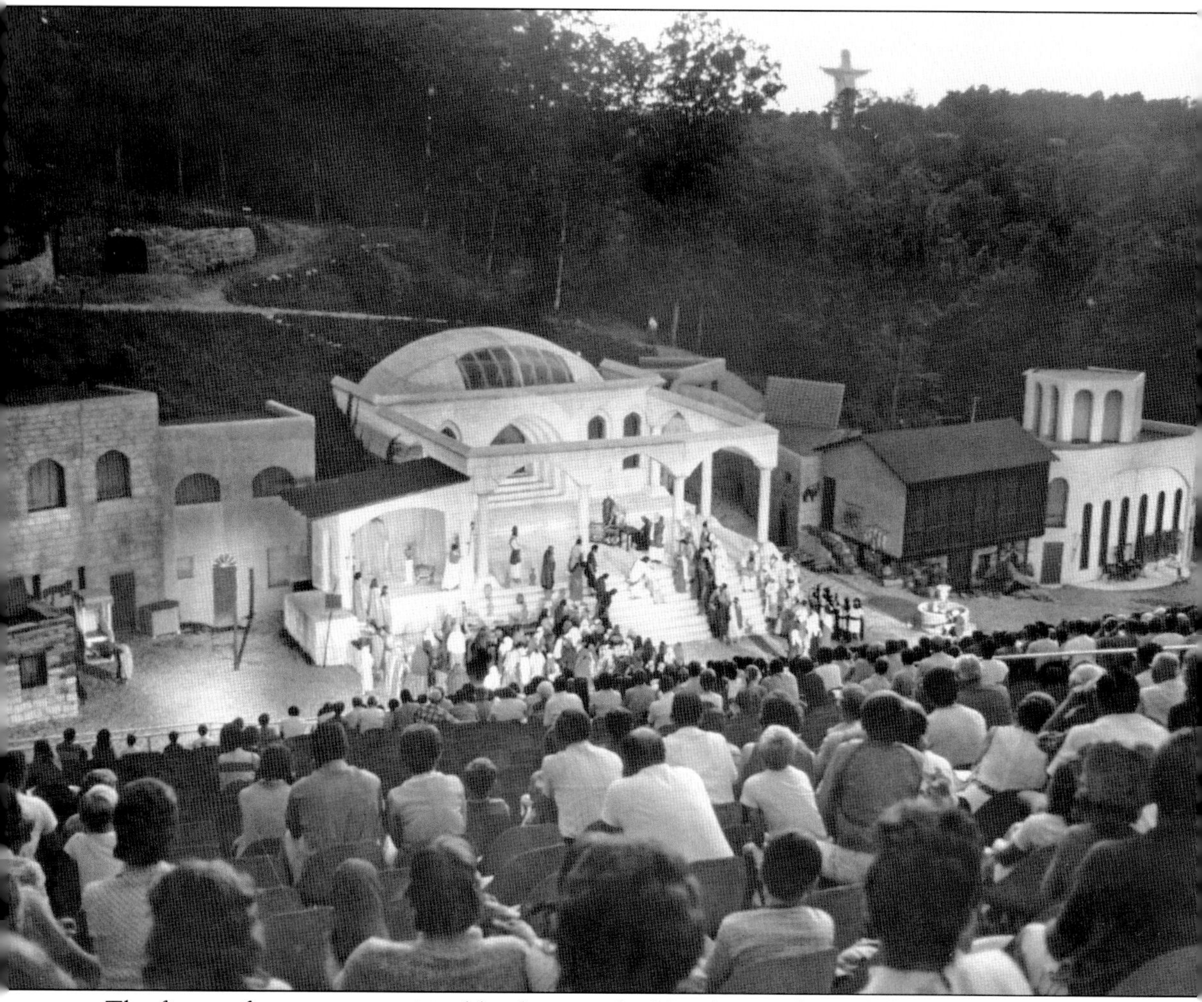

The first performance was visited by distinguished locals, members of the national press, and the genuinely curious. One commentator was quoted, "It is the greatest thing by far of its kind. In fact, it is the only thing of its kind."

Three

Forty Years of Production

The Great Passion Play and its first decade of production were supervised by Robert Hyde. Since that time, numerous changes have occurred. There were three major script changes, as well as multiple new recordings. Nineteen different actors have portrayed Christ. The set was redesigned, and special effects evolved from basic props to elaborate mechanical devices. In short, *The Great Passion Play* continues to develop and evolve as a modern production.

What has not changed is the genius of Elna M. Smith Foundation employees. Local talent continues to be the bedrock of *The Great Passion Play*'s success. *The Great Passion Play* workshop produces props, set changes, special effects, new technology, and general maintenance. It is also local workers who are responsible for the care of livestock, including camels, donkeys, a small flock of sheep, pigeons, and horses.

The Passion play would not be possible without creative ability and ingenuity. Most cast members also serve as technical advisors, designers, and craftsman. Scenes change depending on the cast members who happen to be playing the role, just as scenes change depending upon whom is operating the special effects. Regardless, the individuals involved produce a high-quality drama that maintains its novel approach to theater. In this regard, change is only natural and is even encouraged as part of the production. During the past 40 years, there have been numerous such changes.

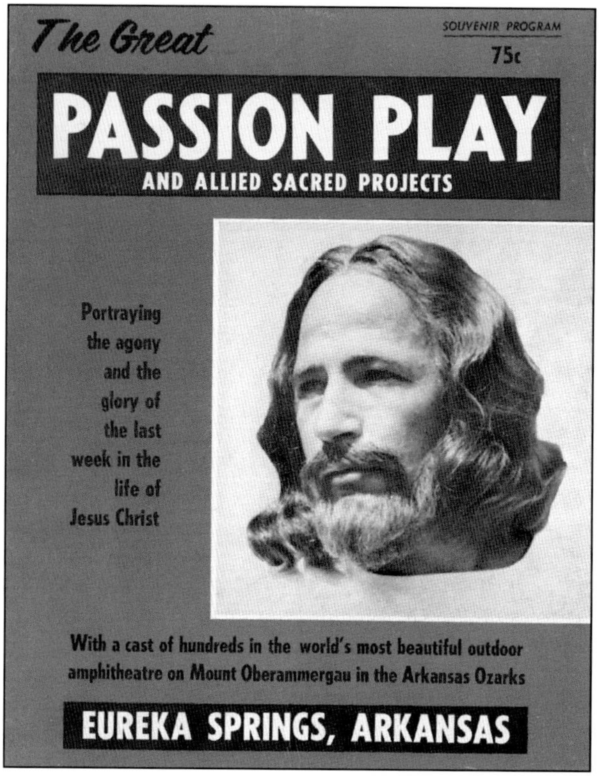

In 40 years, much has changed at the Passion play, and not just the design of the souvenir programs. Robert Hyde was the first Christ figure, and he played the part with only one understudy for more than 10 years. Today there are three Christ figures. However, the unique portrayal of Christ's last week still maintains its novel approach. (Photographs courtesy of Mary Murray.)

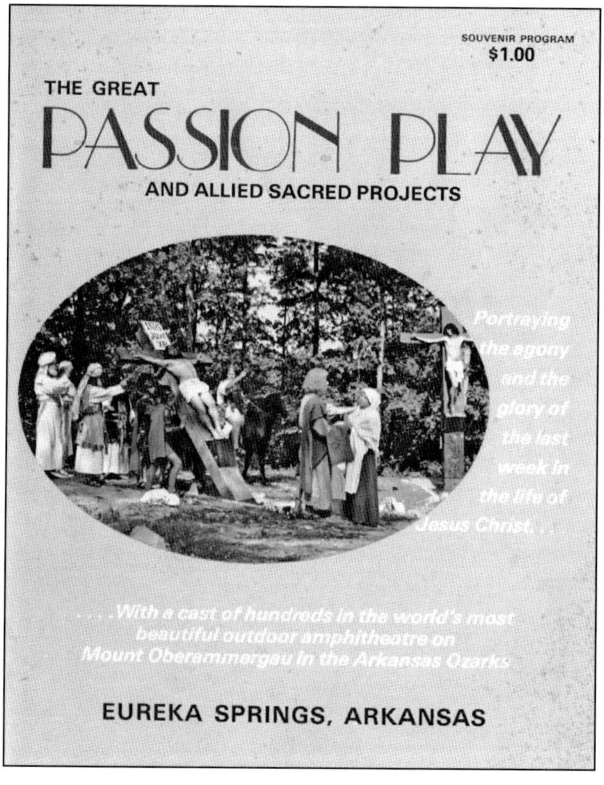

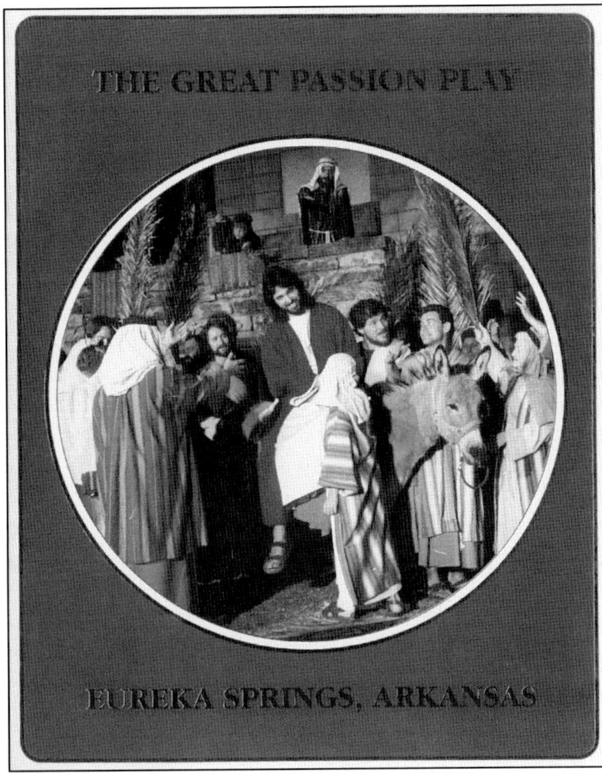

Although the Passion play changes from year to year, depending upon cast members, props, or, in some cases, the soundtrack, current programs still boast of the original, unique elements. They highlight the live action, the exotic animals, and authentic costuming. More importantly, they focus on the Christ figure and the story of his last week on earth.

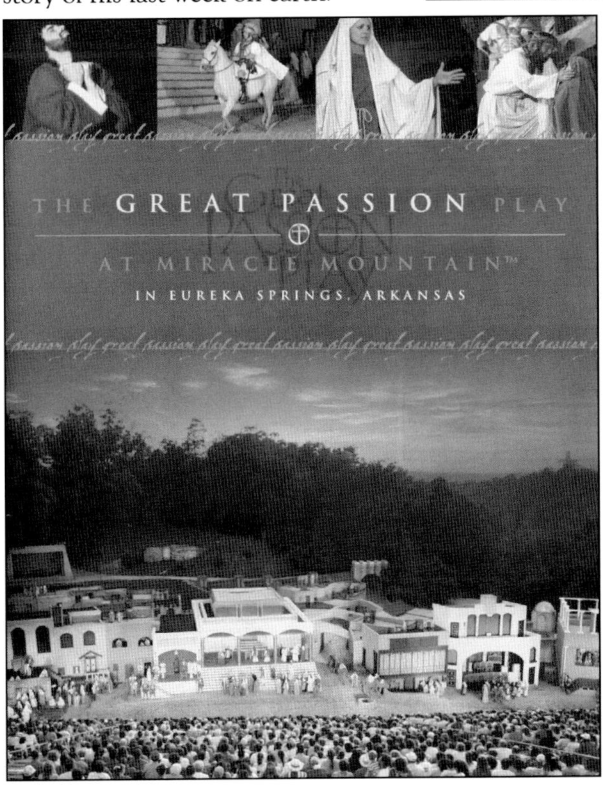

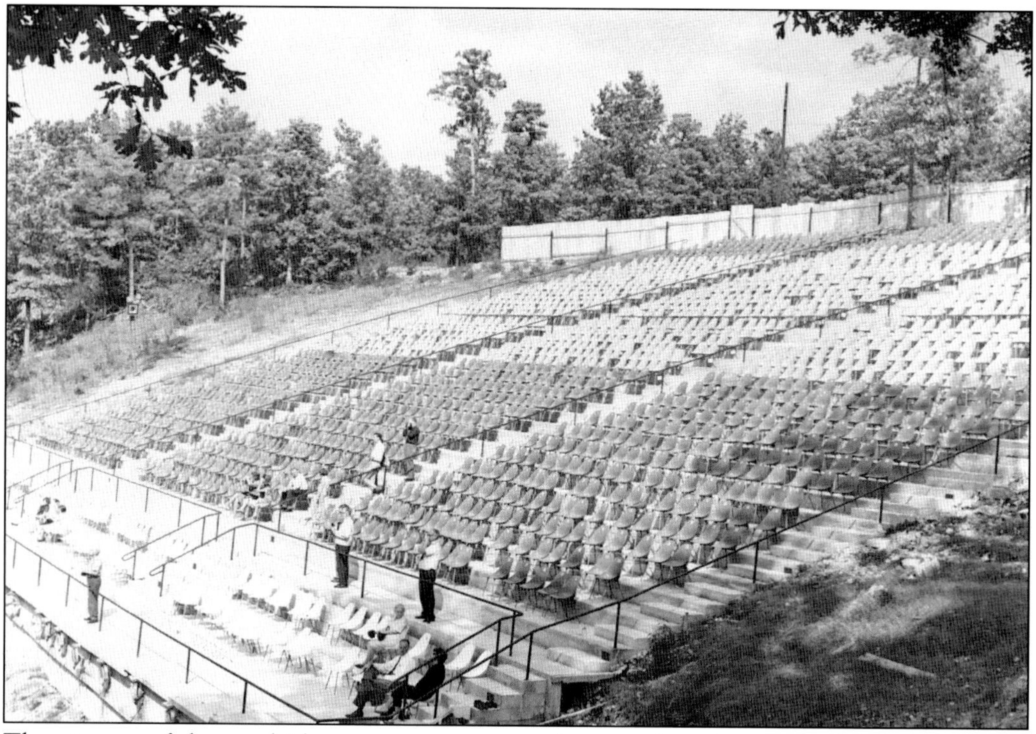

The pictures of the amphitheater seats represent the growth and success of the Passion play. The original theater, pictured above, had three sections and could seat approximately 3,500 attendees. Today's theatre, pictured below, has an added section and can accommodate more than 4,500 visitors.

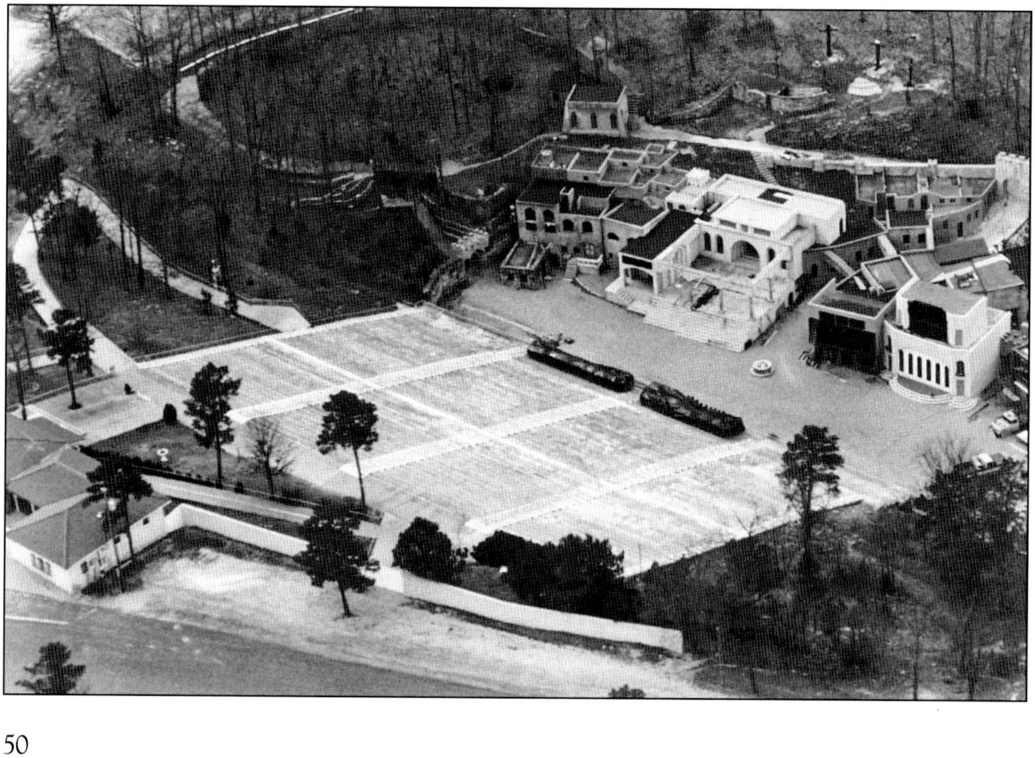

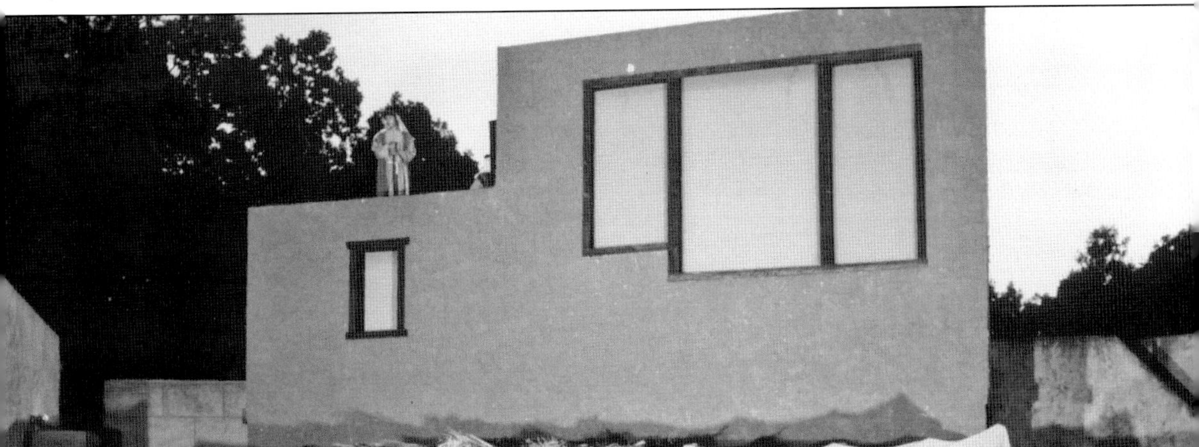

Street scenes and their elaborate props are a major part of the production. In this particular scene, there is a canopy made of palm branches, as well as carts, beggars, baskets, loaves of bread for sale, pottery, merchants, shoppers, and more. Ironically this part of the set no longer exists. In the late 1980s, it was transformed from a market into Herod's porch.

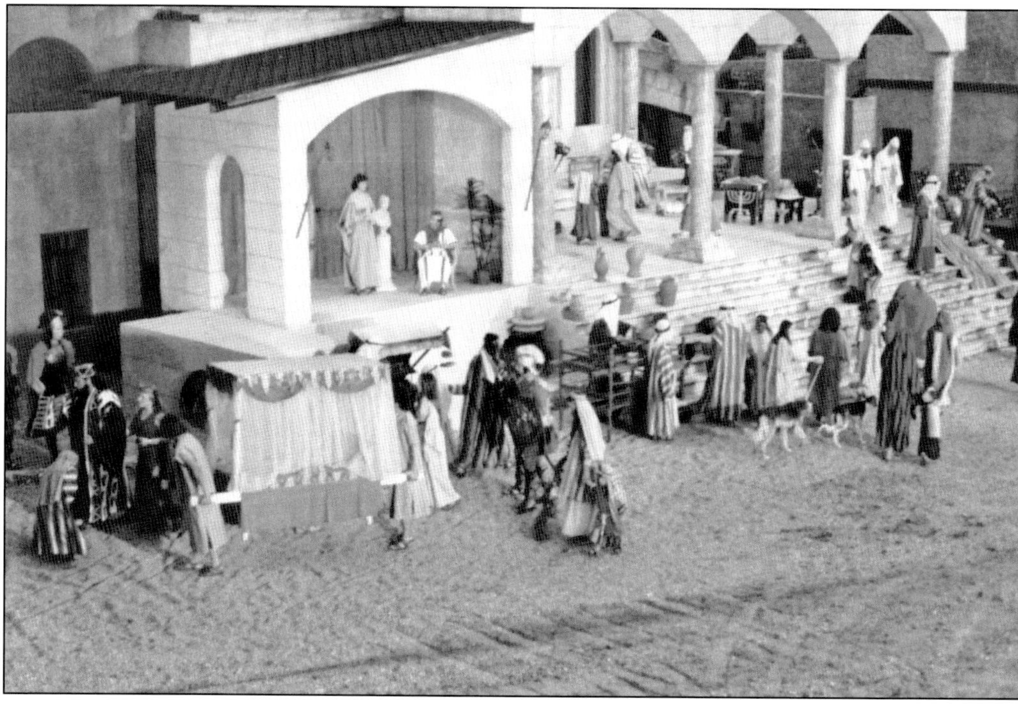

The busy street scenes have transformed themselves over the years. In these two photographs, there are children on camels, a walking Herod, dogs on a leash, and an extra door on Pilate's porch. None of these remain. The camels no longer carry children; Herod now enters the set on a chariot; the dogs were the personal property of cast members; and Pilate's porch was redesigned.

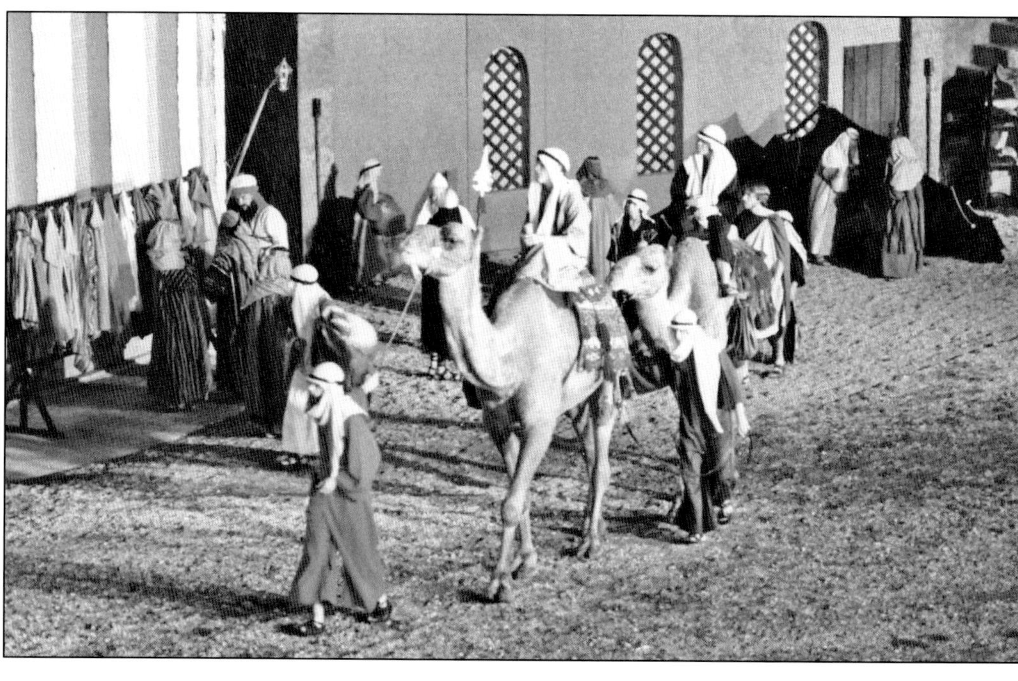

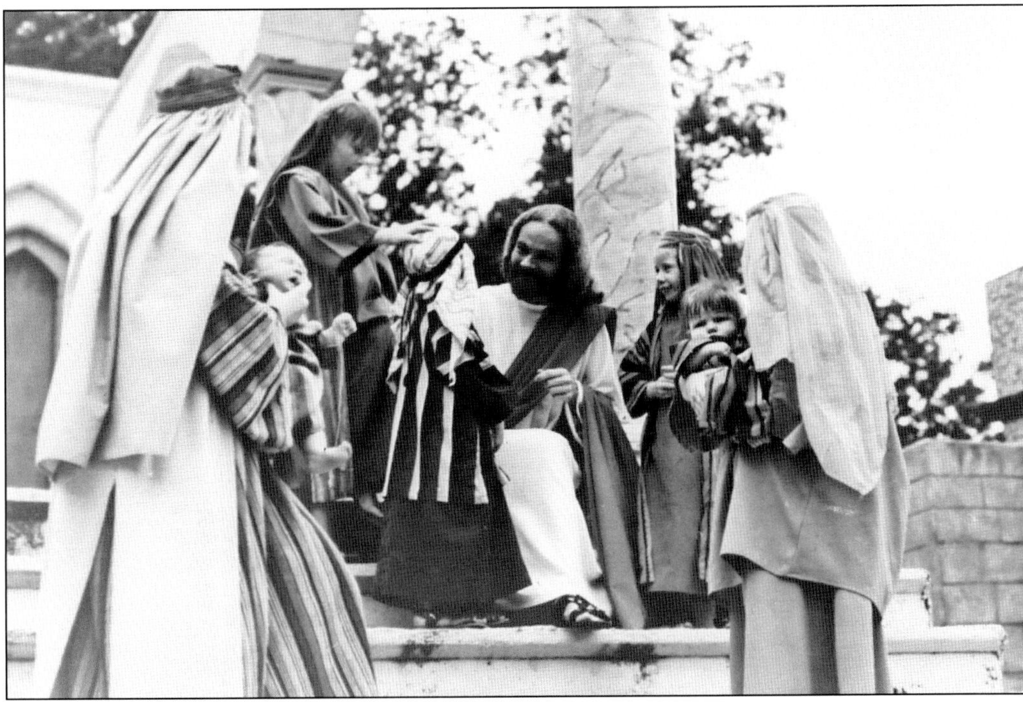

A major component of the Passion play is the establishment of scenes that represent Biblical verses. One of these scenes is Matthew 18:3, which begins, "Unless you become as little Children . . ." It has changed little over the years.

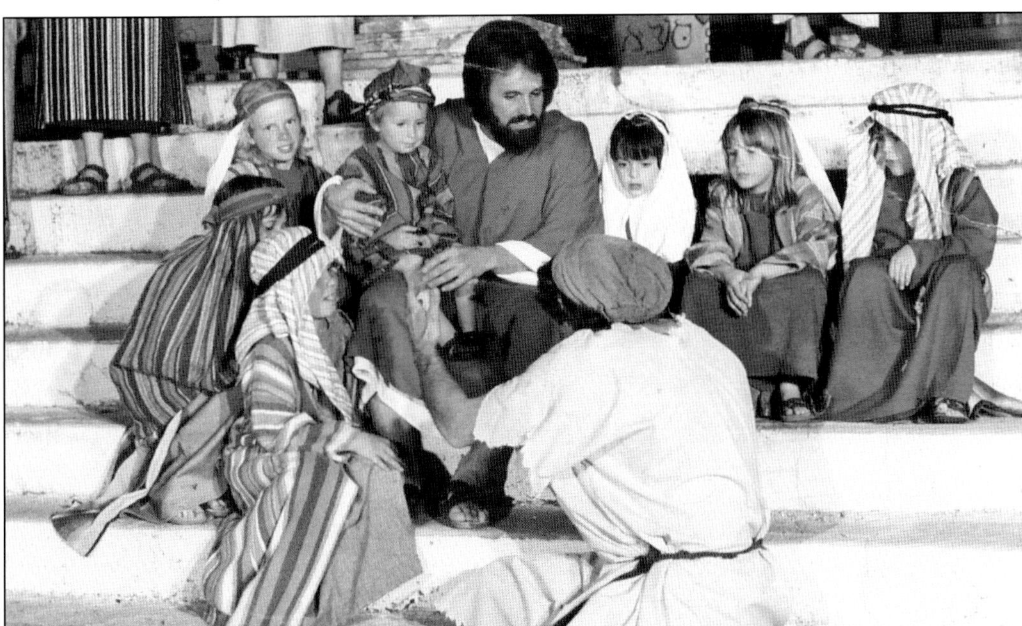

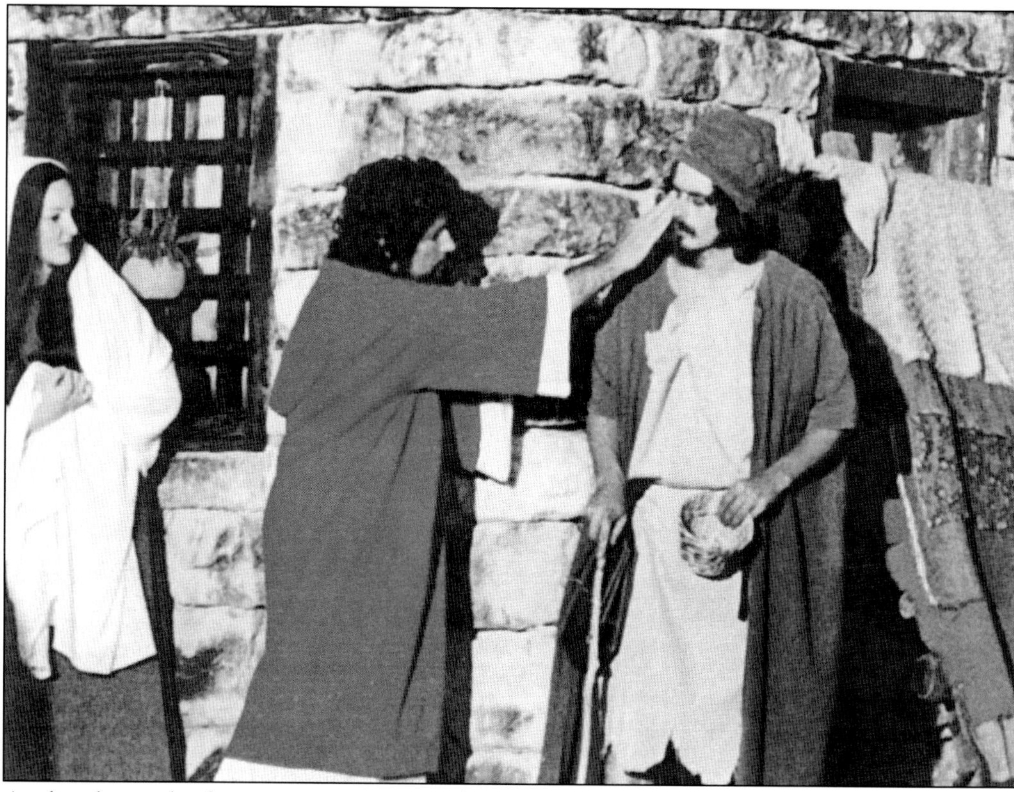

As the play evolved, some scenes necessarily were transformed. Represented in these pictures is the scene of the healing of the blind man. Both scenes, which prominently appeared in souvenir programs, took place on different parts of the set.

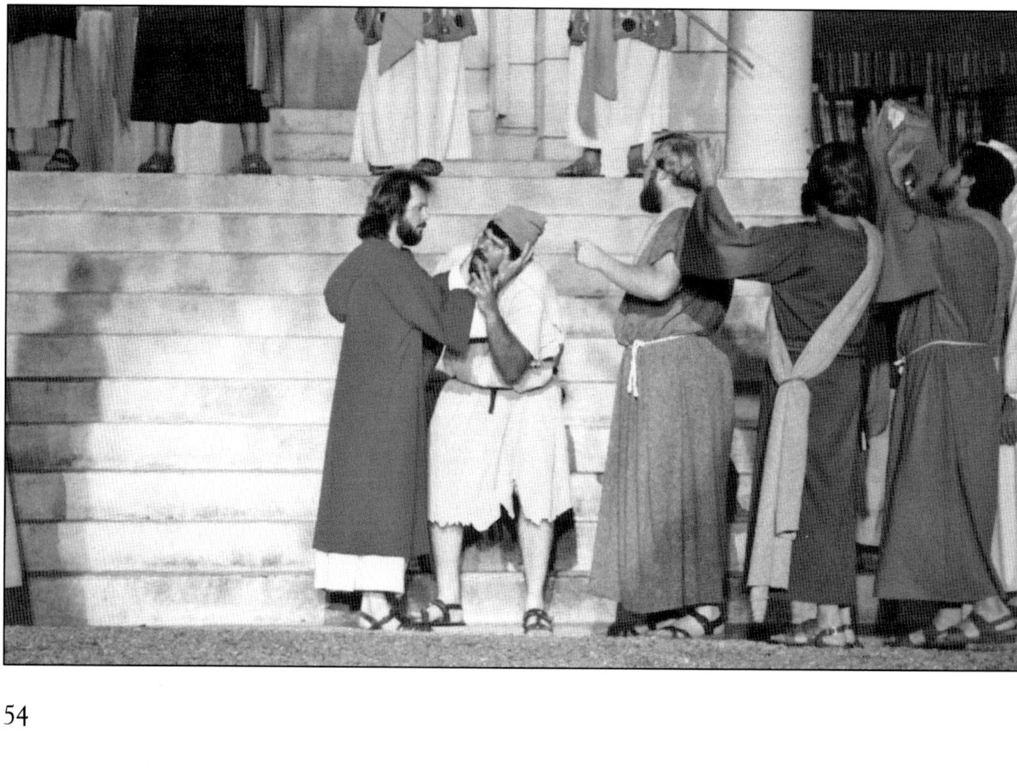

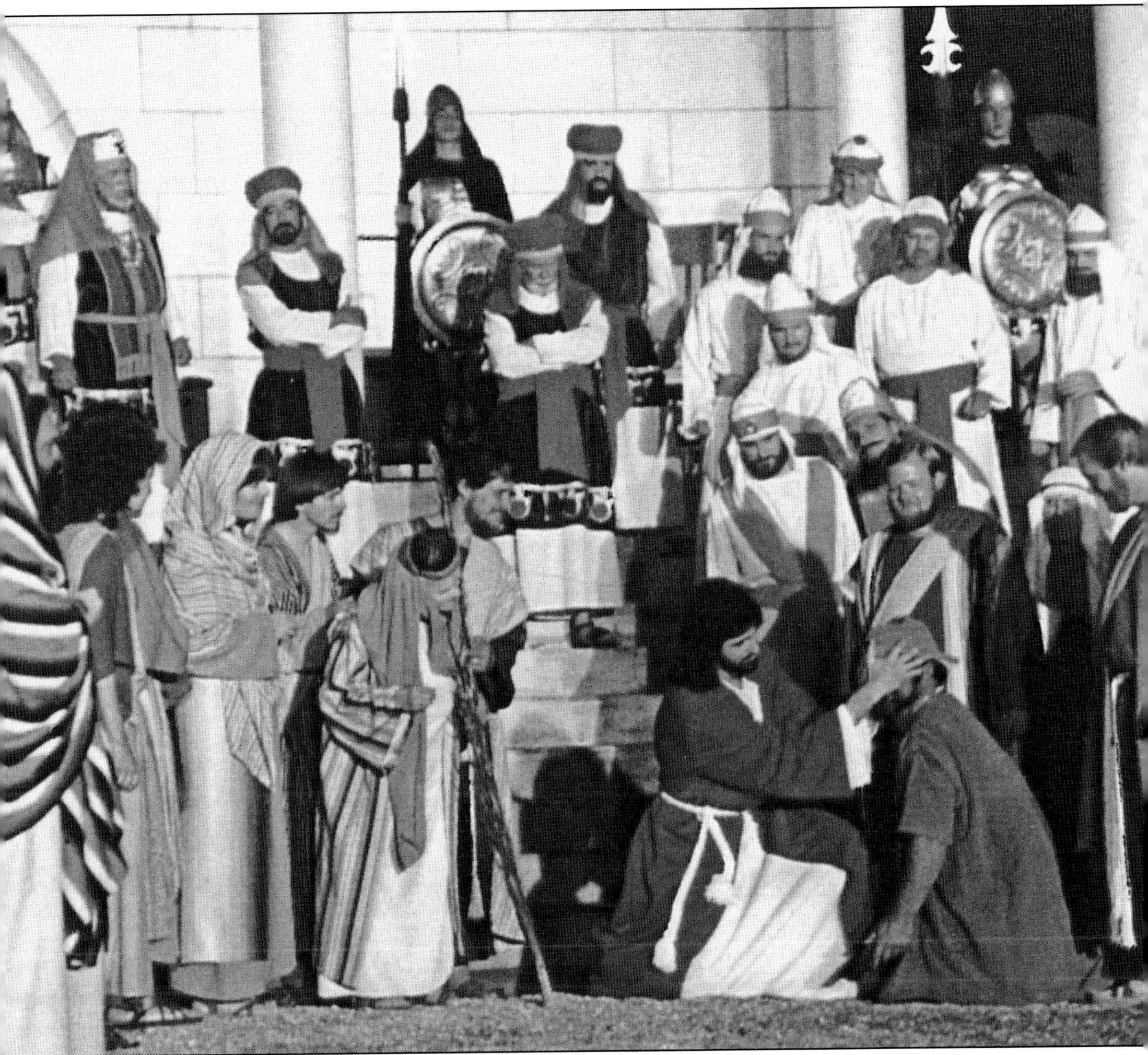

This photograph is another example of how staging changes from year to year. Even more ironic is the fact that the healing of the blind man is no longer even part of the play.

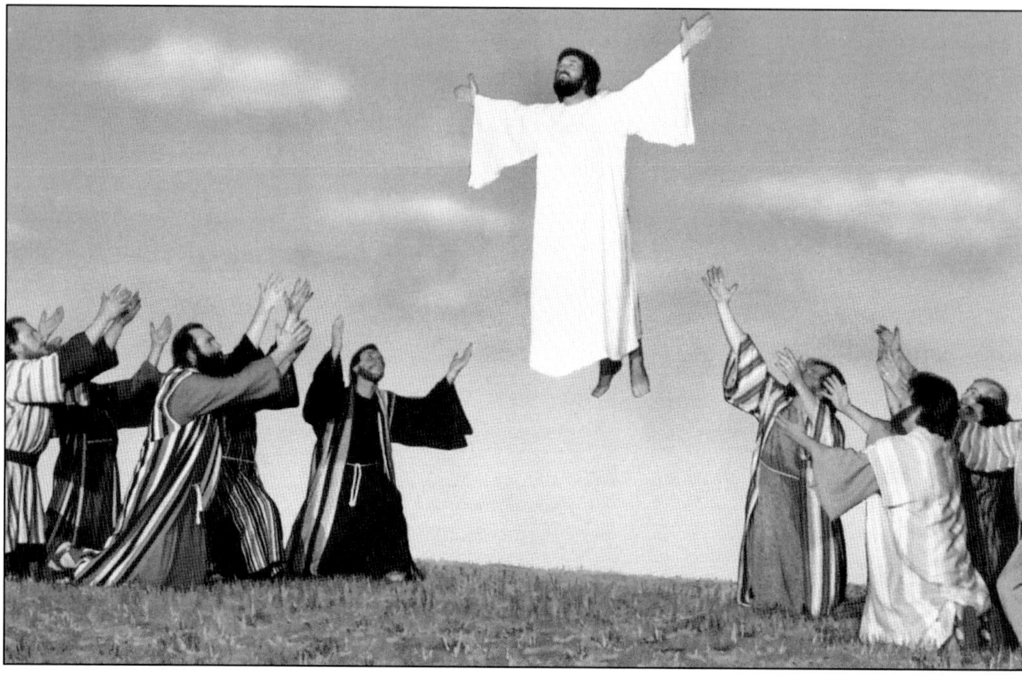

Special effects have to be creatively applied. Promotional materials advertised the ascension of Christ. Initially this happened in an enclosed building on the set. Christ was lifted out of sight behind a special screen, which helped hide the wiring. However, in the 1980s, ascension wires were added to the top portion of the set. Christ is now lifted 40 feet into the air and carried into the trees, where he disappears from sight.

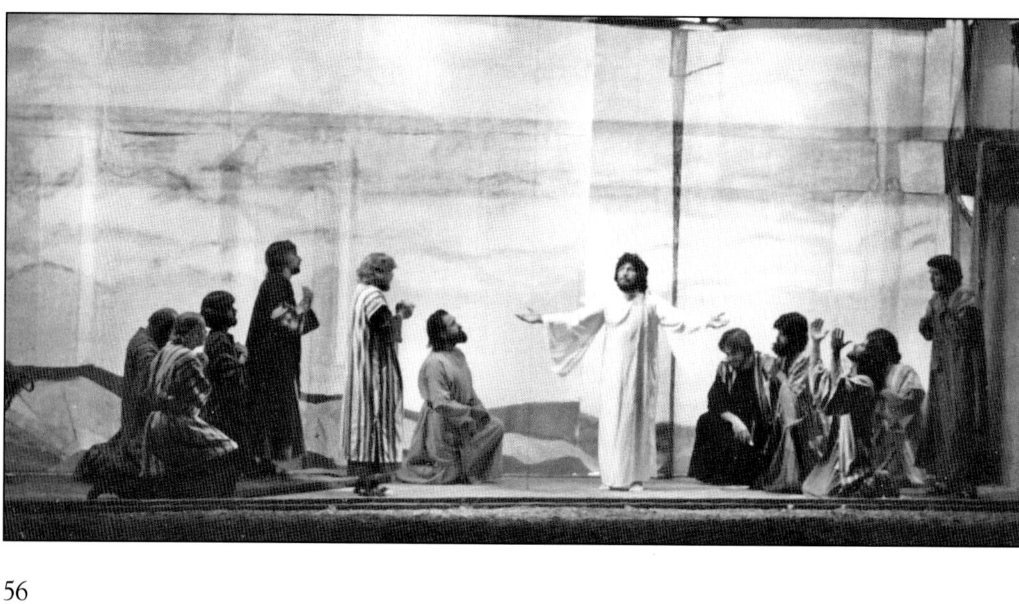

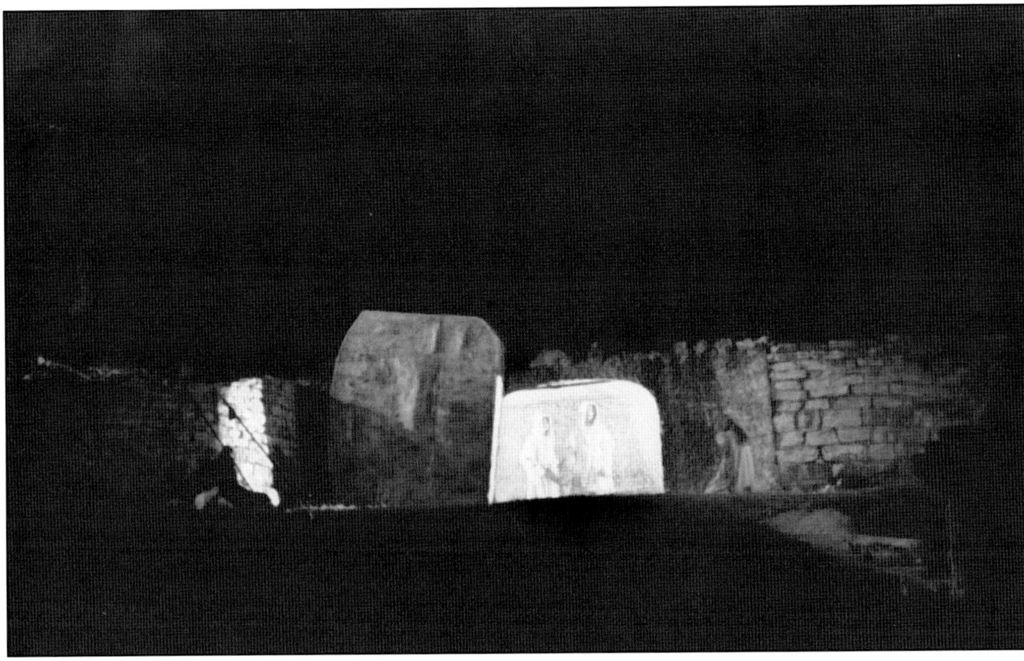

Another special effect that has changed over time is the resurrection. The original tomb was replaced in 1984. Smoke and lighting changes are now frequent, but more importantly, the costuming and position of the angel continues to develop.

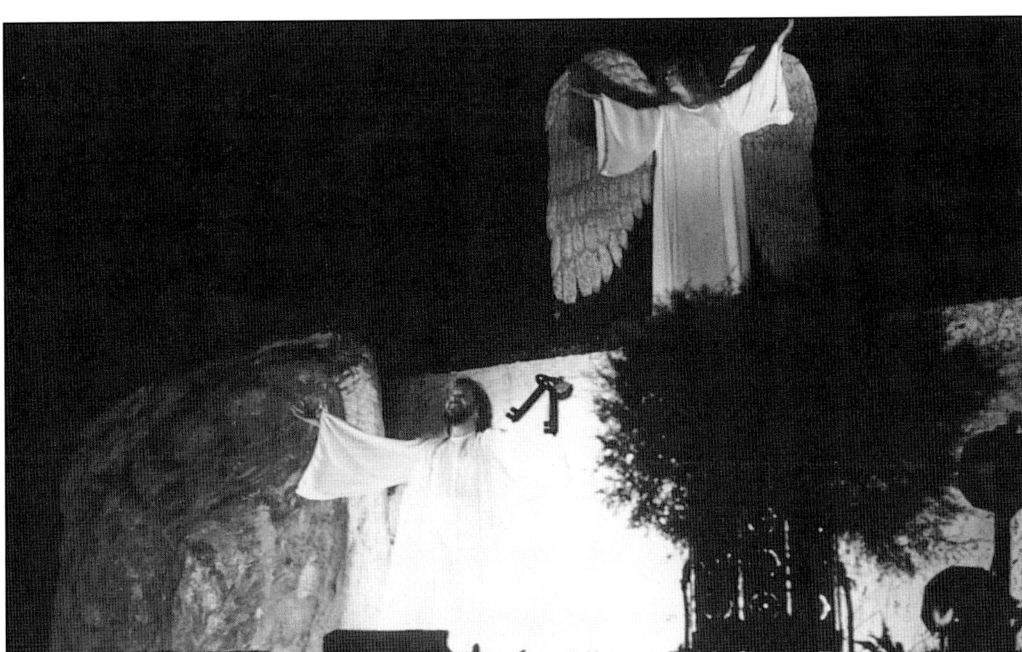

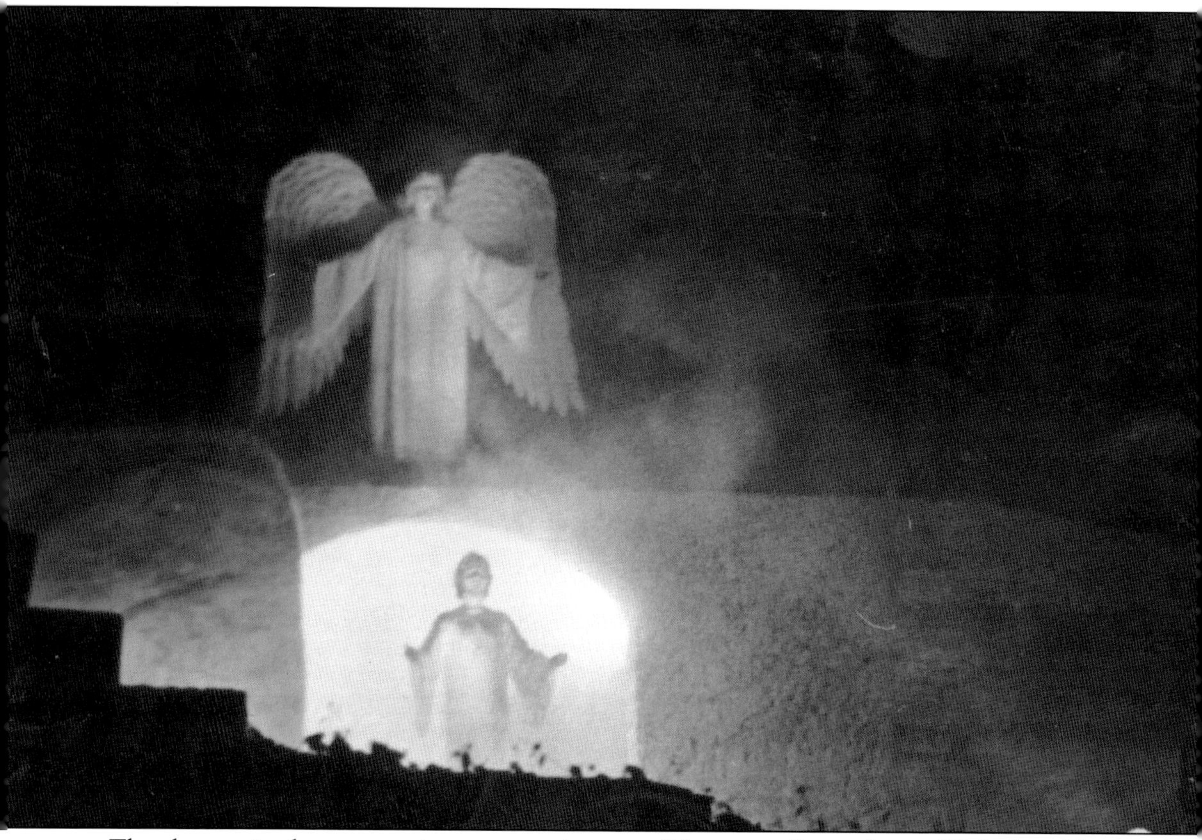

The changes in the resurrection are sometimes small but are still significant. With the addition of smoke and lightening, the soundtrack also had to be adjusted. To portray the miracle, the ground shakes; thunder roles; and sounds of a spiritual struggle can be heard throughout the amphitheater. At that moment, Christ appears.

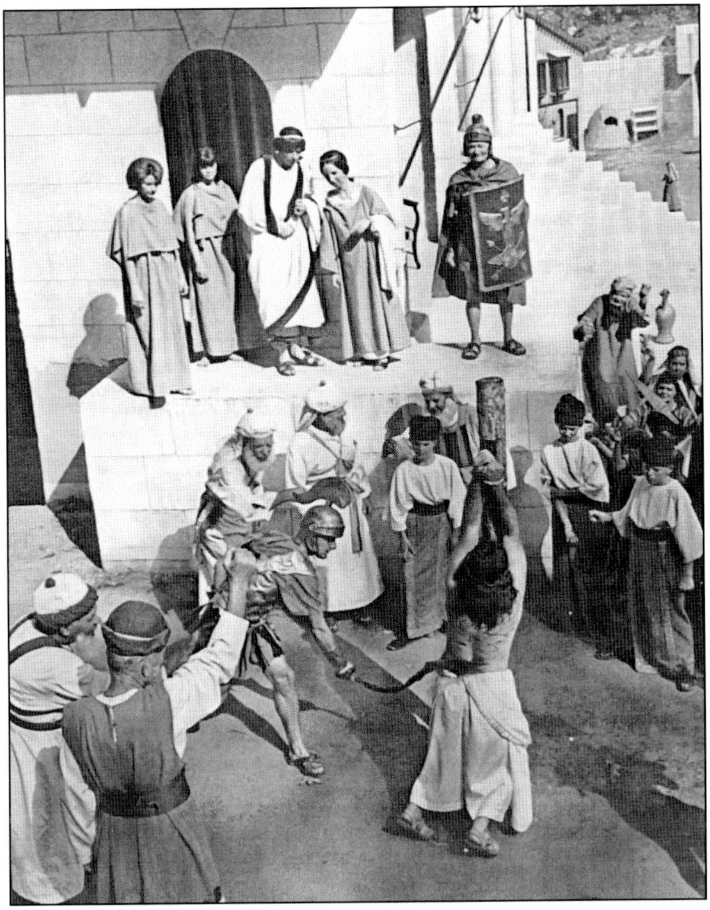

The scourging of Christ requires dramatic timing. The crack of the whip on stage has to match the soundtrack. Furthermore, the makeup representing the Christ figure's scars cannot be revealed until after the appropriate scene. This is usually accomplished with tear away clothing. In some cases, the scars were made with lipstick and smeared by the stage whip.

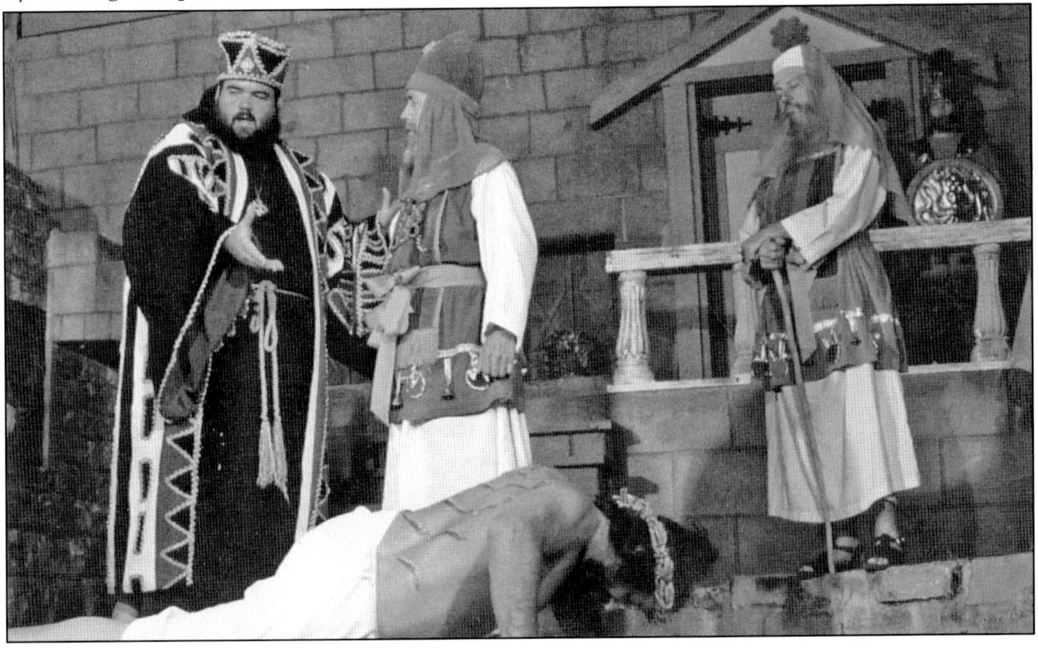

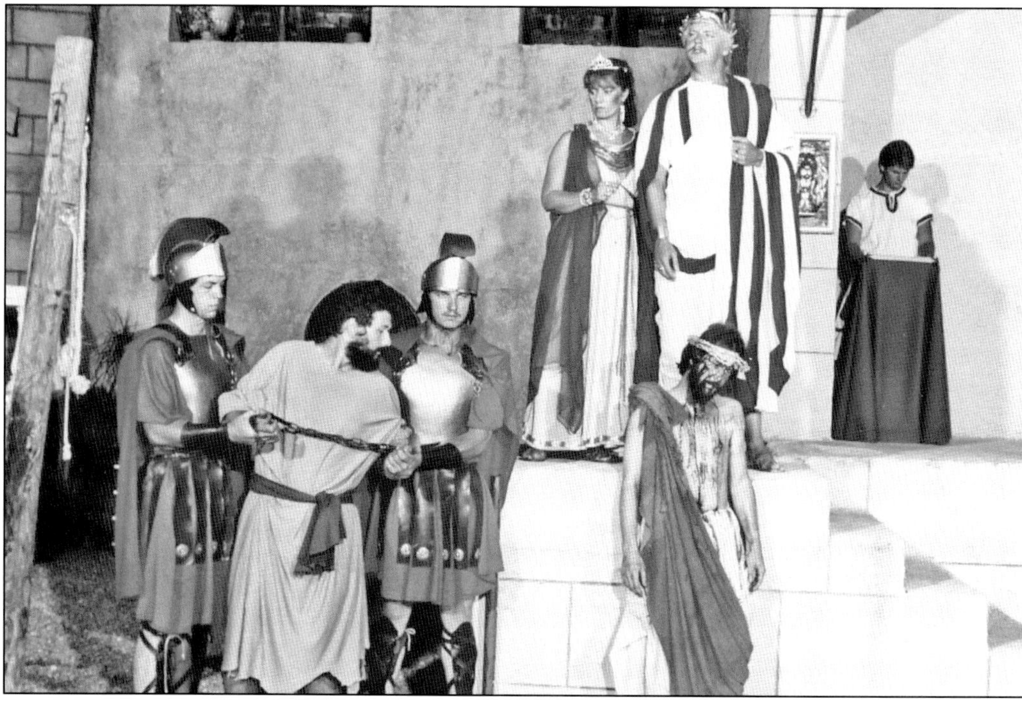

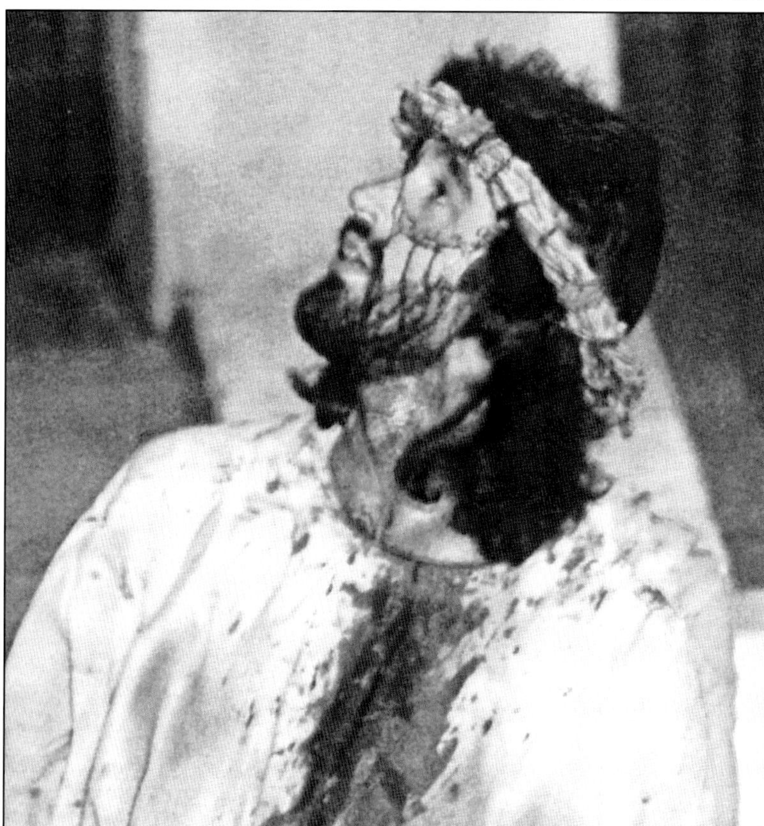

Stage makeup for the abused Christ figure was not added until after decades of production. The blood is rapidly applied backstage. In some cases, as represented below, a pre-stained robe is used. Furthermore, as the Christ figure changes, so does the crown of thorns, which are custom-made for each actor.

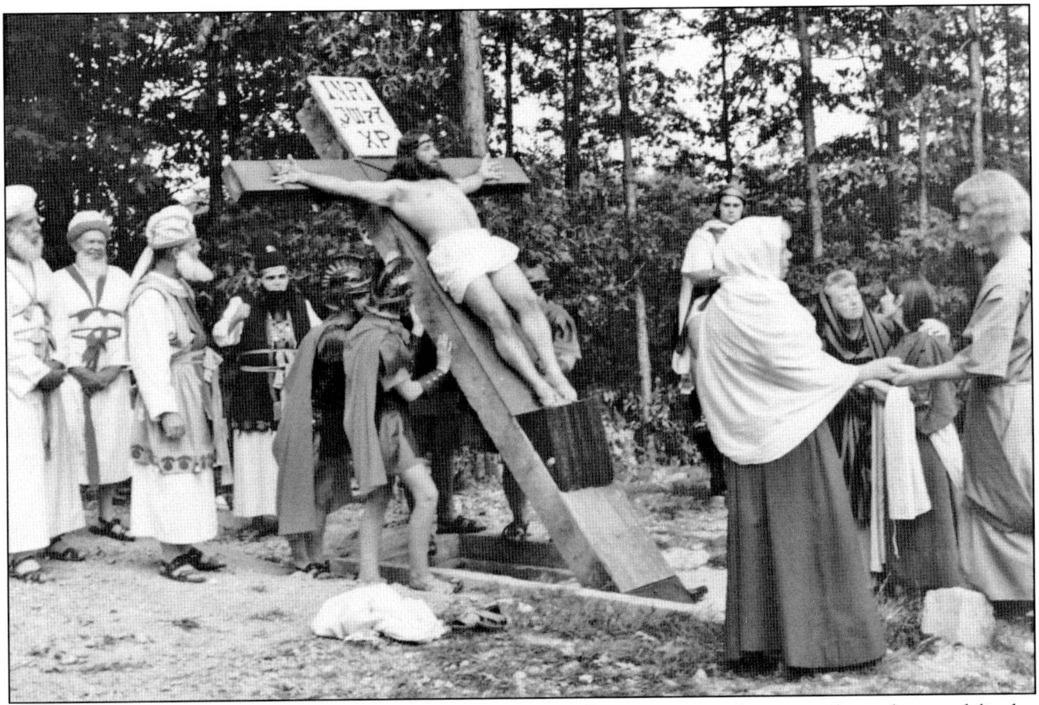

While some scenes have changed numerous times, the scene on the cross has changed little. Makeup and the timing of lines have changed, but the effect is the same. Actors portraying Christ hold on to two nails, and the platform is slightly slanted. The dimensions of the cross have also not changed. Shorter Christ figures have to stretch to the nails and platform. Taller figures have to remain on the cross in a bent fashion.

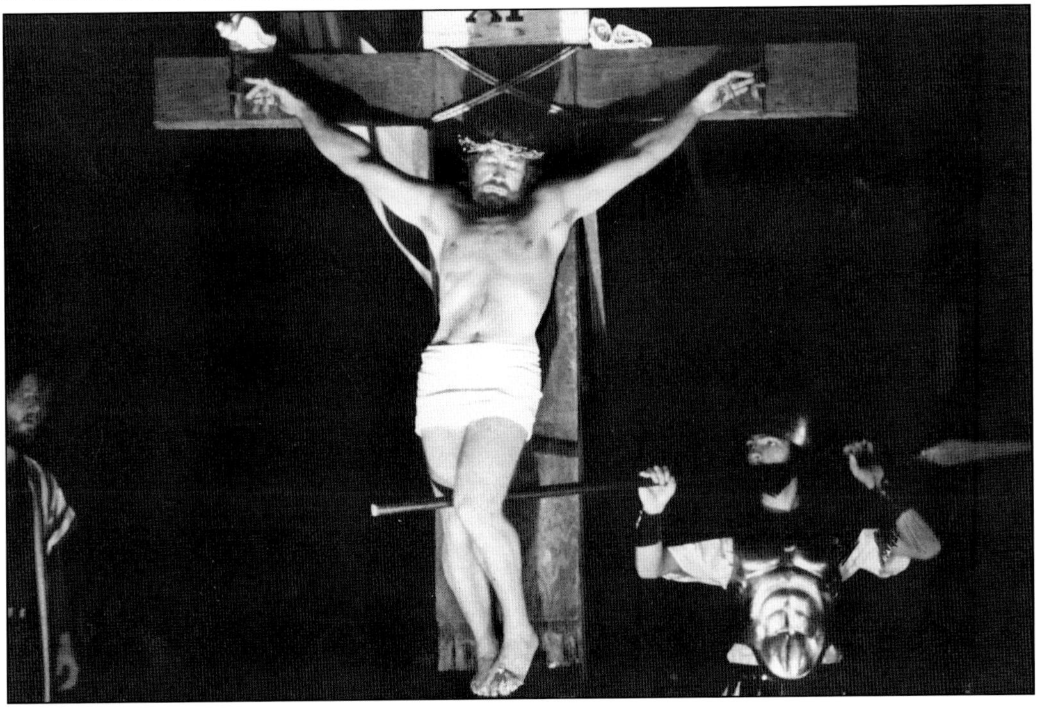

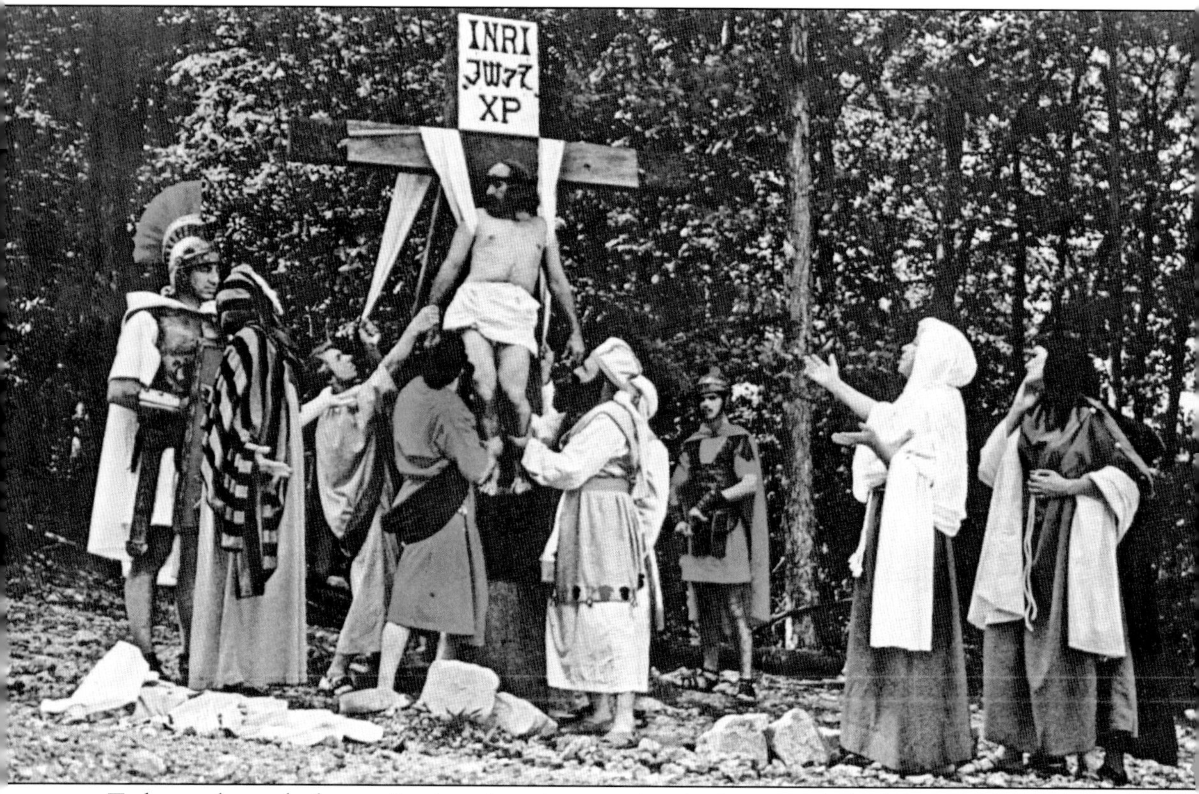

Today at the end of every Passion play, the cross is raised as a symbol of victory. Hanging from the cross are two strips of the white linen that were used to take the Christ figure off of the cross. The design of this effect belongs to the original Christ figure, Robert Hyde.

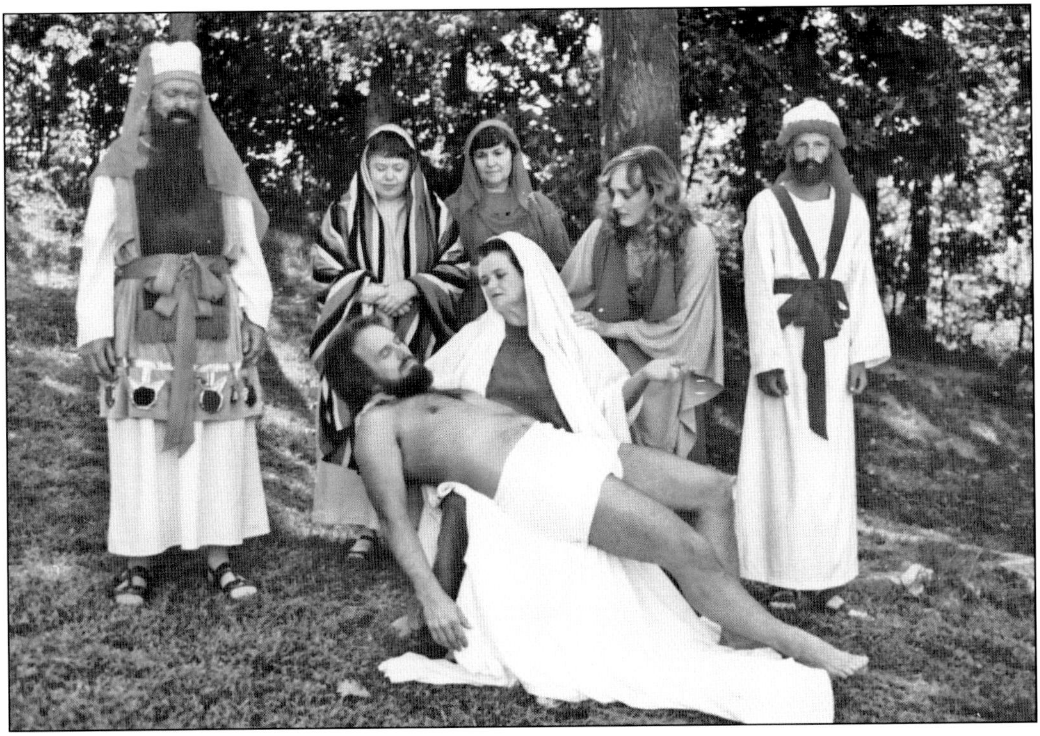

This particular scene was inspired by Michelangelo's *Pieta*. It is another scene that has changed little over the decades.

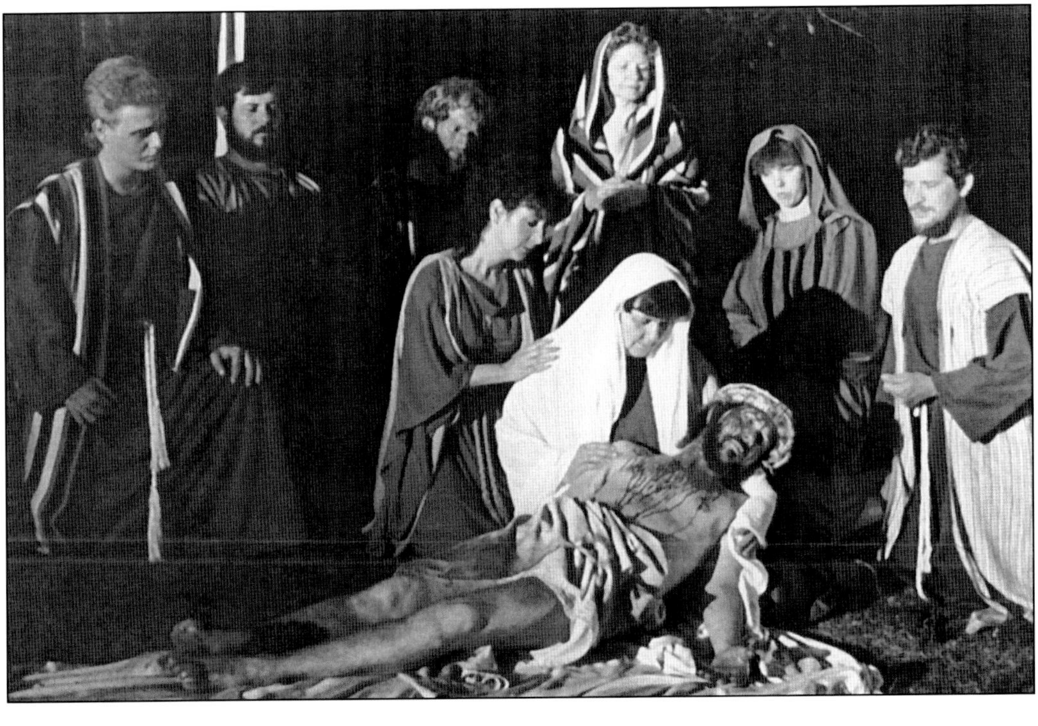

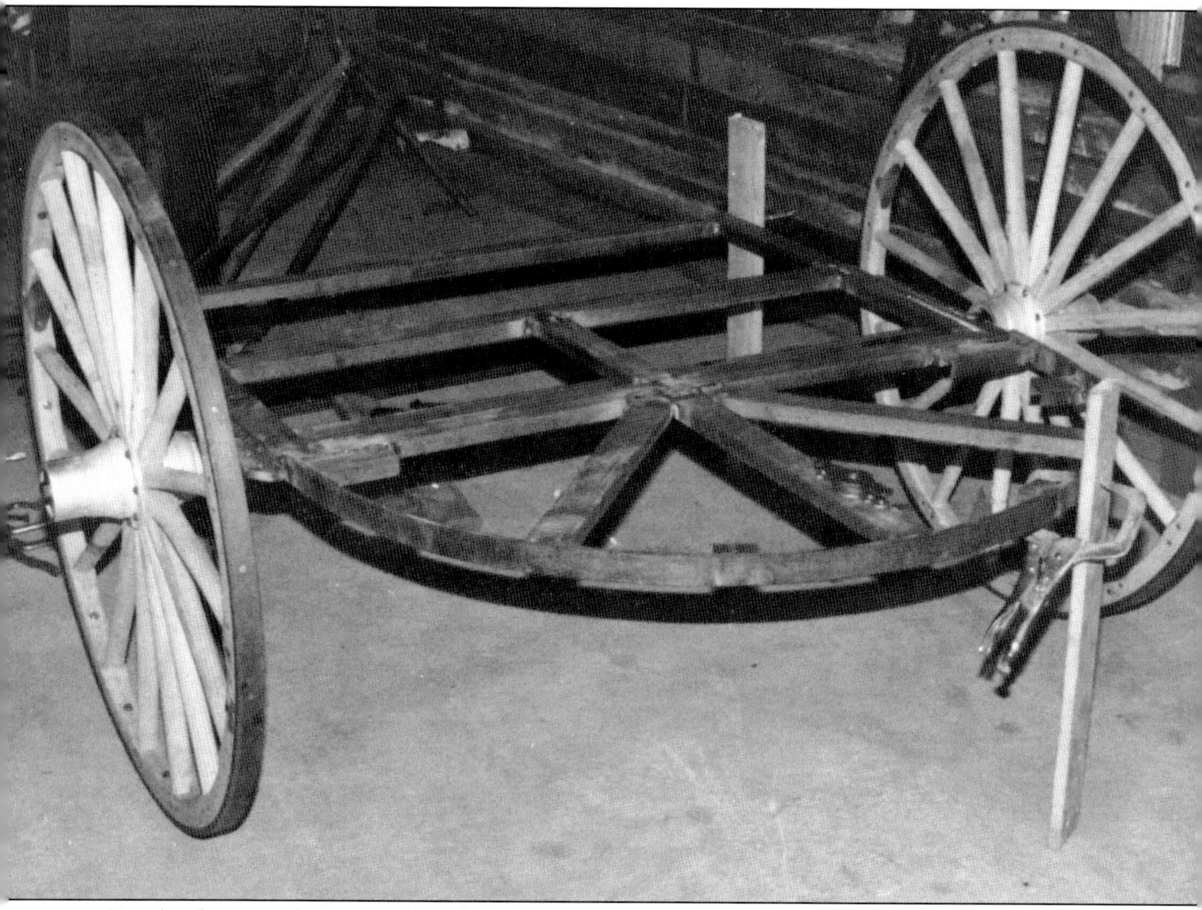

Besides the critical staging of the play, major additions were added in the area of props. Among these additions was Pilate's chariot, which was designed and produced in the workshop of the Elna M. Smith Foundation. In fact, most of the props have been custom-built by foundation employees.

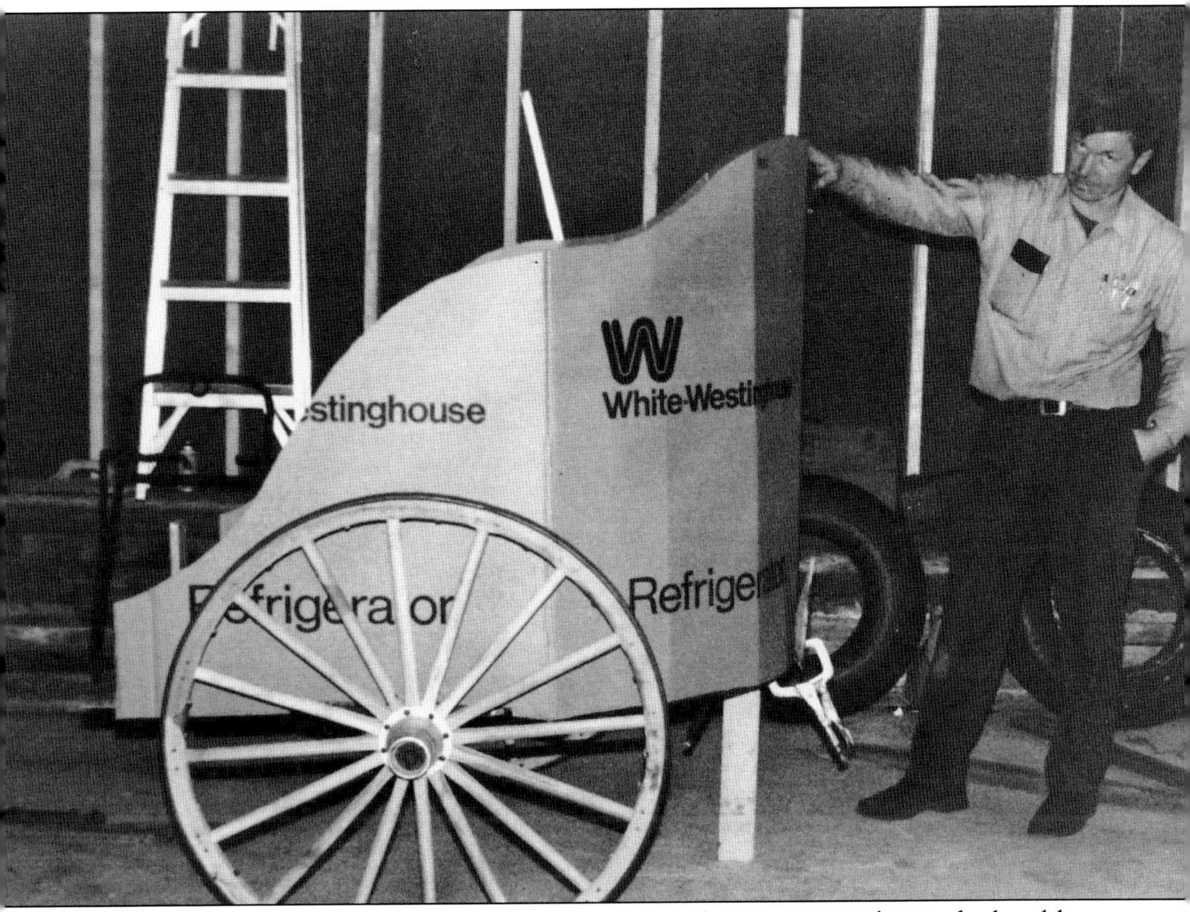

As the frame of Pilate's chariot took shape, its front plate was carved out of a box-like material. The felt and exterior designs were added after the chariot was determined to be of adequate dimensions.

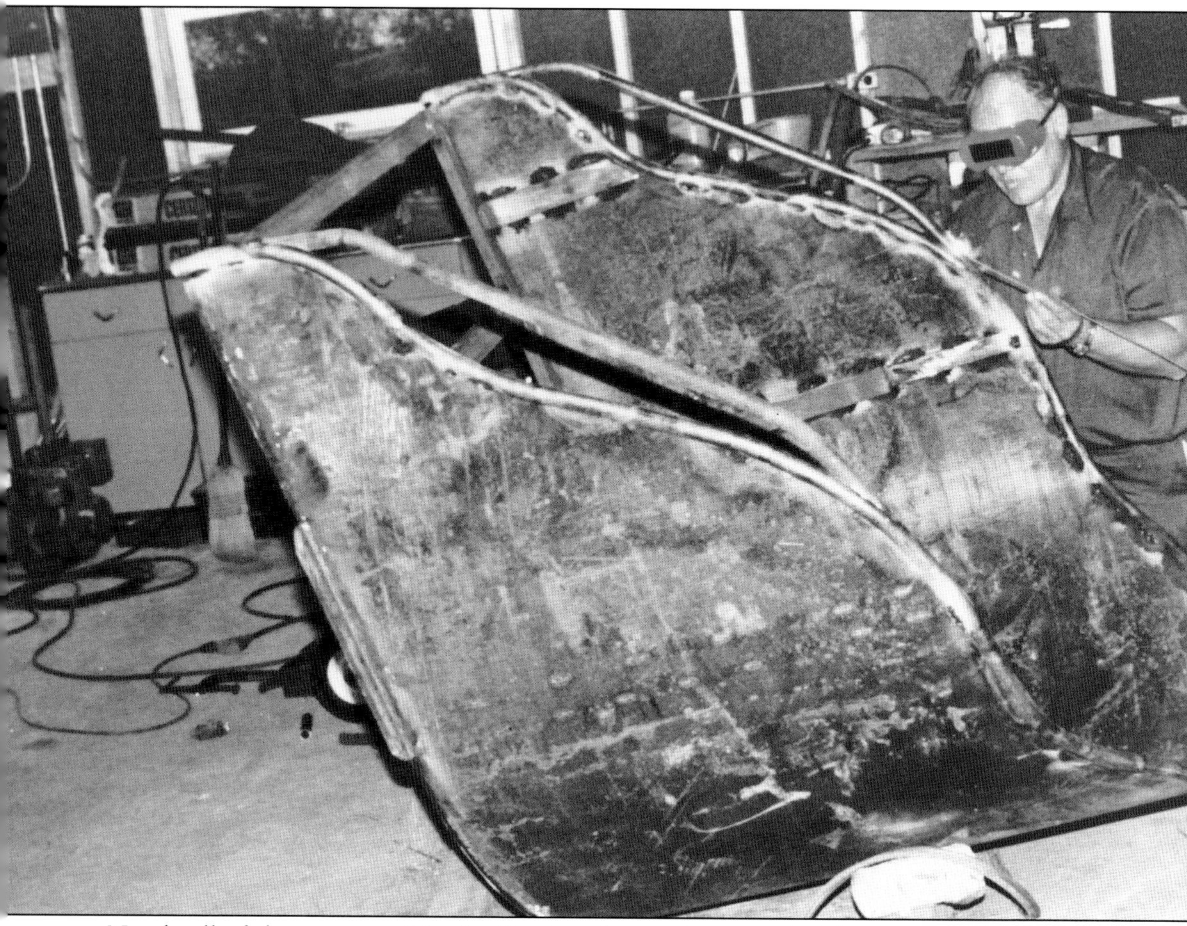

Nearly all of the props used in the Passion play are homemade. The Passion play workshops incorporate artists, seamstresses, sculptors, construction crews, and welders, as shown here.

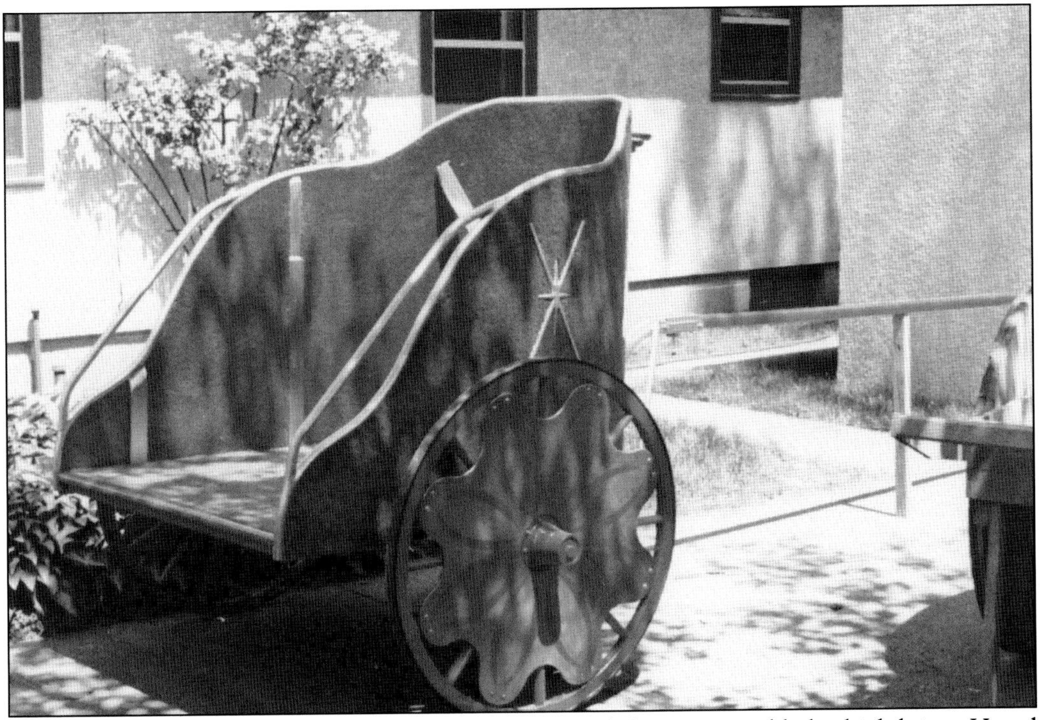

The chariot brings Pilate onto the set. In 1988, a second chariot was added, which brings Herod onto the set. For many years, there remained a single chariot driver. Between Pilate and Herod, the driver simply switched helmets in order to appear different.

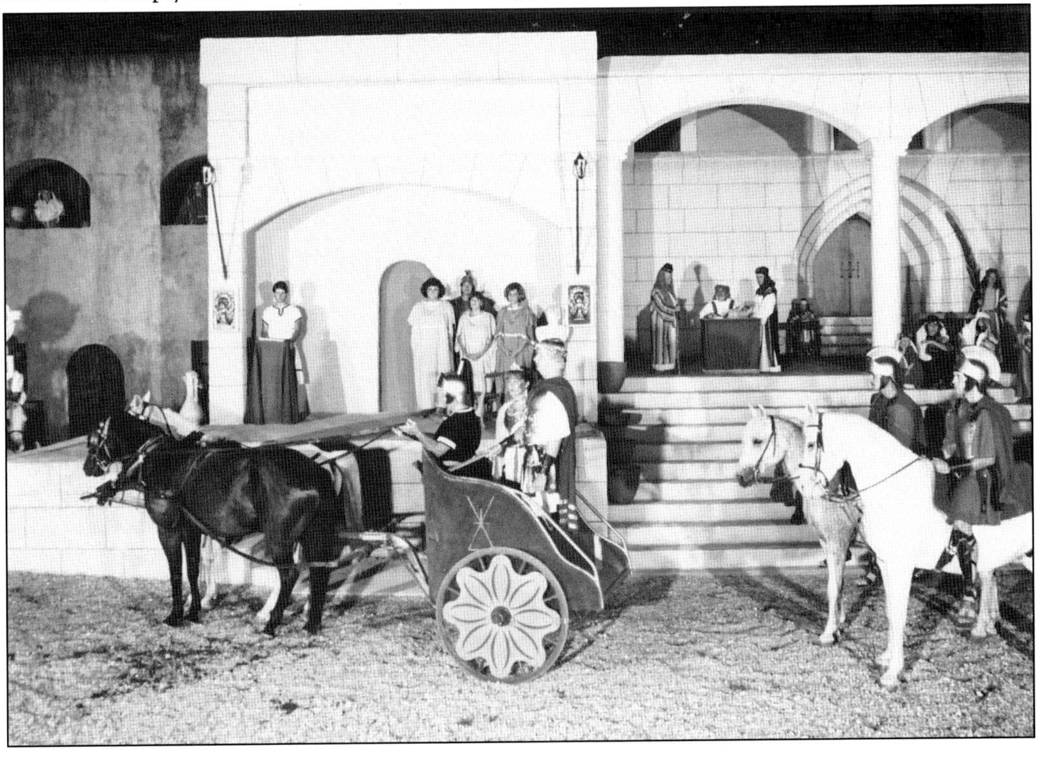

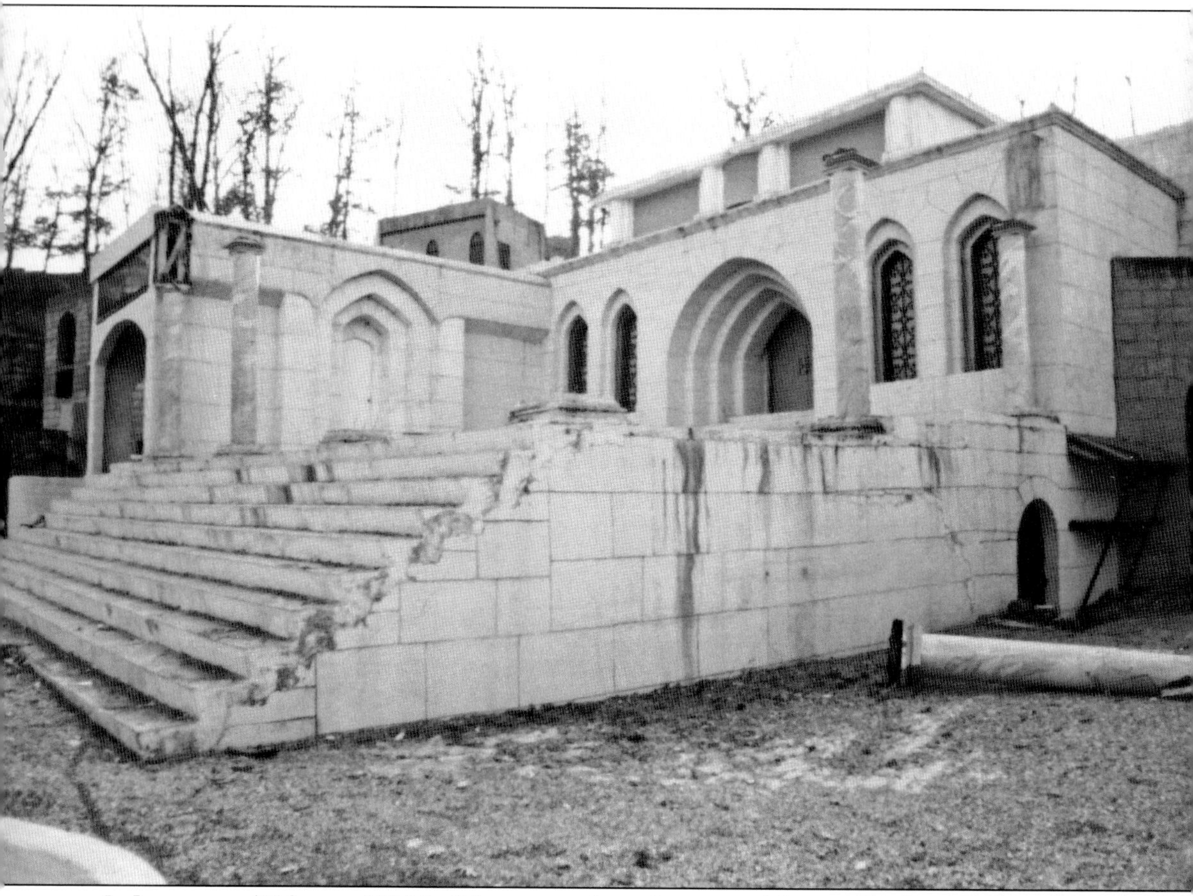

In January and February 1984, bulldozers were brought on set. After nearly 17 years of production, the set was slowly deteriorating. The temple at center stage was the first priority. A team of workers set out to redesign and replace the temple porch.

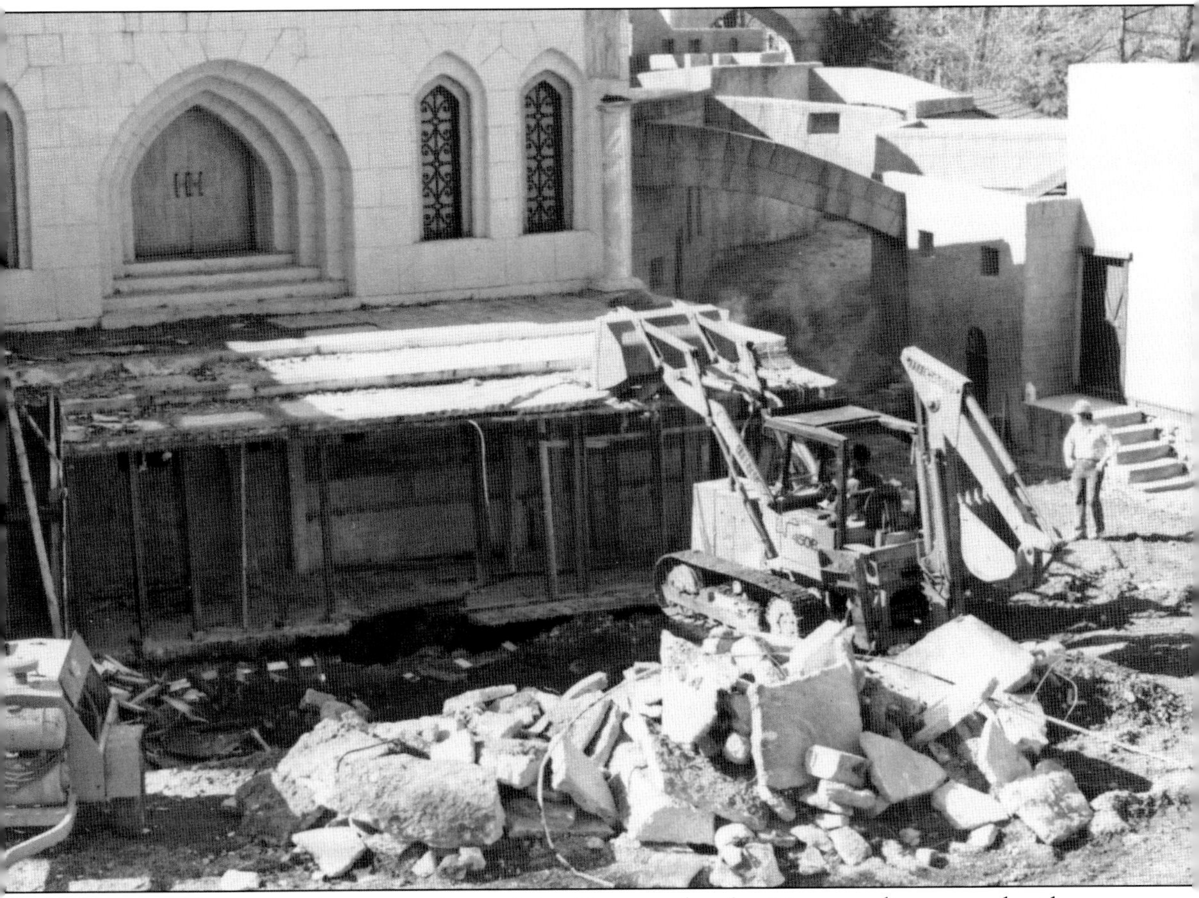

The original temple, the centerpiece of the Passion play for 16 years, disappeared rather undramatically. A bulldozer simply took it apart, piece-by-piece.

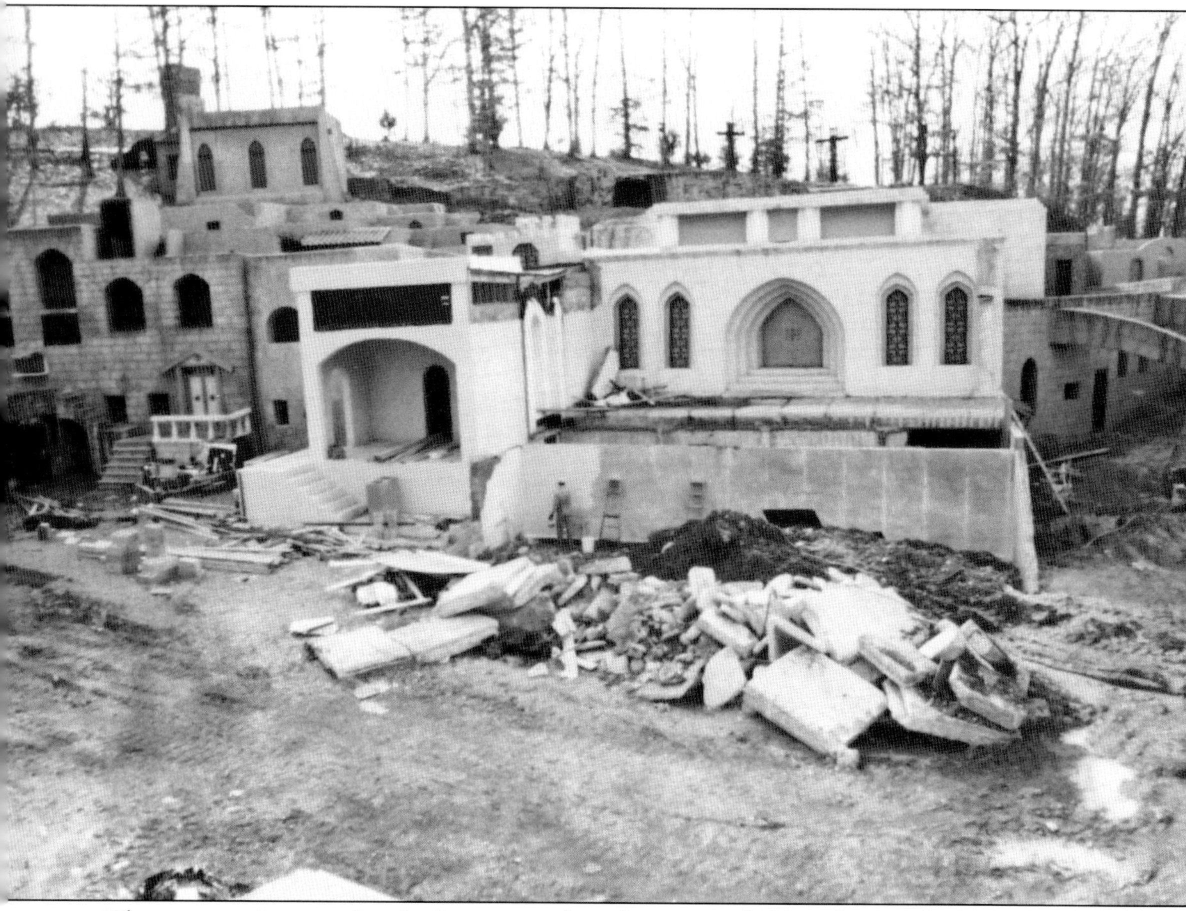

The construction crew faced a daunting task in the winter of 1984. The crew had to destroy parts of the previous set and rebuild it in only two months. This picture reflects the enormous effort of coordinating time and materials.

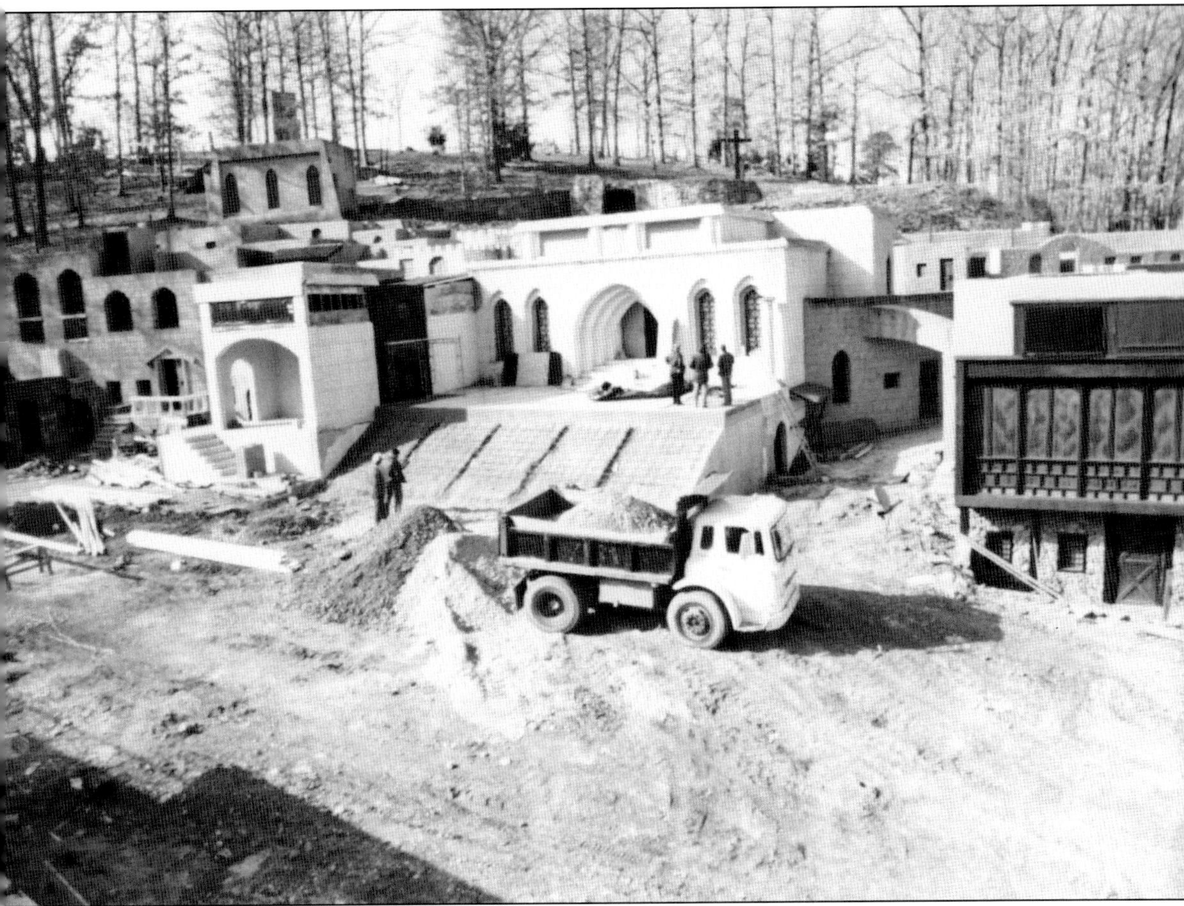

It took two months of destruction before replacement steps could be constructed. Methodically the workers put together a new staging area that would withstand the elements.

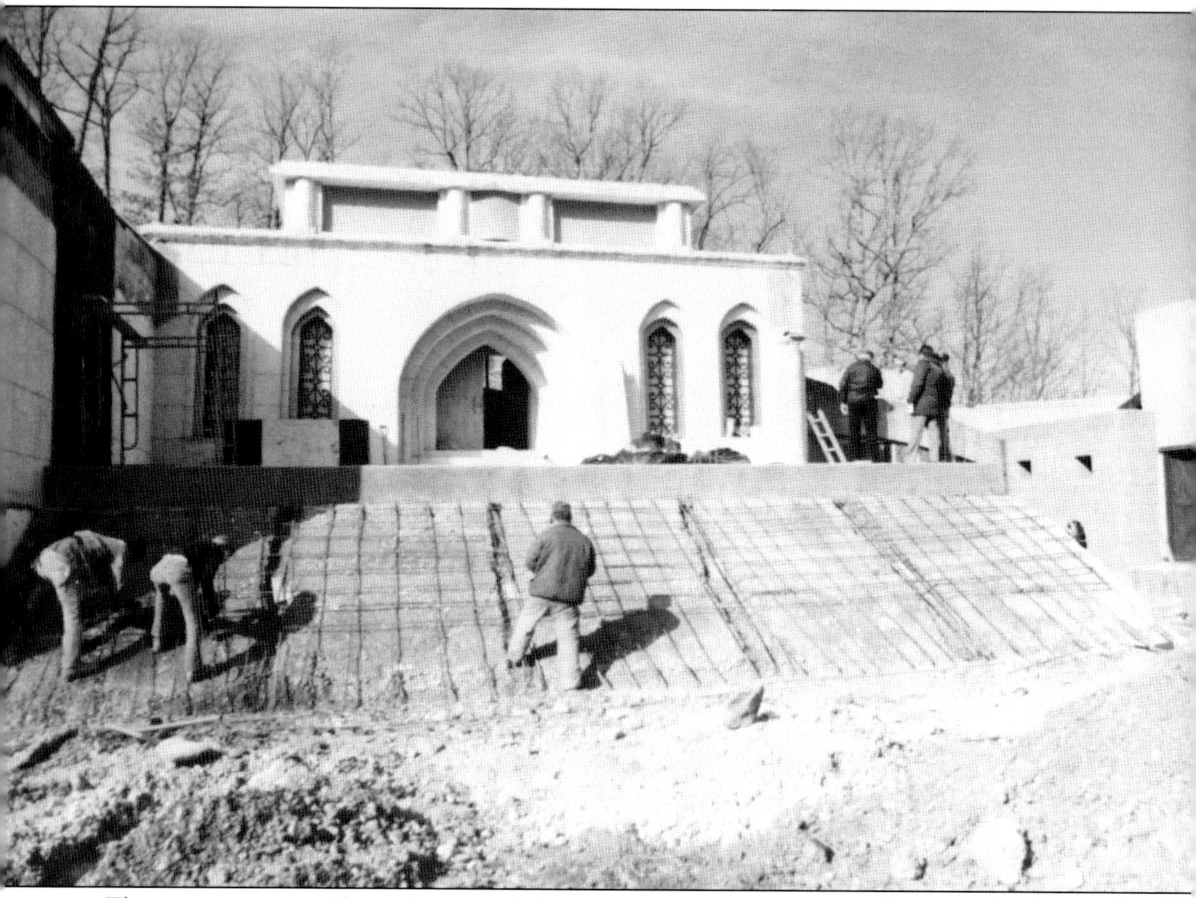

The new steps were wider and stronger. More importantly, they maintained their original purpose: they looked authentic but were also a stage.

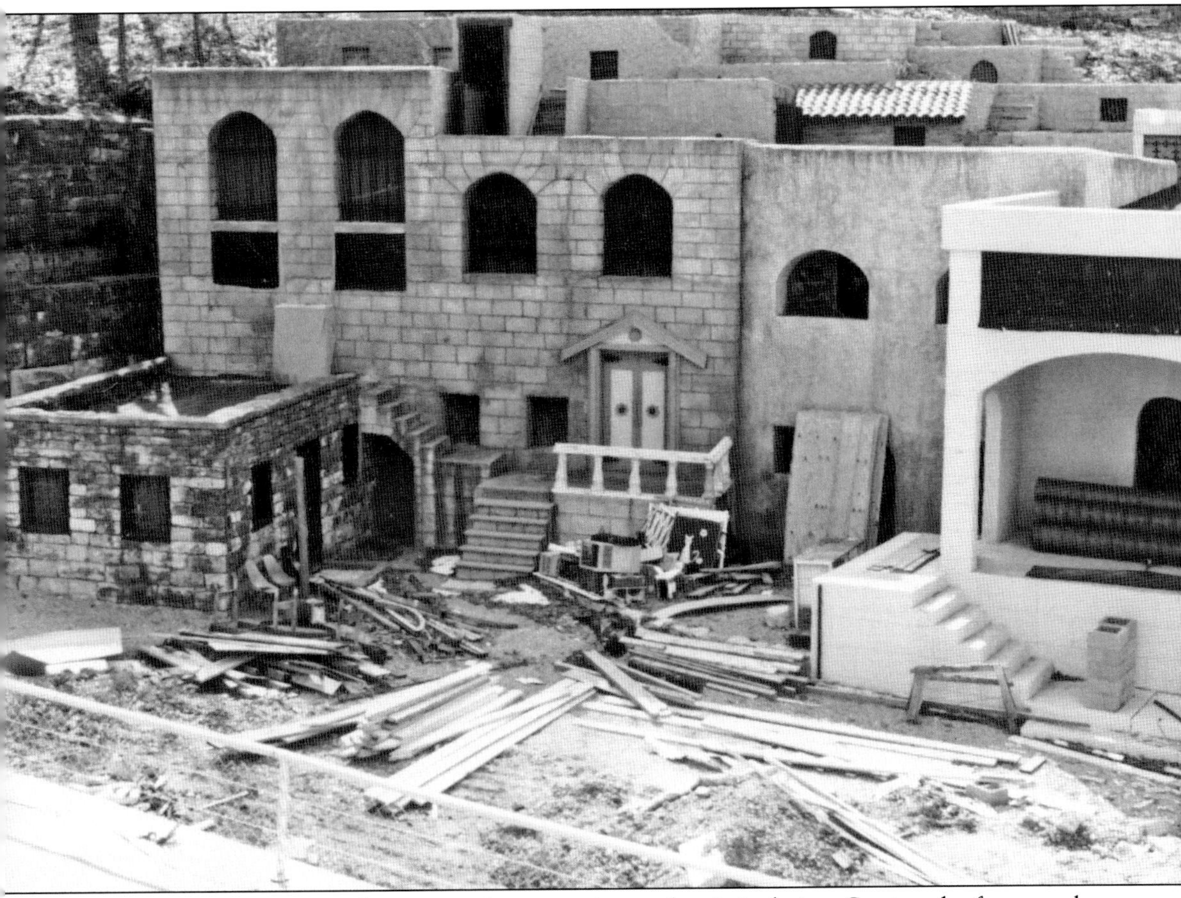

As the set was reconstructed, it required engineering and artistic design. Setting the framework was just as important as the final, authentic outcome.

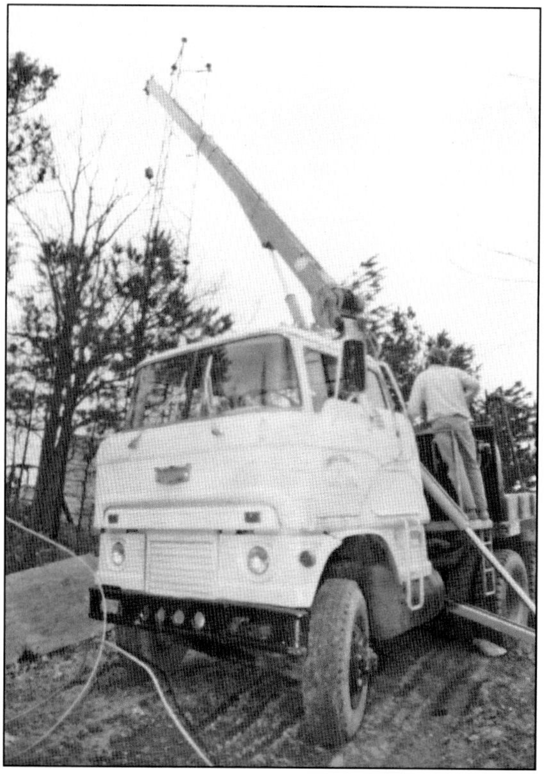

By April 1984, the new temple was complete. The attention of the talented construction crew was turned to smaller but still significant projects. Among these projects was the construction of the ascension tower. The tower sits behind Golgotha and raises Christ more than 40 feet into the air.

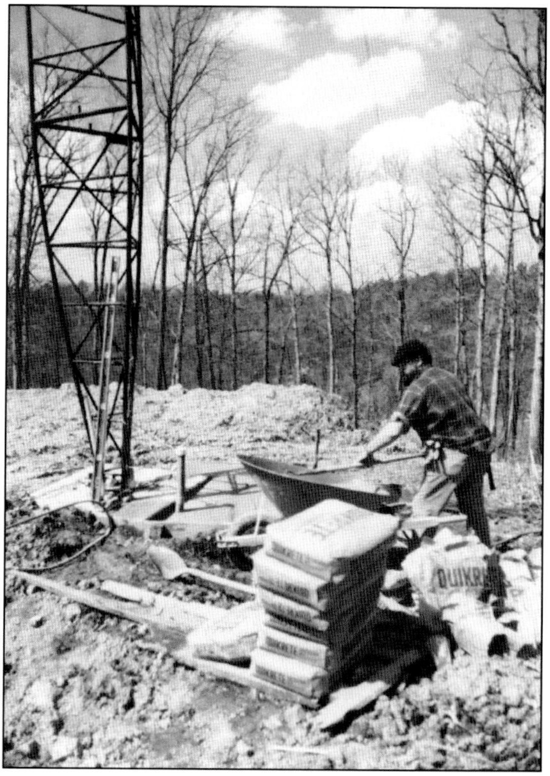

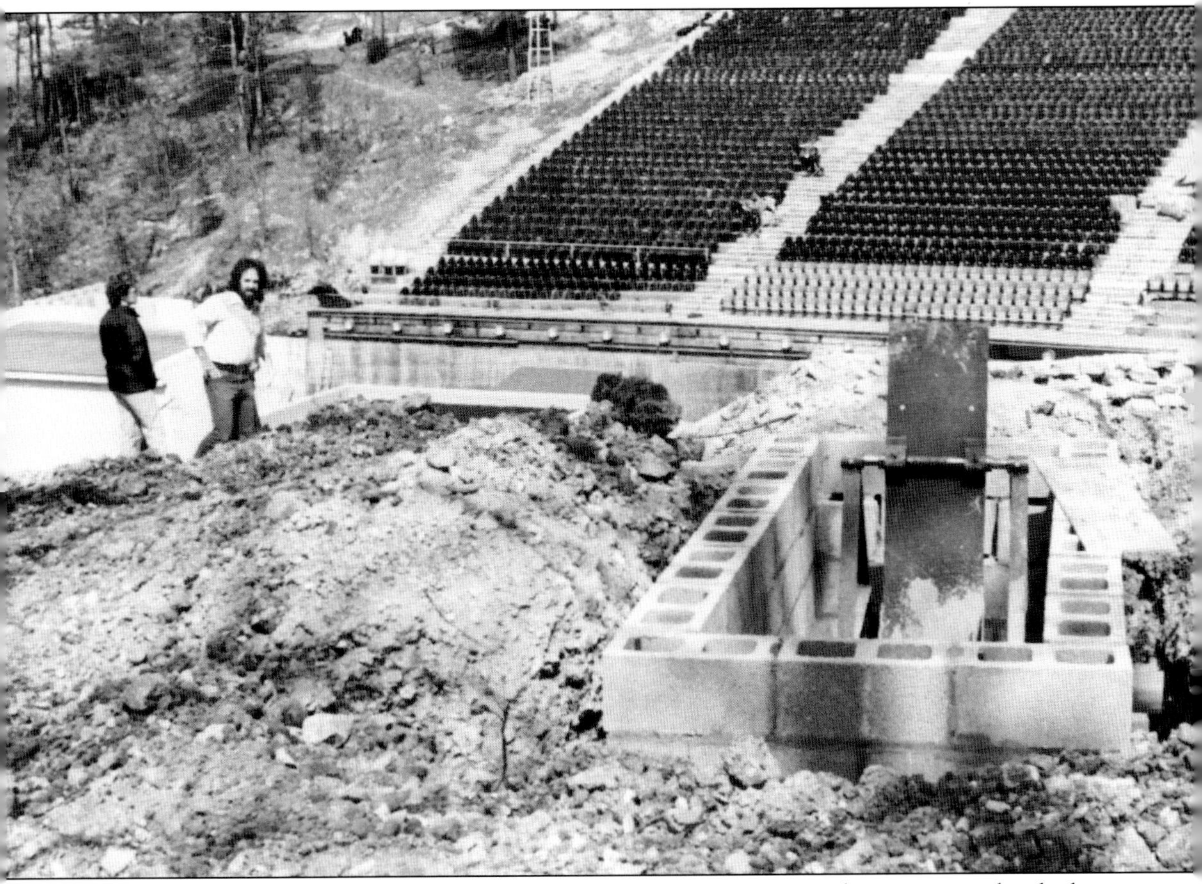

A new footing for the cross was added in 1984. The crosses operate on a hinge system that locks into place when a cross is raised. Characters in the play can quickly lower the crosses simply by pulling a string and guiding the cross to the ground.

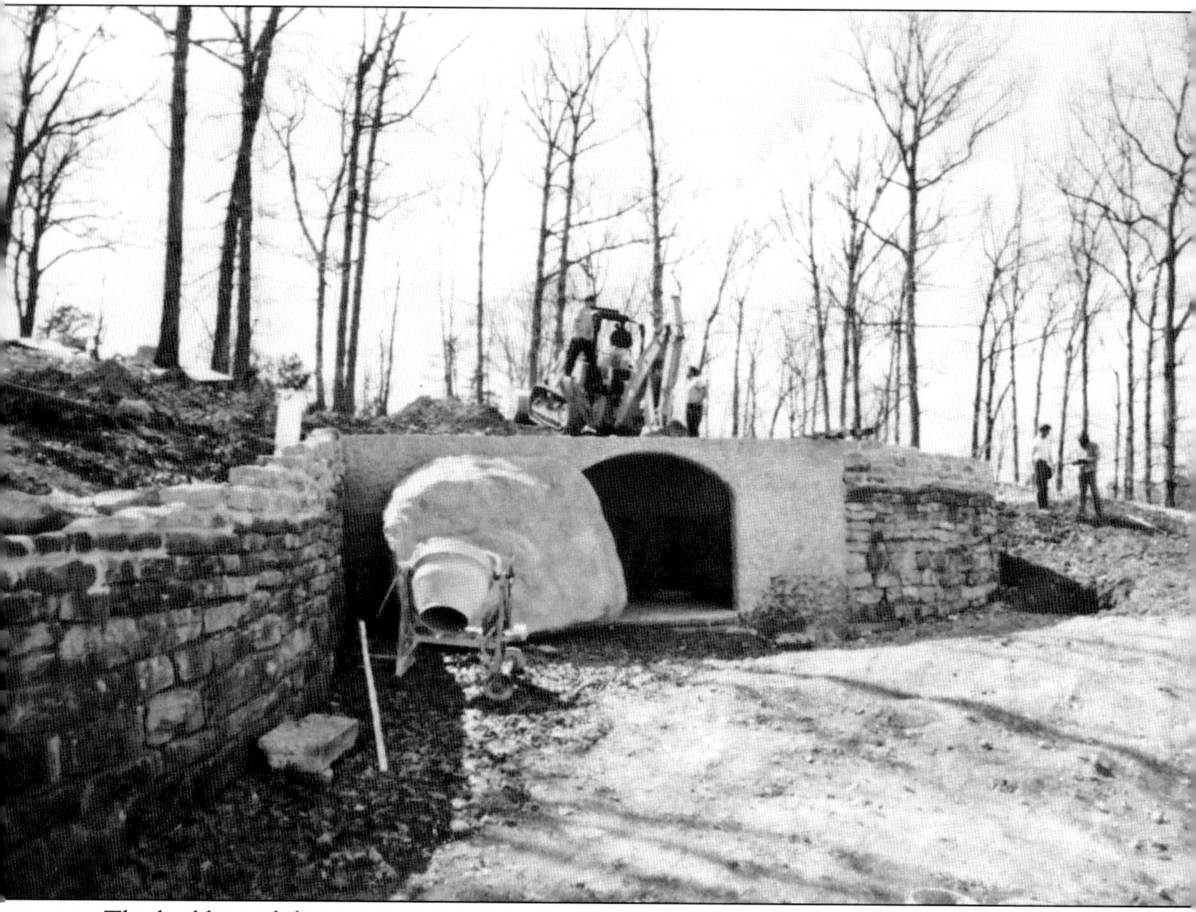

The building of the ascension tower necessitated a new tomb. The ascension wires require a remote operator, one who is close to the ascension. The control room was built into the new tomb, which is adjacent to the lifting point.

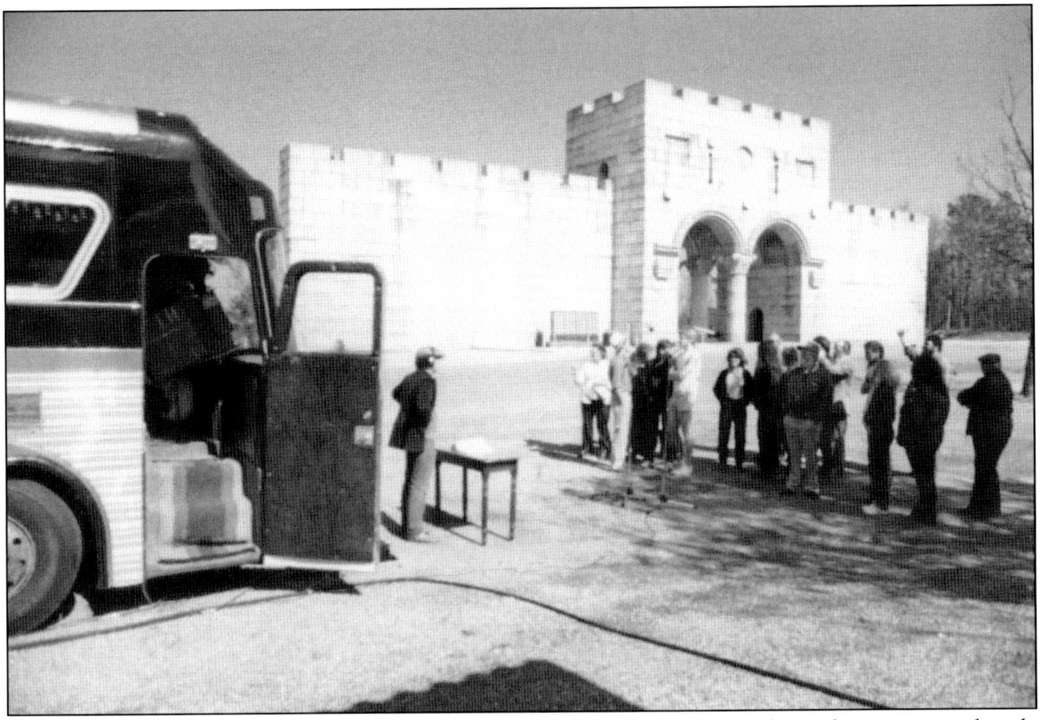

The soundtrack has undergone several reformations. In keeping with tradition, many locals participated in such productions. In this case, recordings were carried out on the Elna M. Smith Foundation grounds. Microphones were set up as part of a mobile recording studio, and cast members recorded background dialogue for street scenes.

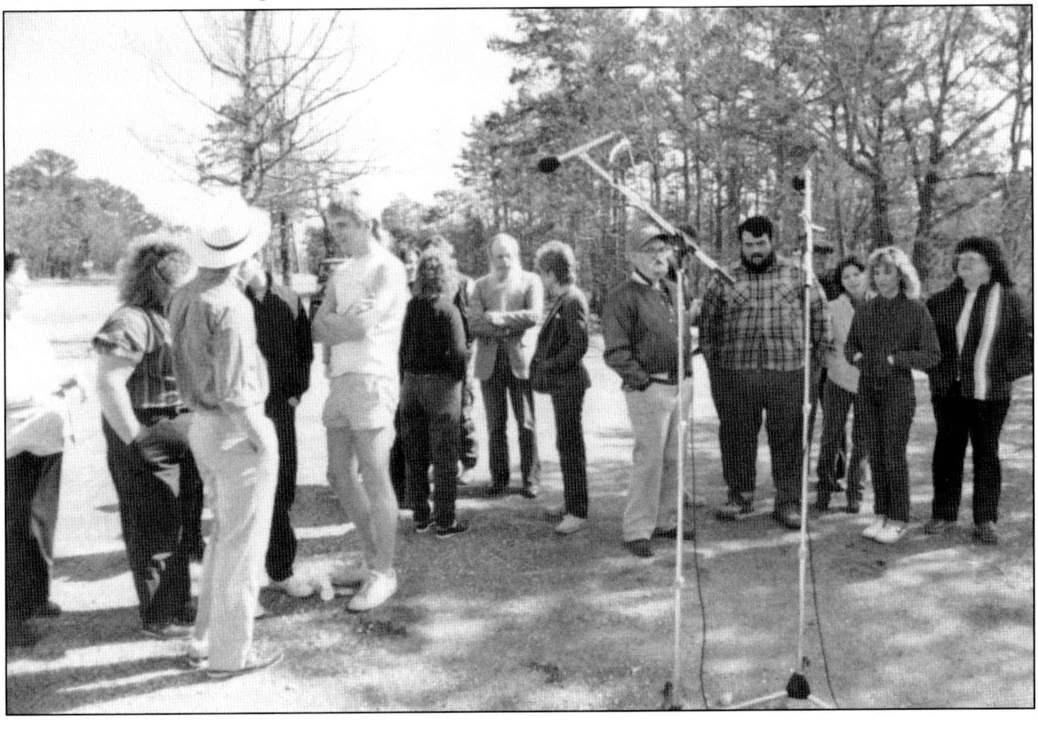

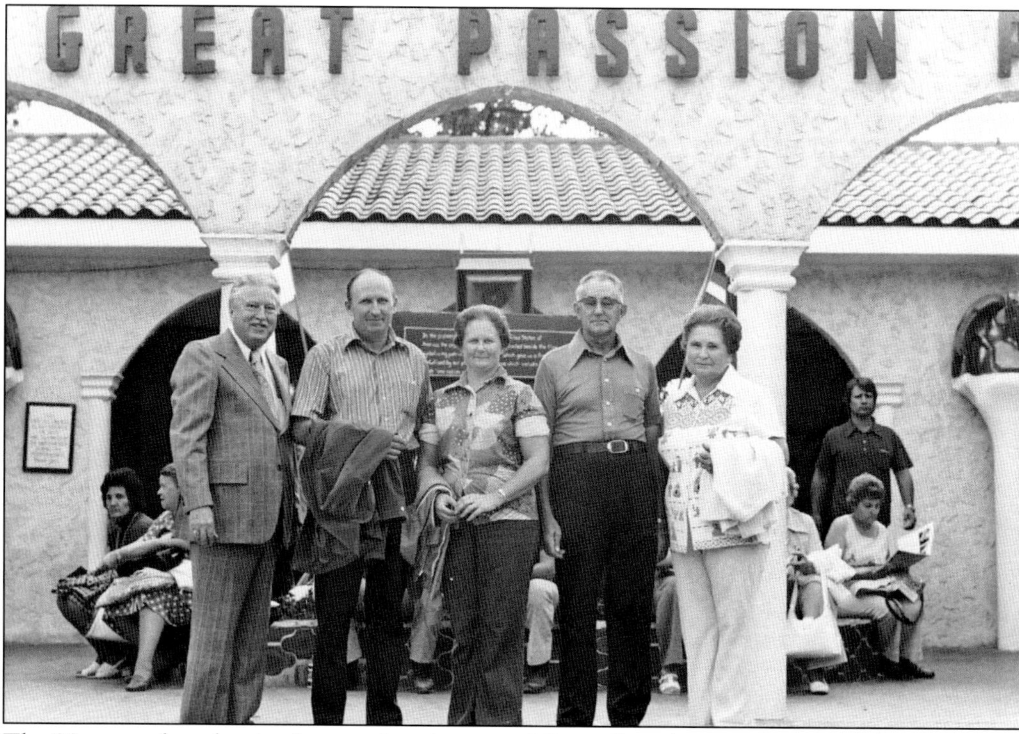

The 20 years of production has produced success. The millionth visitor was recorded in October 1976, shown above. The celebration of the two-millionth visitor came only five years later. Over the years, there have been numerous celebrations, and more than seven million visitors have attended since 1968.

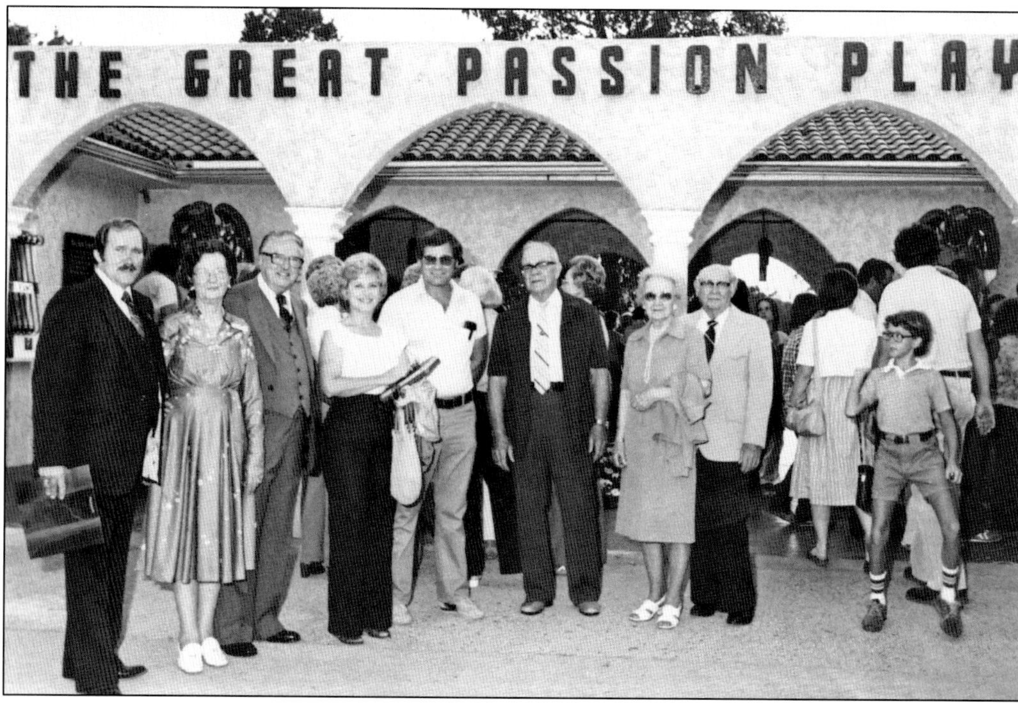

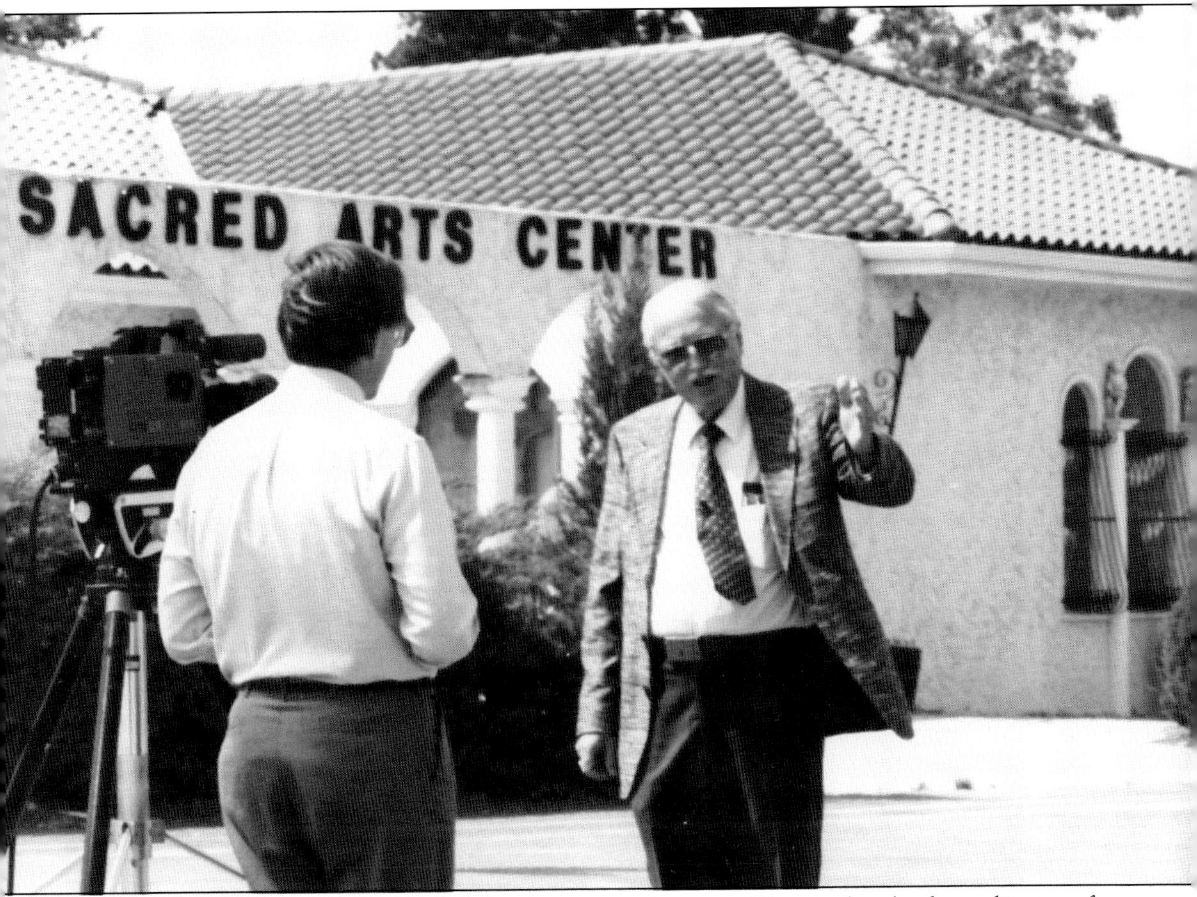

Charles F. Robertson gave numerous interviews over the years. He was the chief coordinator of the Elna M. Smith Foundation for more than 20 years, and under his leadership, the Passion play expanded from the *Christ of the Ozarks* statue to the five Sacred Projects.

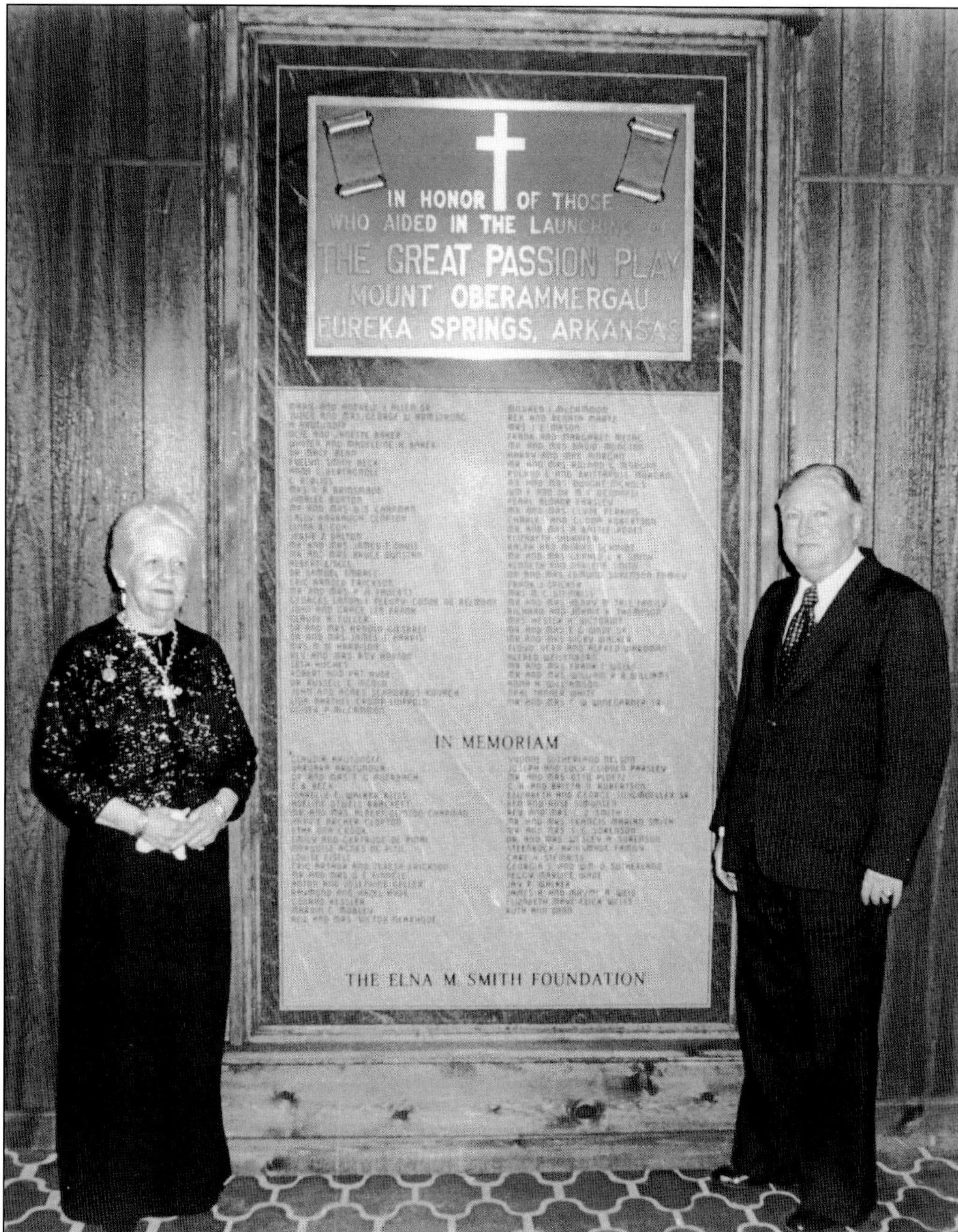

In the early 1980s, Elna M. Smith and Charles F. Robertson stood next to a new plaque commemorating the hard work of donors and participants from the early period of *The Great Passion Play*. It was and still is a symbol of a multifaceted project that reshapes, modernizes, and revitalizes itself to this day.

Four

The Sacred Projects

The Great Passion Play and the *Christ of the Ozarks* statue are the main attractions at the Elna M. Smith Foundation. But they are only part of a much larger endeavor. In fact, there are five Sacred Projects: the *Christ of the Ozarks* statue, the Passion play, the Bible museum, the Sacred Arts museum and the New Holy Land. Each of these projects was developed separately and was added to the foundation between 1965 and 1972.

Once again, the projects represent the interests of Gerald L. K. and Elna M. Smith. In the case of the Bible and Sacred Arts museums, many of the pieces came from Elna's private collection. It was her personal desire that the treasures of her life be available to the public.

The New Holy Land is the largest project at the foundation. It was originally designed to replicate ancient Jerusalem. Only part of this grand city has been reconstructed, the stonewall entrance. Over time, the focus of the New Holy Land was centered less on buildings, and the project evolved into a complex of holy land sites, including a small Sea of Galilee, a replica tomb and Golgotha, a Biblical watchtower, a full-scale tabernacle replica, and numerous other items of Biblical significance.

The five Sacred Projects receive the greatest amount of attention, but the Elna M. Smith Foundation maintains an eclectic array of religious artifacts. On the grounds, visitors can look at a fully restored country chapel, see a piece of the Berlin wall, tour a creationist museum, and witness free productions of Biblically themed dramas.

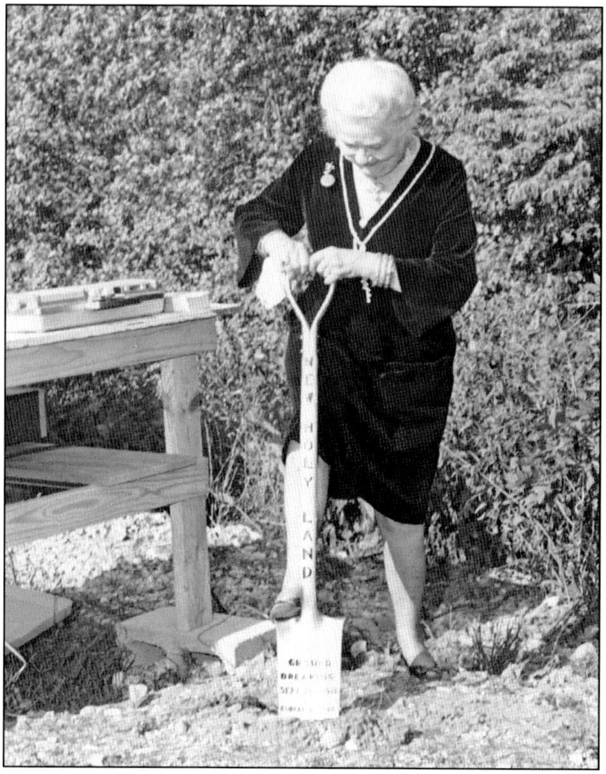

Elna M. Smith broke ground for the New Holy Land in September 1971. The dedication represented the most ambitious of the Elna M. Smith Foundation's projects. It was estimated that the New Holy Land would require 10 years to build at the cost of millions.

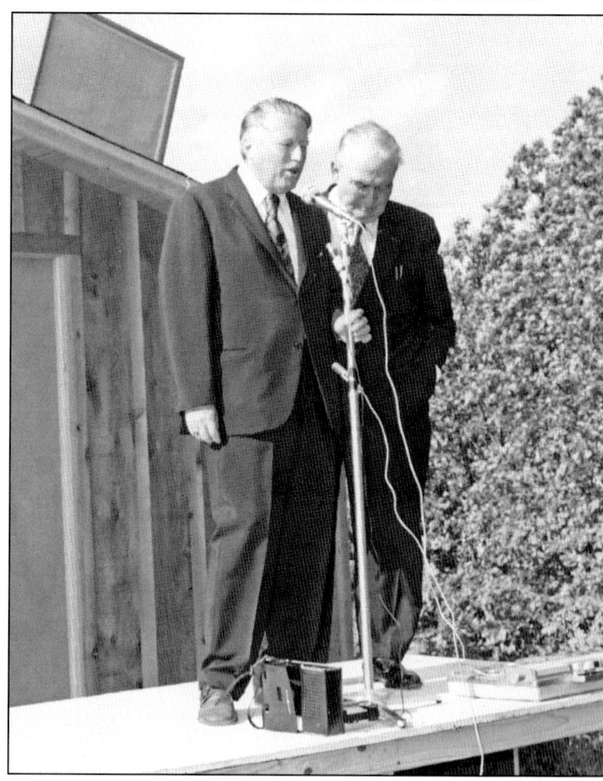

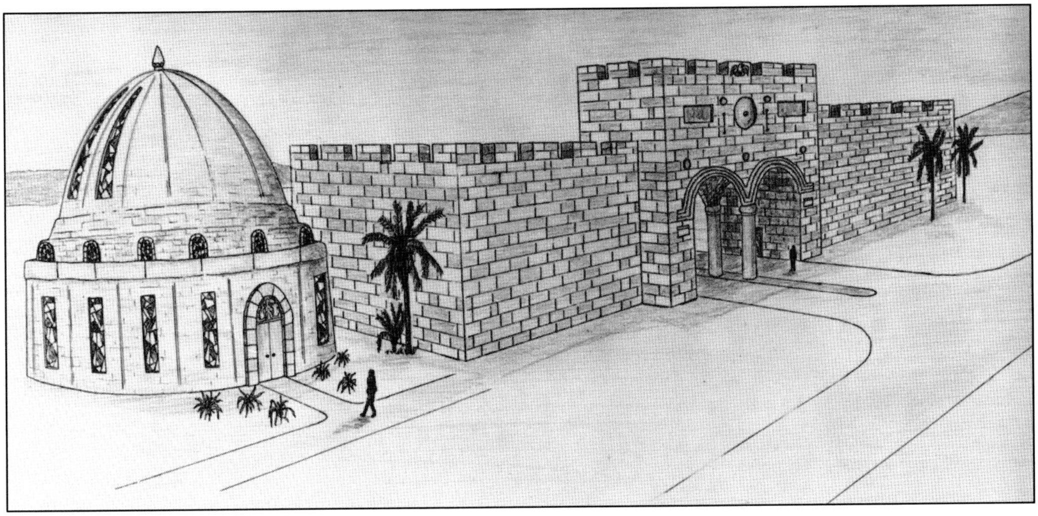

The original sketch of the New Holy Land called for a massive stone entrance and a rotund chapel at one end. The wall was erected within a year, and the chapel was added within the decade.

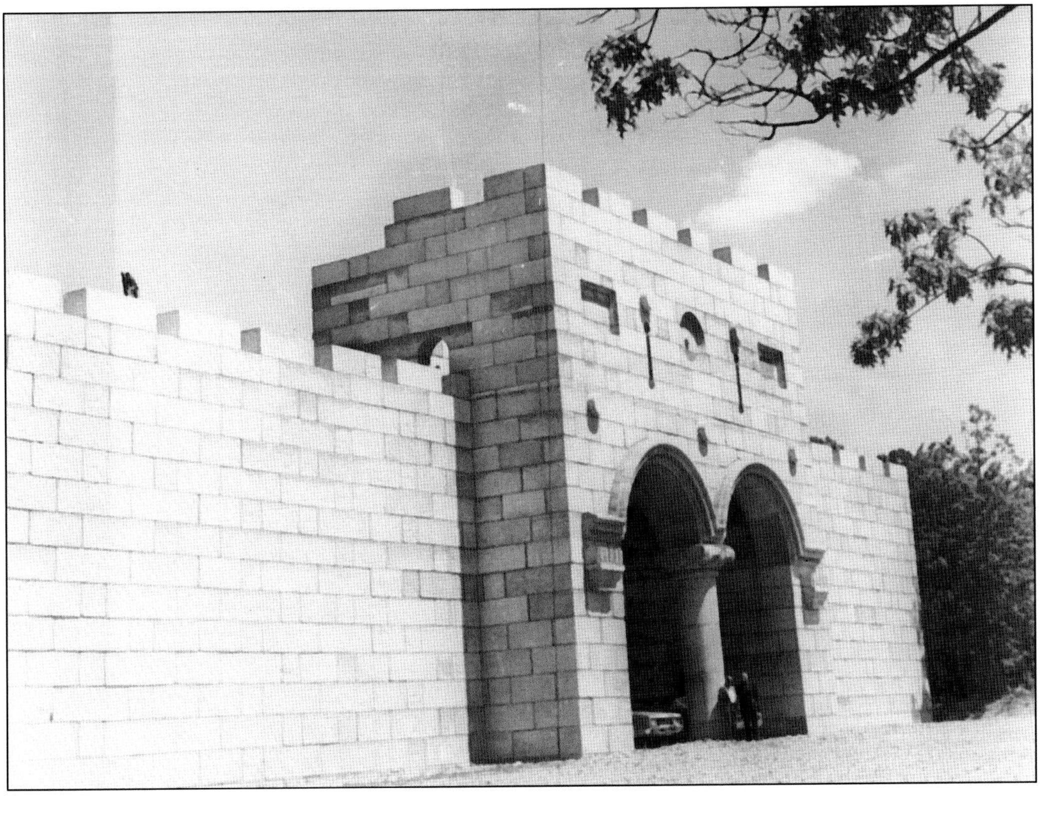

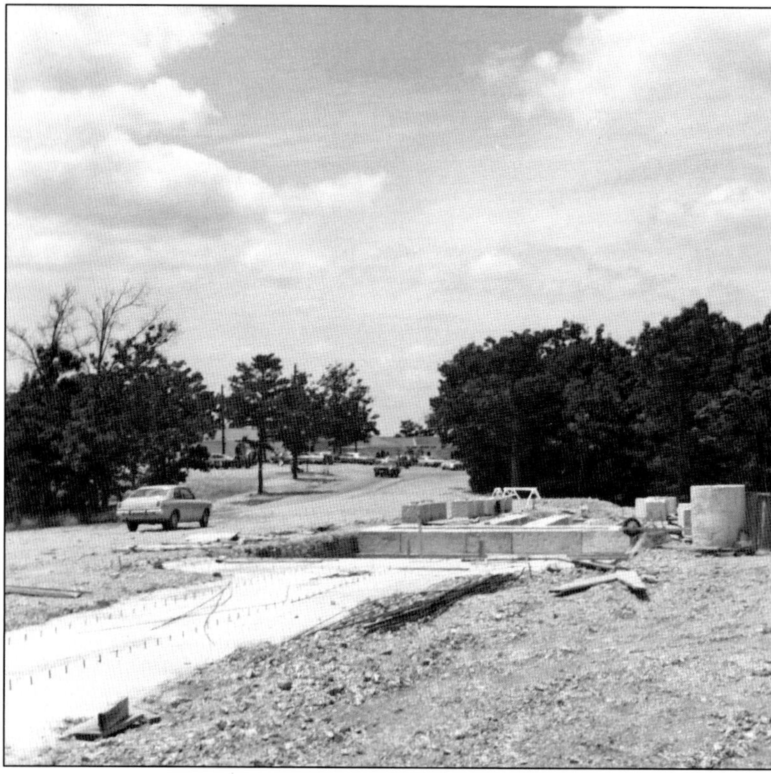

The New Holy Land entrance was composed of solid cement blocks. Two rows of blocks were set below the surface and composed a solid foundation. These blocks, which each weigh close to half a ton, could only be moved with heavy equipment.

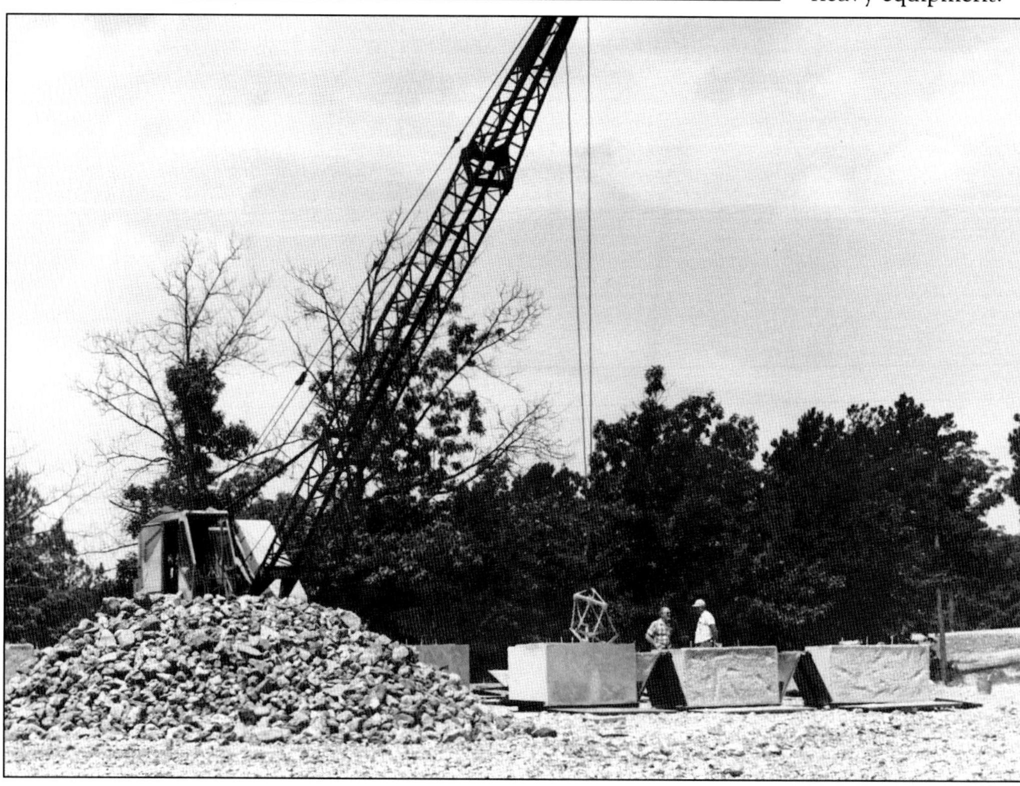

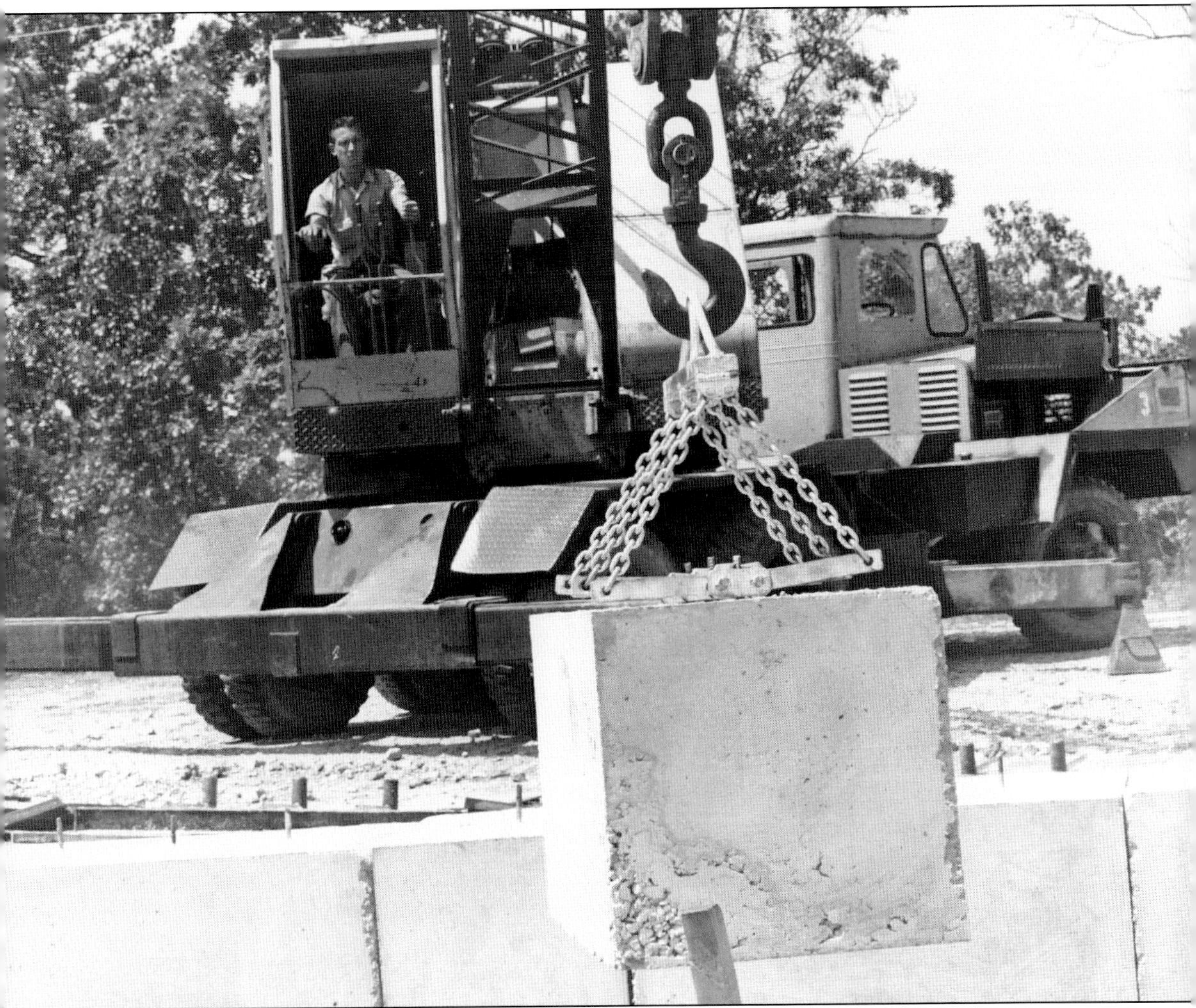

With the help of a crane, the cement blocks were carefully put into place. Workers had to precisely align the blocks, row after row. In order to keep the blocks in place, massive steel bars connected the levels.

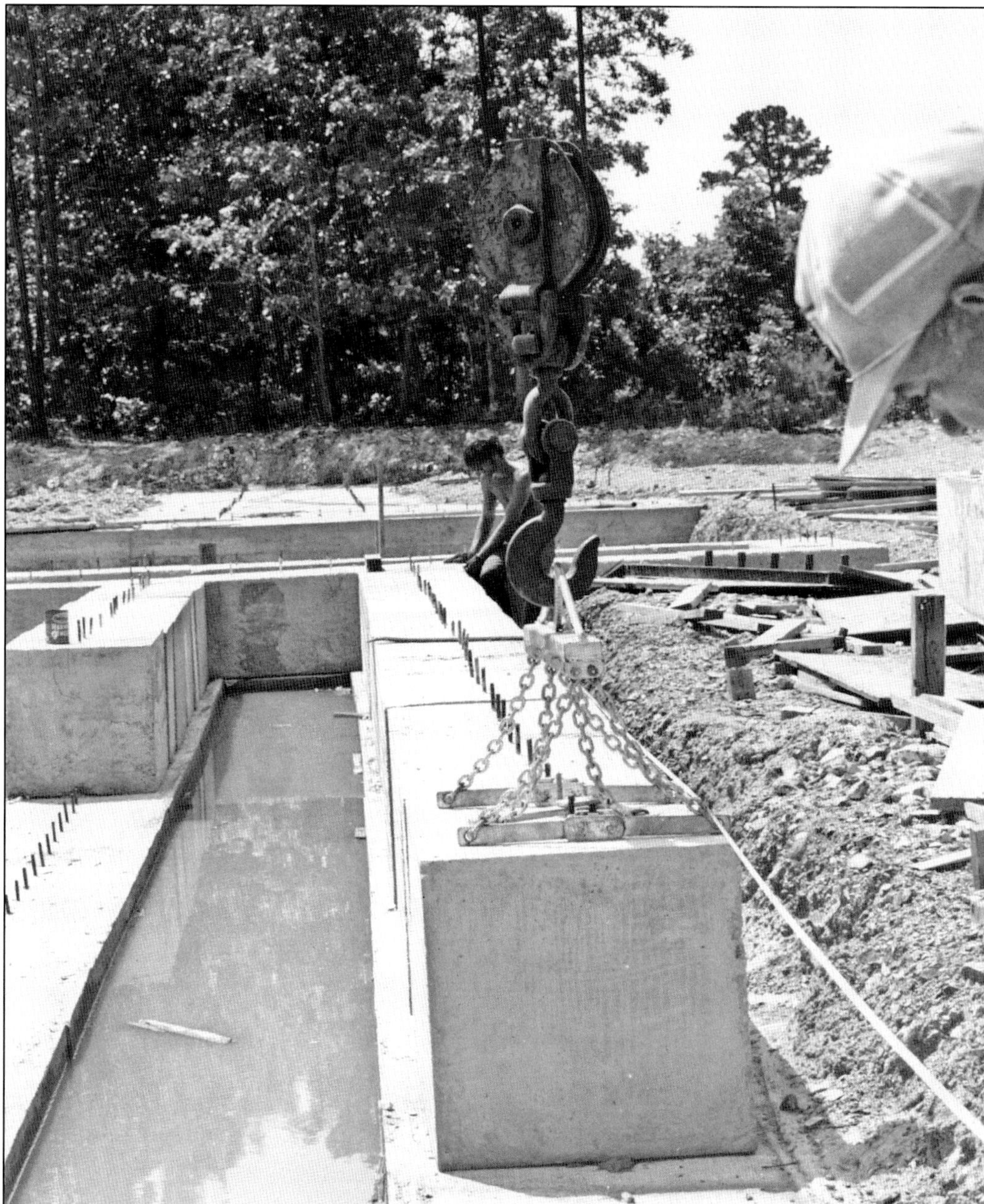

The blocks weighed over a ton. They came together slowly but efficiently thanks to the design and implementation of the construction crew.

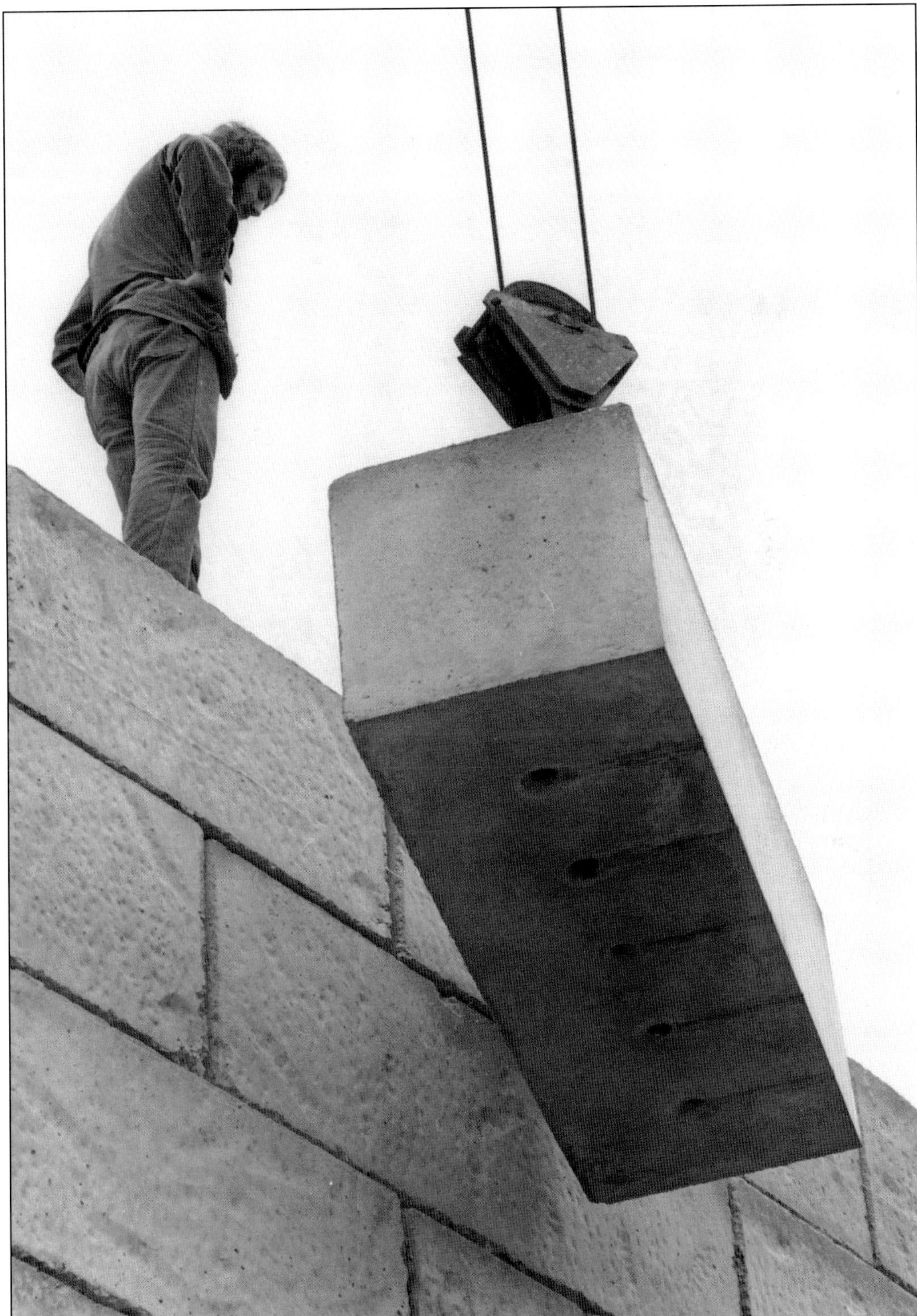

The blocks were held together with a series of steel bars. Each row is connected to the row below it and above it.

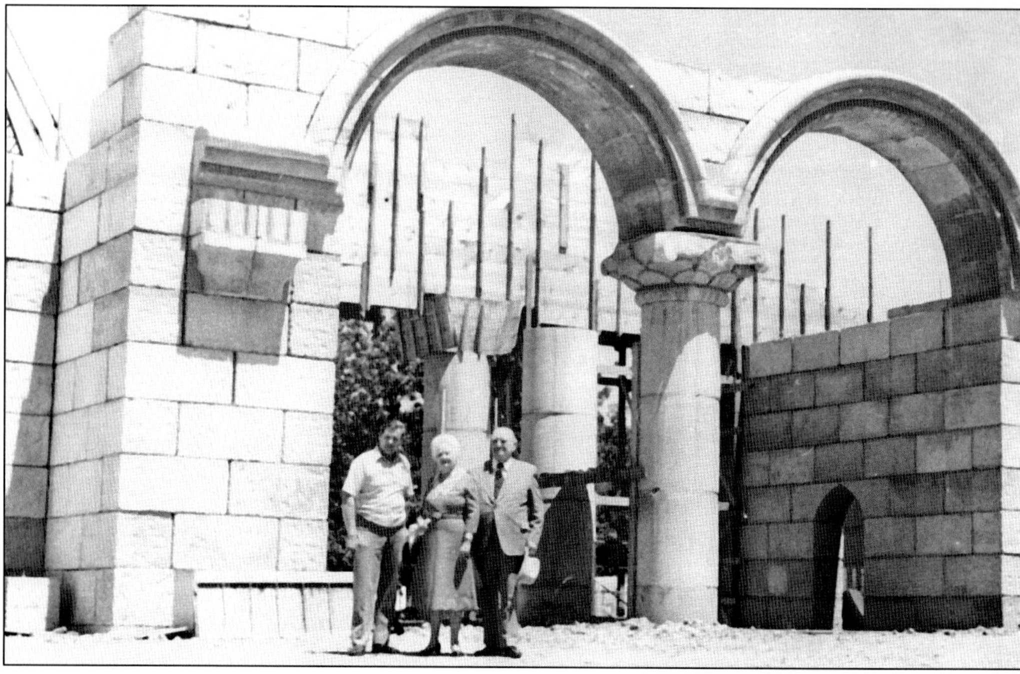

Elna M. and Gerald L. K. Smith inspected the progress on a regular basis, as shown above. The original vision of the New Holy Land included a complex of stone buildings that would represent the city of Jerusalem, pictured below. This idea was later abandoned in favor of sights that could be easily adapted to the Ozark landscape.

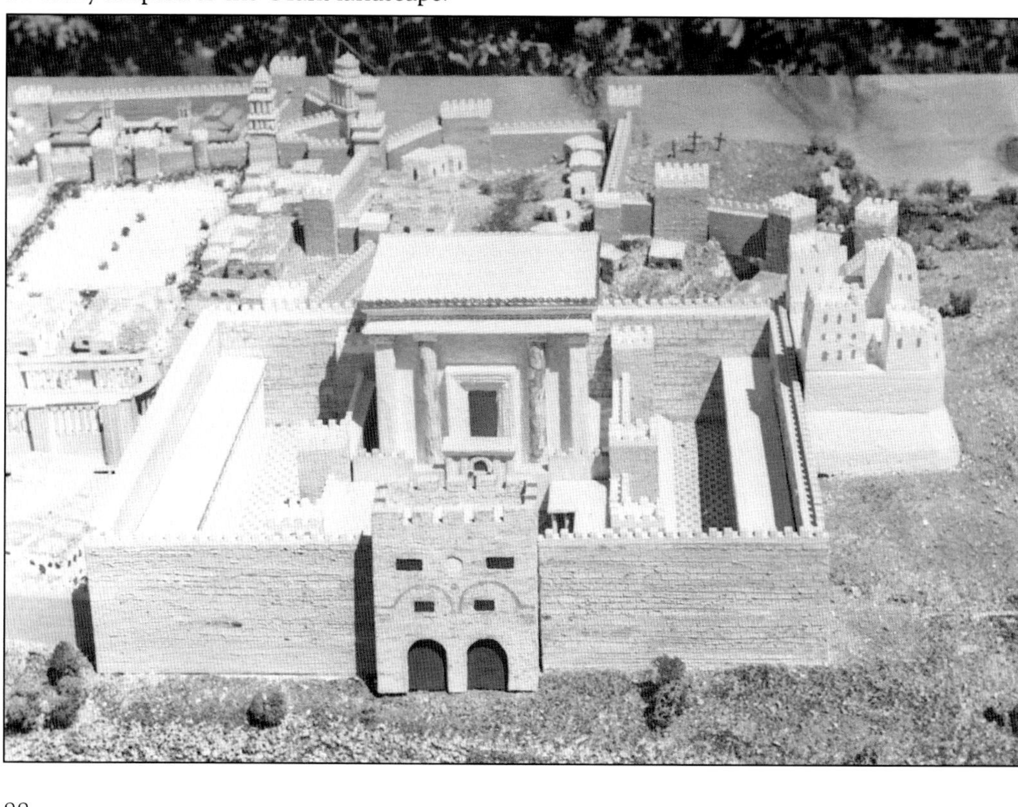

A rotund chapel was added to the grounds in the late 1970s. It was originally designed as part of the New Holy Land, but it eventually served many purposes. After Gerald L. K. Smith's death in 1976, it was dedicated as a memorial chapel, and its downstairs became the new Bible museum. Today the Bible museum is still on the lower level, but the upstairs chapel has been transformed into the museum of earth science.

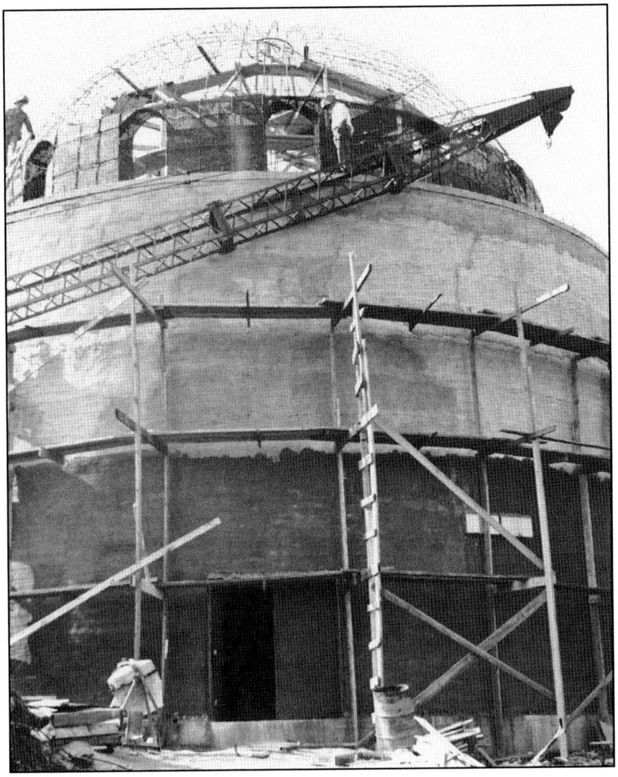

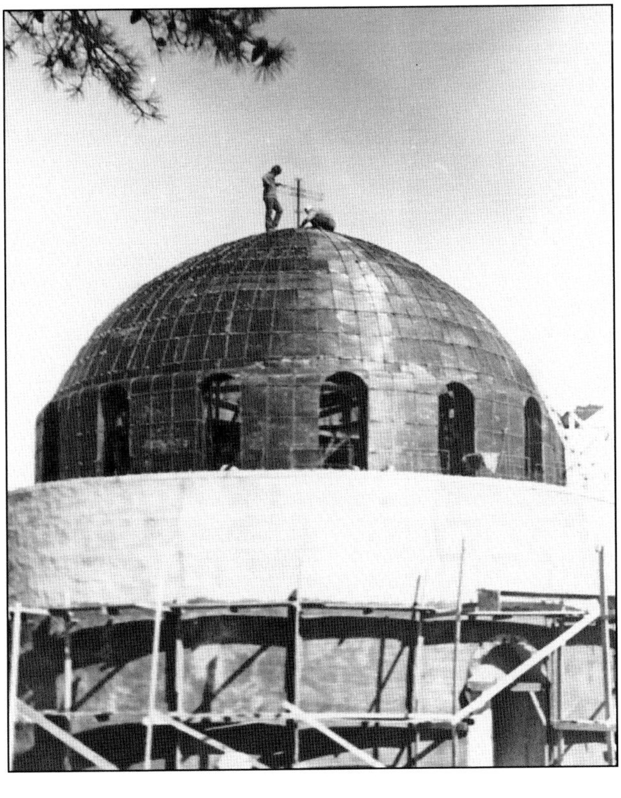

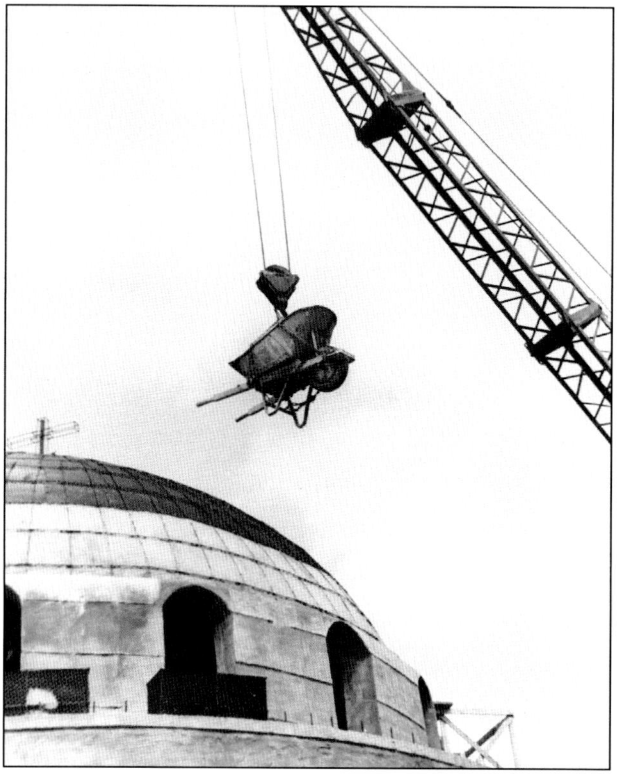

Setting the cross to the Smith Memorial Chapel required ingenuity. Workers could not lift buckets of cement high enough to reach the cross, so a crane lifted the entire wheelbarrow to the top. In the picture below, the wheelbarrow teeters close to the edge, held in place only by the crane.

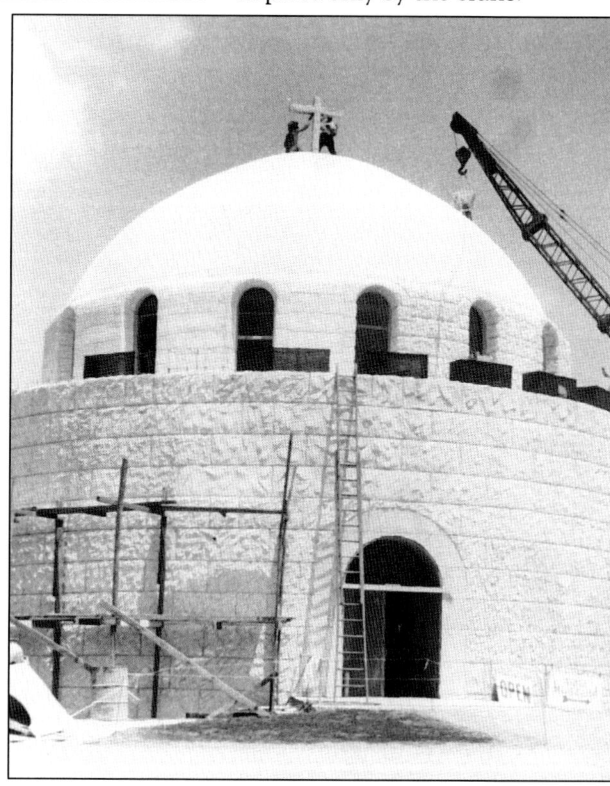

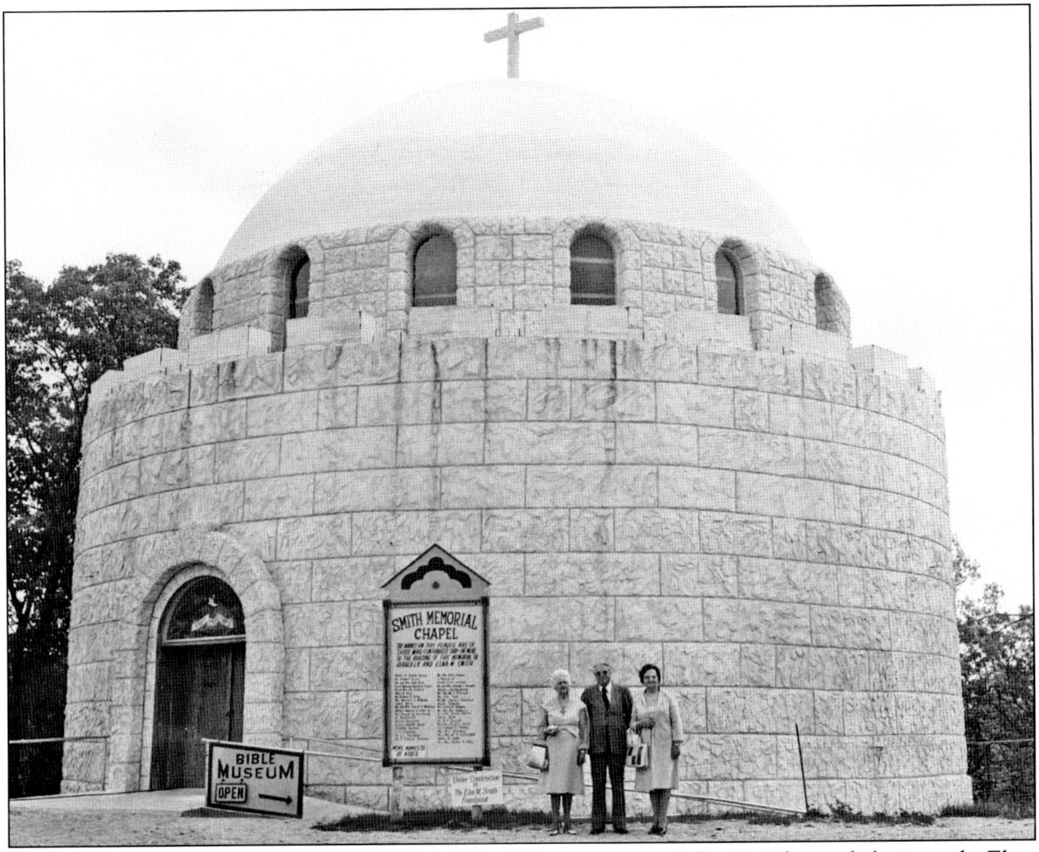

The Smith Memorial Chapel was dedicated to the memory of the Smiths and their work. Elna M. Smith was alive to witness its completion. Standing in the photograph is Elna and her dear friends Charles F. and Gunda C. Robertson.

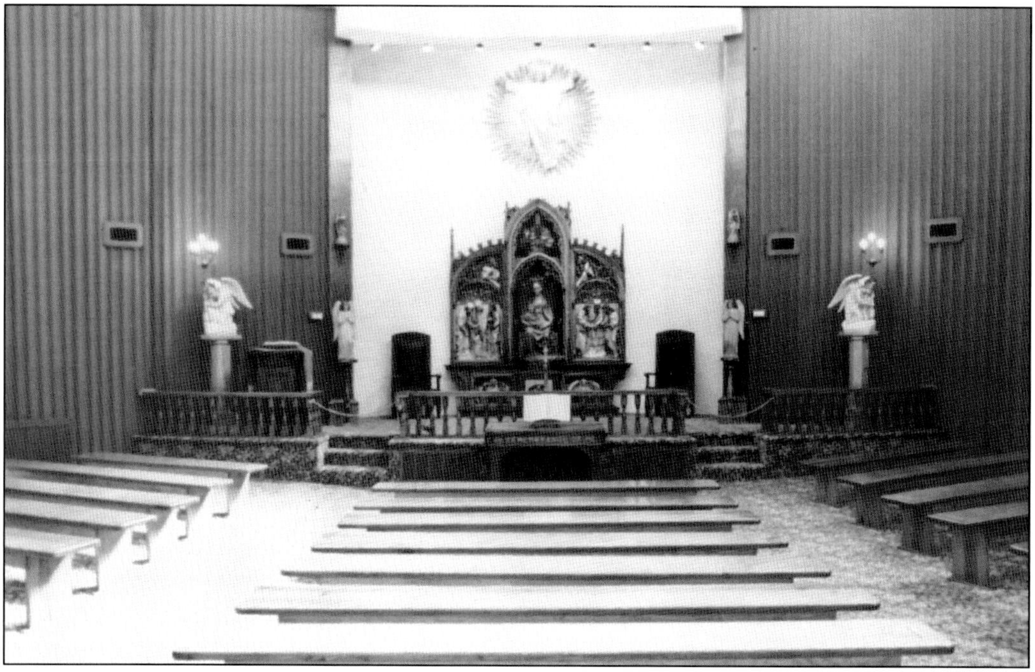

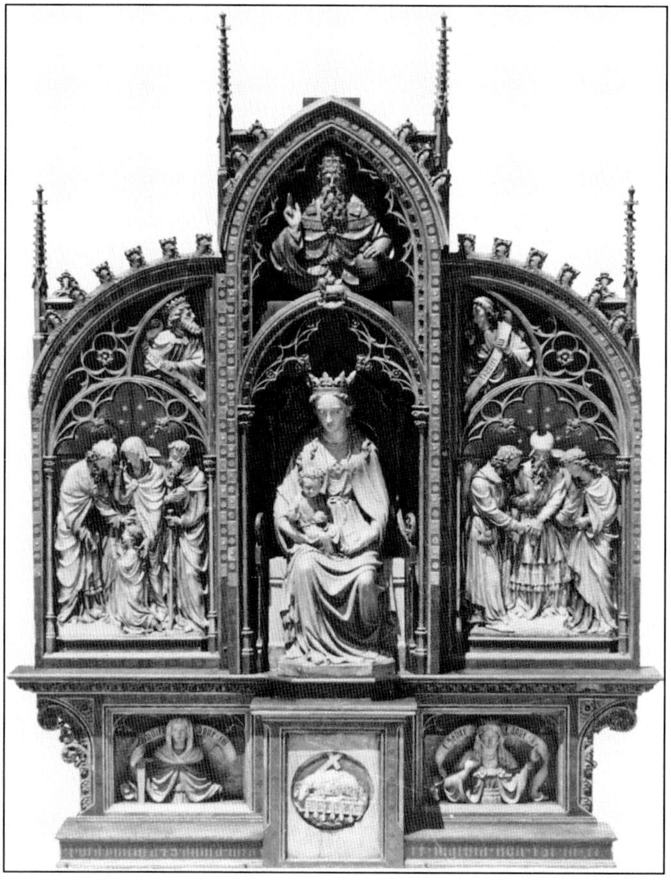

The interior of the Smith Memorial Chapel reflected the artistic taste of the Smiths. The centerpiece of the chapel was an ornate alter screen, purchased in Europe and transferred to Eureka Springs.

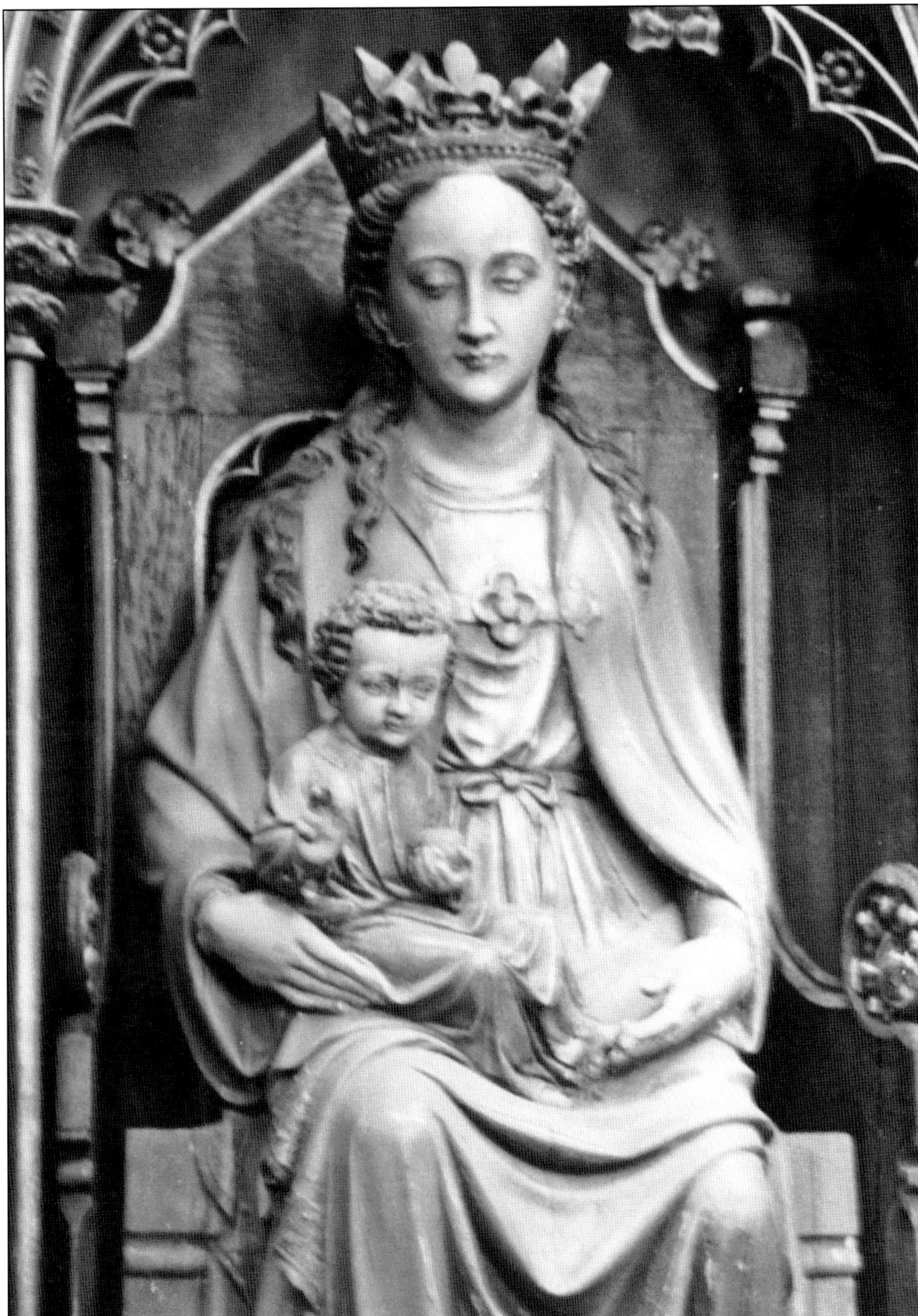

Elna M. Smith wanted the chapel to reflect a non-denominational prayer chapel. As such, it was both modern and traditional.

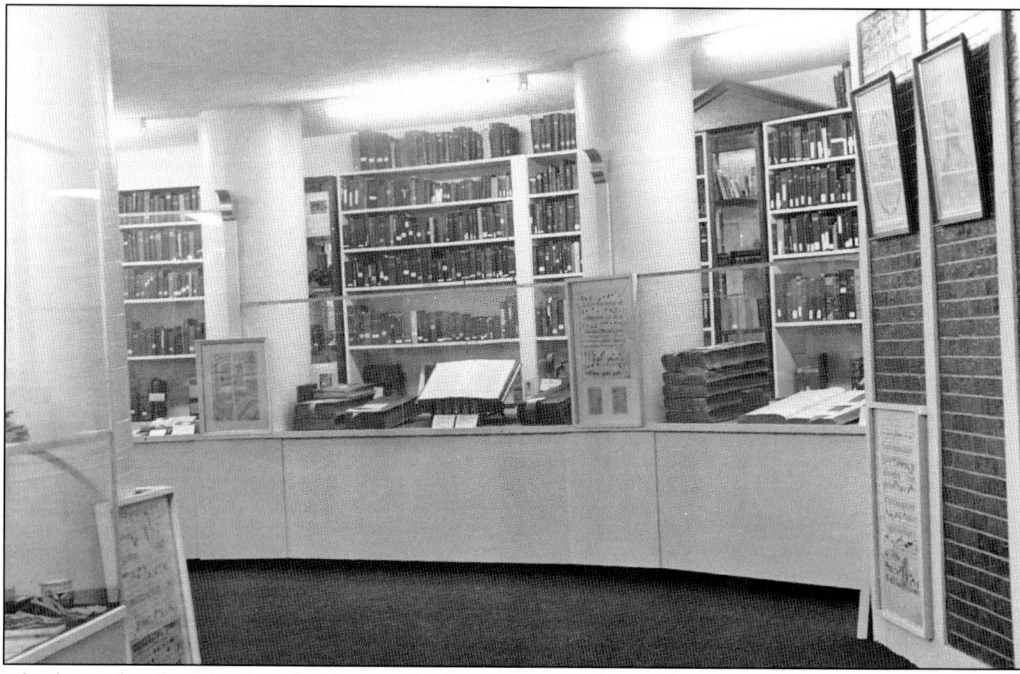

The lower level of the Smith Memorial Chapel houses the Bible museum. Bible collecting was a passion of Elna M. Smith long before the Smiths moved to Eureka Springs. When the foundation expanded its Sacred Projects, Elna Smith opened her Bibles to the public. Today the museum boasts one of the largest collections of Bibles in the world, including original King James Bibles, rare first-print editions, and the only Bible signed by all of the original Gideons.

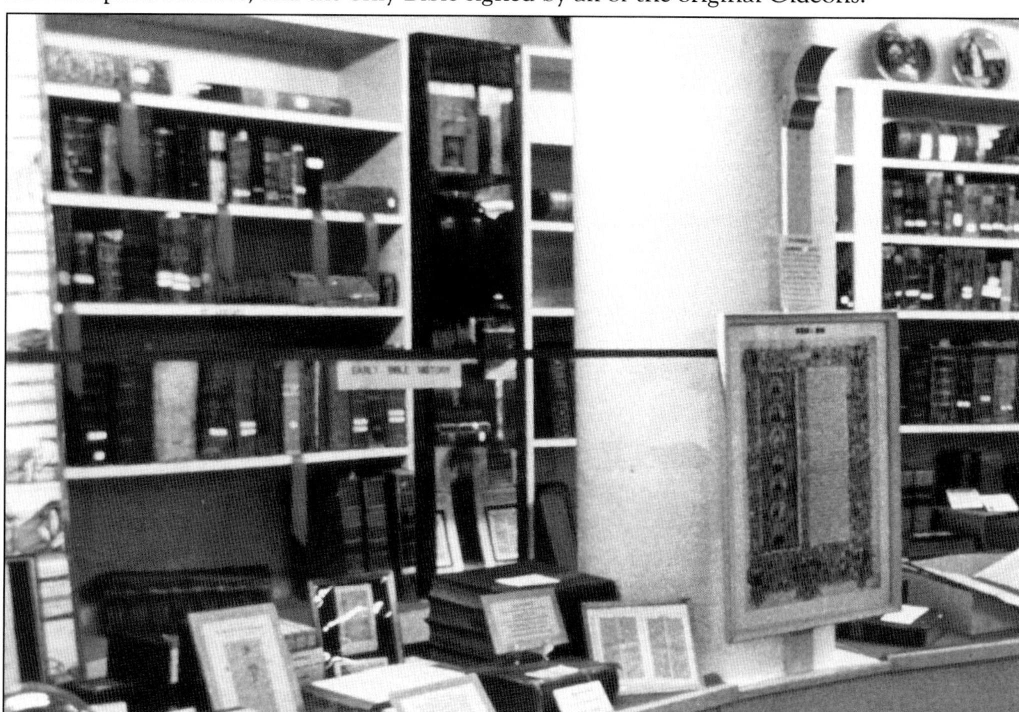

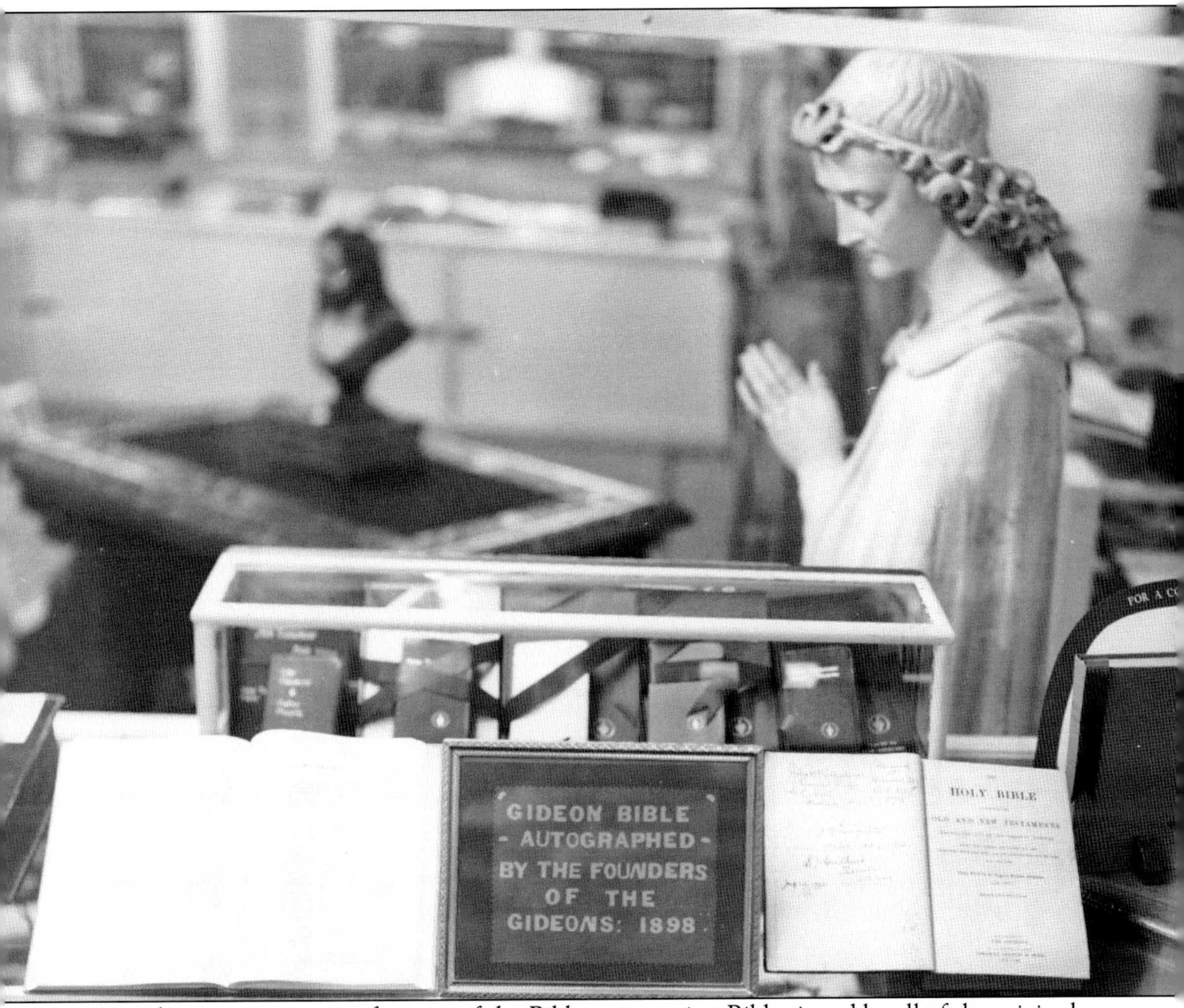

Among the most interesting features of the Bible museum is a Bible signed by all of the original Gideons. This is the only Bible of its kind.

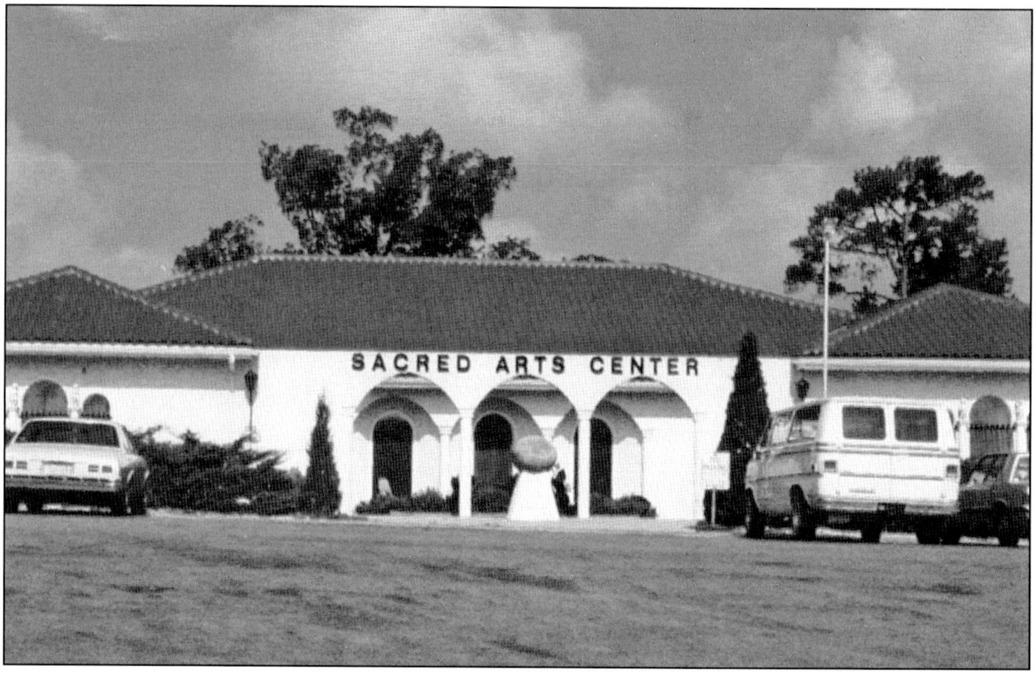

The Sacred Arts Gallery was first entitled the Christ Only Art Gallery. It opened in 1967 in downtown Eureka Springs. As its popularity grew, so did its collection, which included all forms of Biblical art. Today there are thousands of rare works and items that come from all over the world.

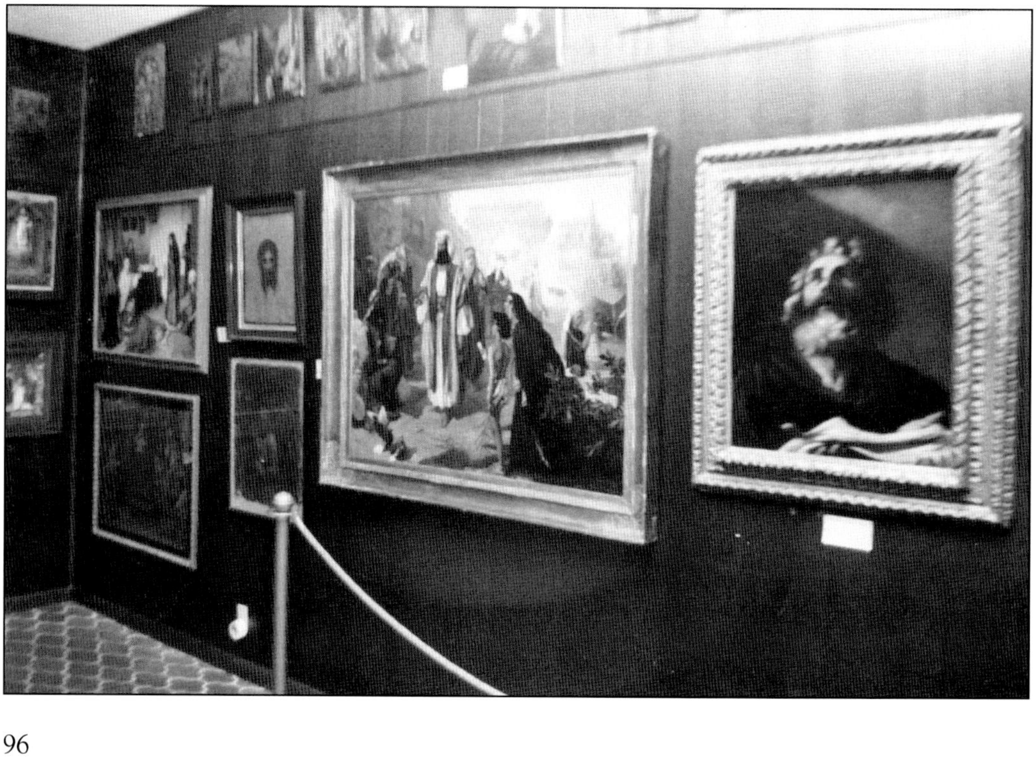

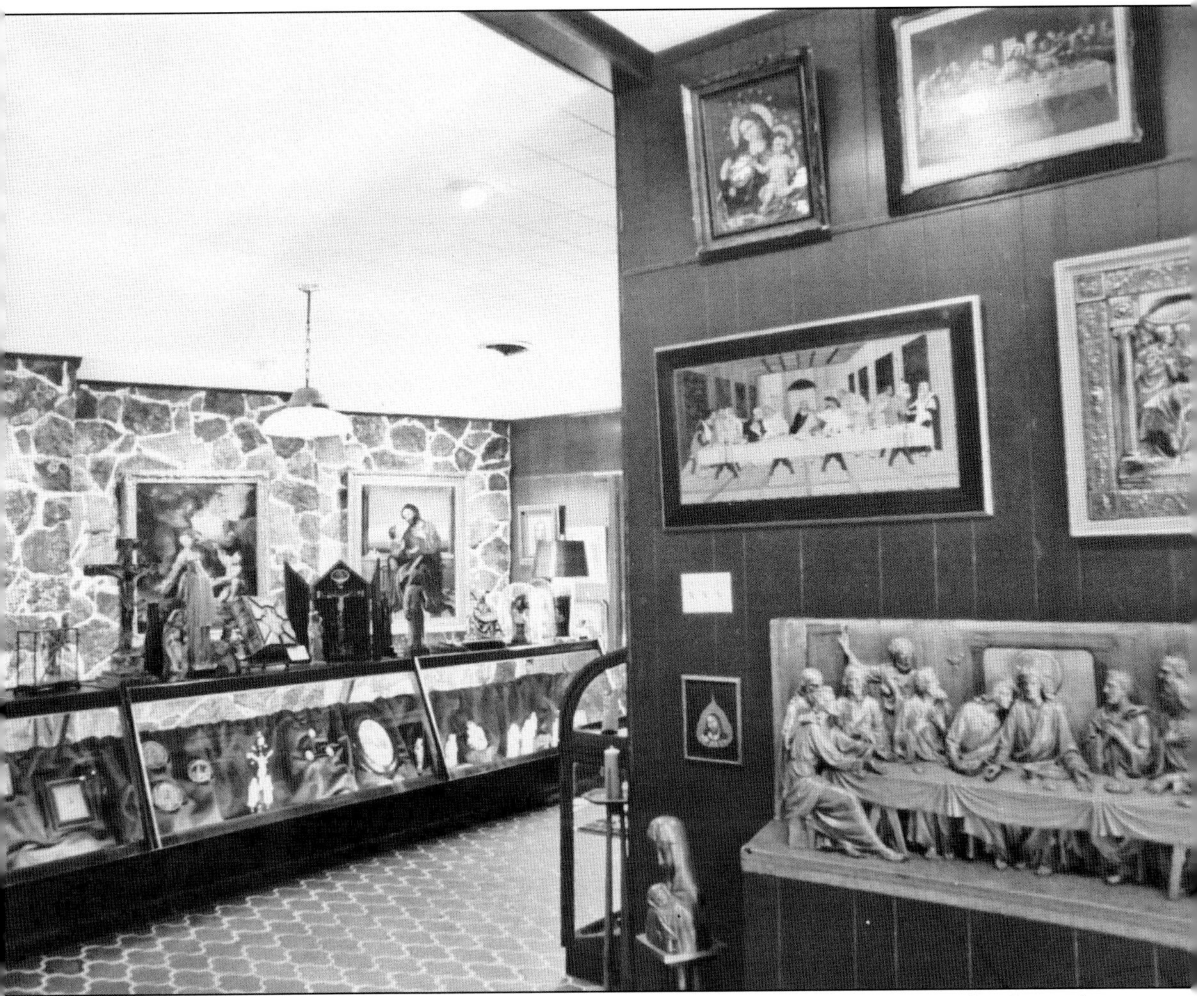

The Sacred Arts museum is an eclectic array of spiritual items. From the beginning, it has housed all forms of artistic design.

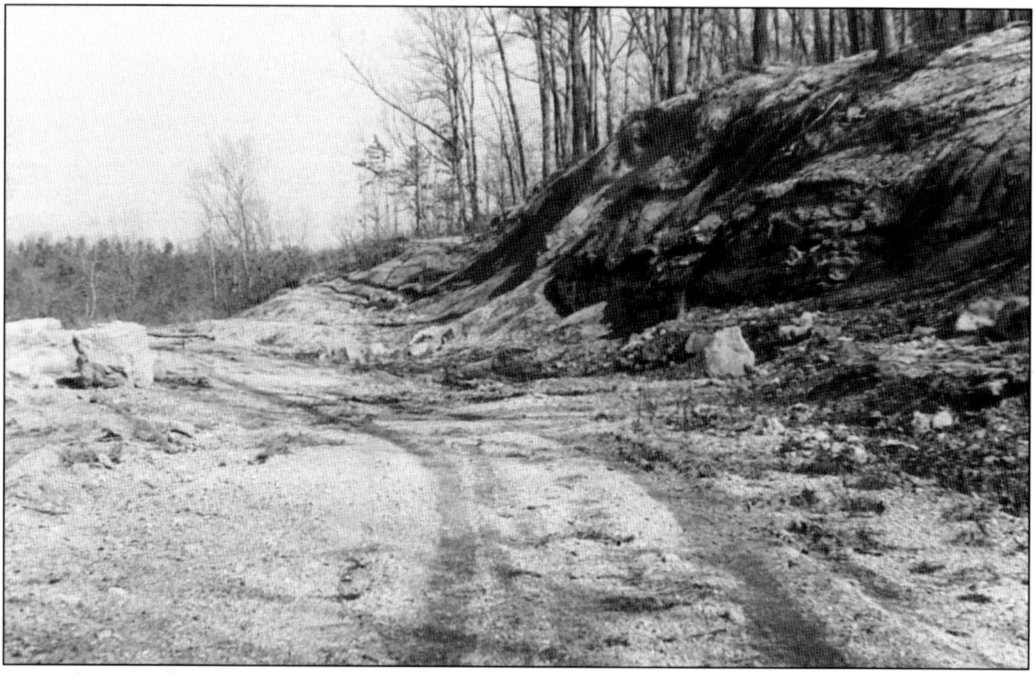

Several years after the New Holy Land entrance was constructed, work began on the new Sea of Galilee. Before the work could begin, roads had to be carved out of the Ozark wilderness, and rough terrain had to be surveyed. The work was hard but fruitful. The creek bed, seen below, was transformed into a lake in several months.

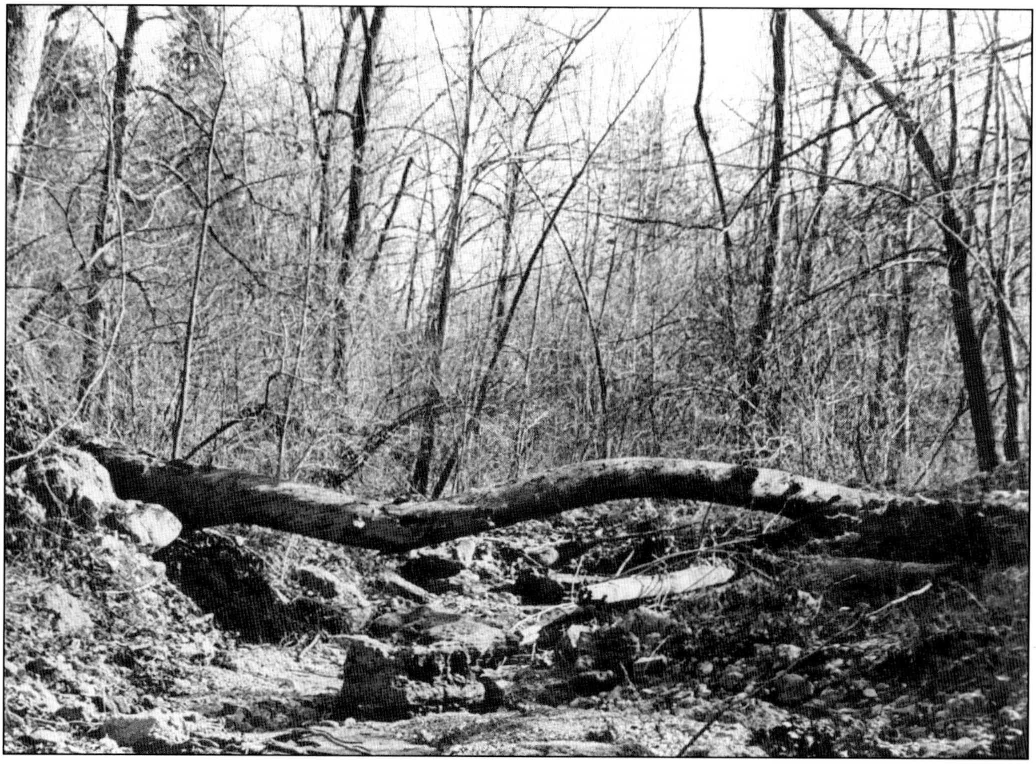

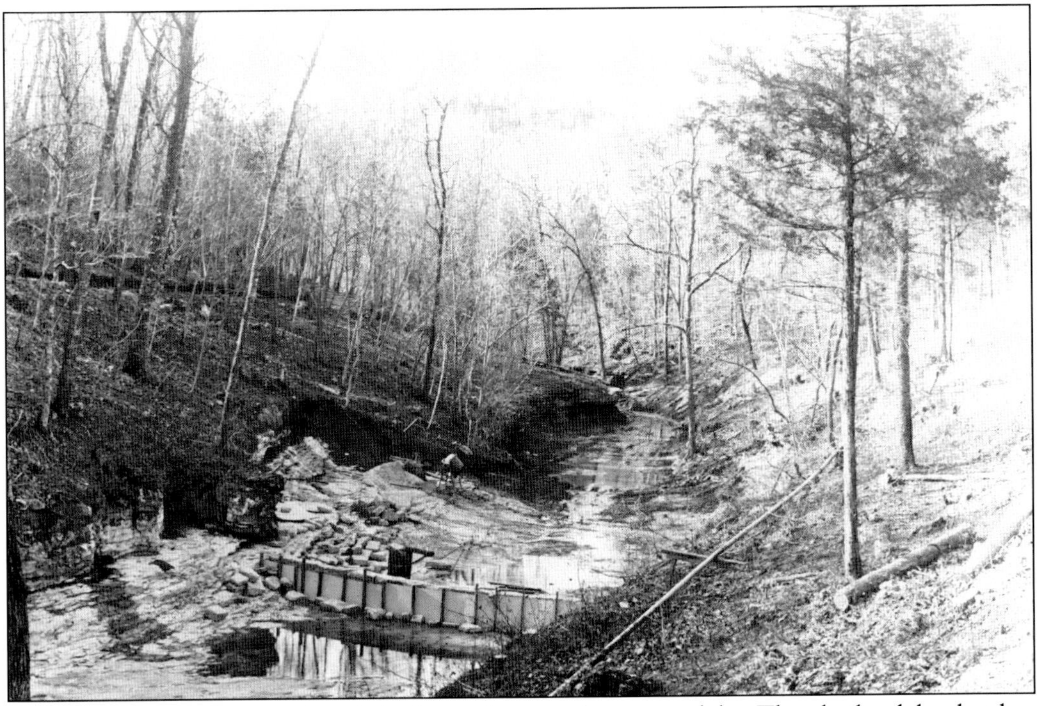

The engineers of the new Sea of Galilee built more than just a lake. They built a lake that has features similar to the original sea. In some cases, this required the removal of bluffs and hard earth. In other cases, rock and cement walls were added in order to reshape the creek bed.

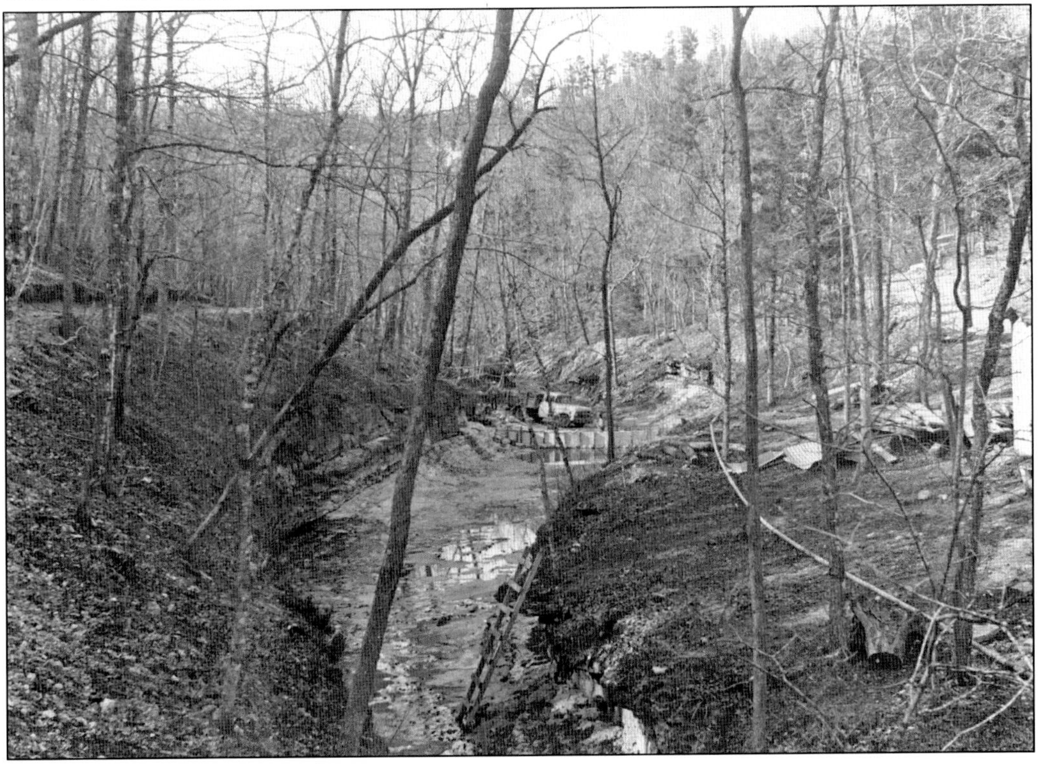

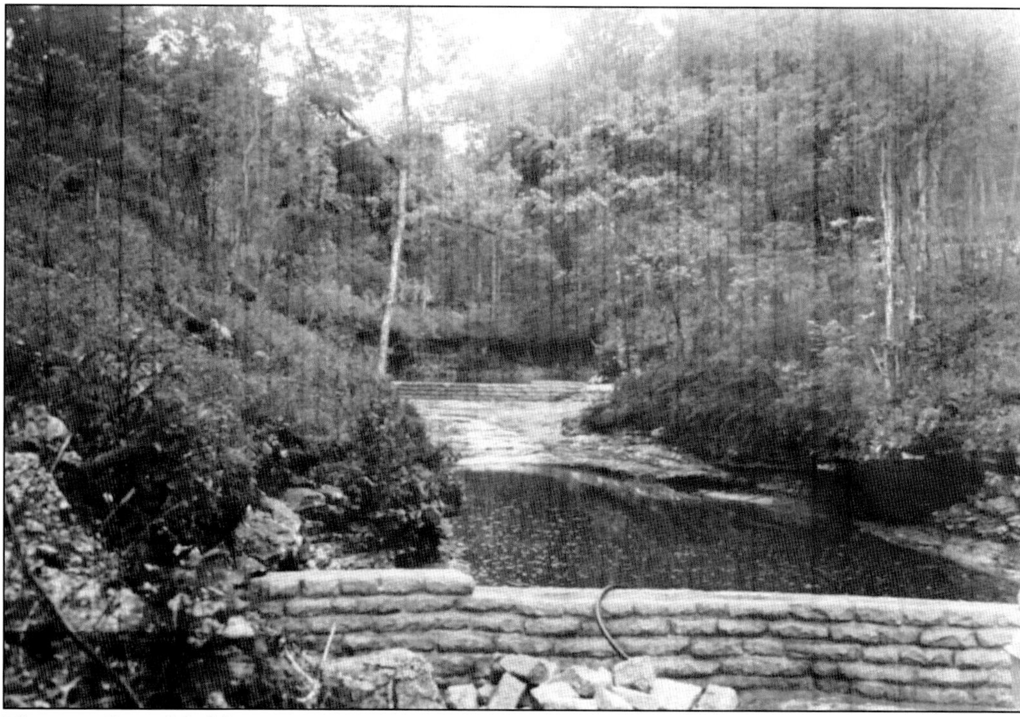

The new Sea of Galilee was an engineering success. Two walls at either end of the creek formed a retaining system that remains to this day.

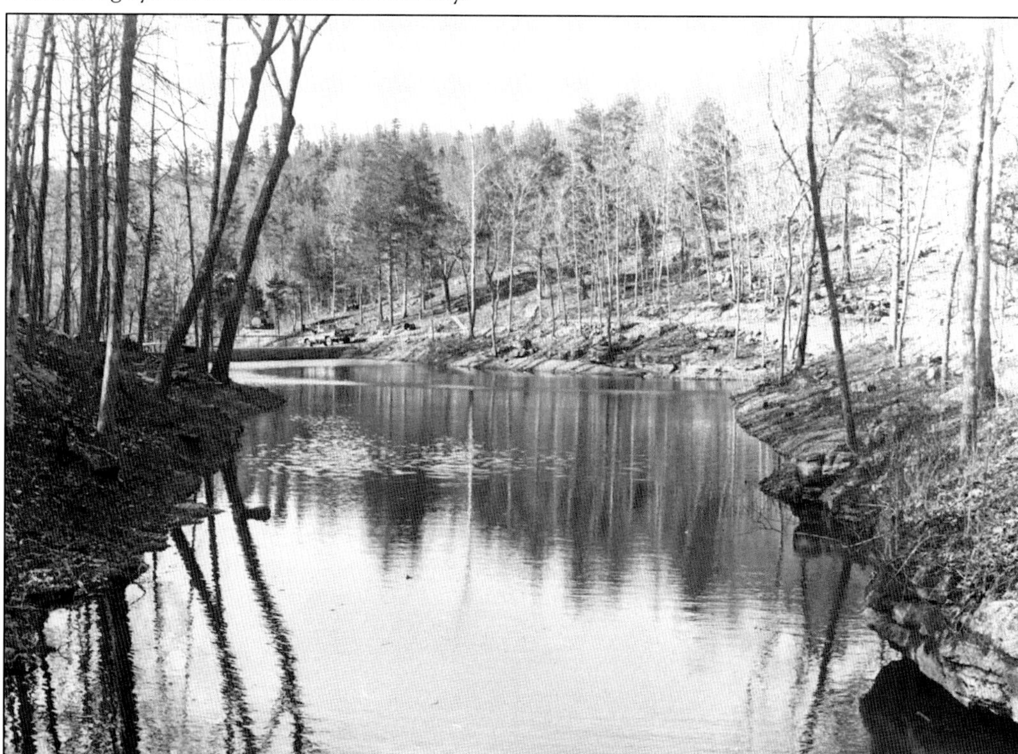

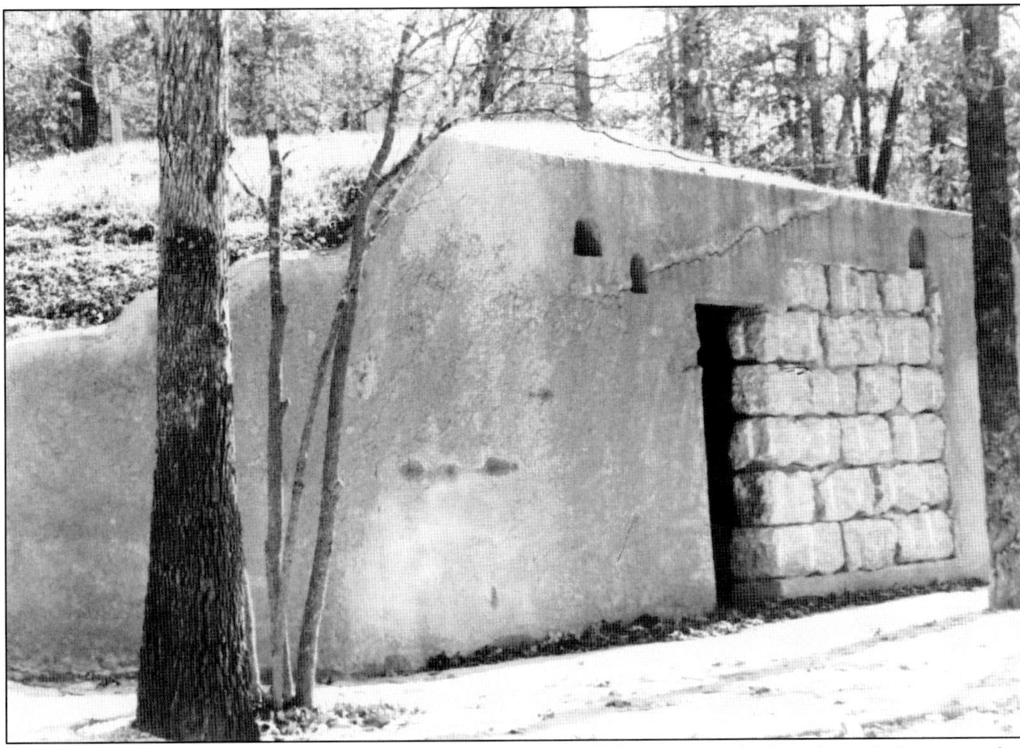

Surrounding the new Sea of Galilee are other pieces of the New Holy Land, including a replica of Christ's tomb and Golgotha. These sites were created to be precise and authentic. Their dimensions were taken directly from Jerusalem sites.

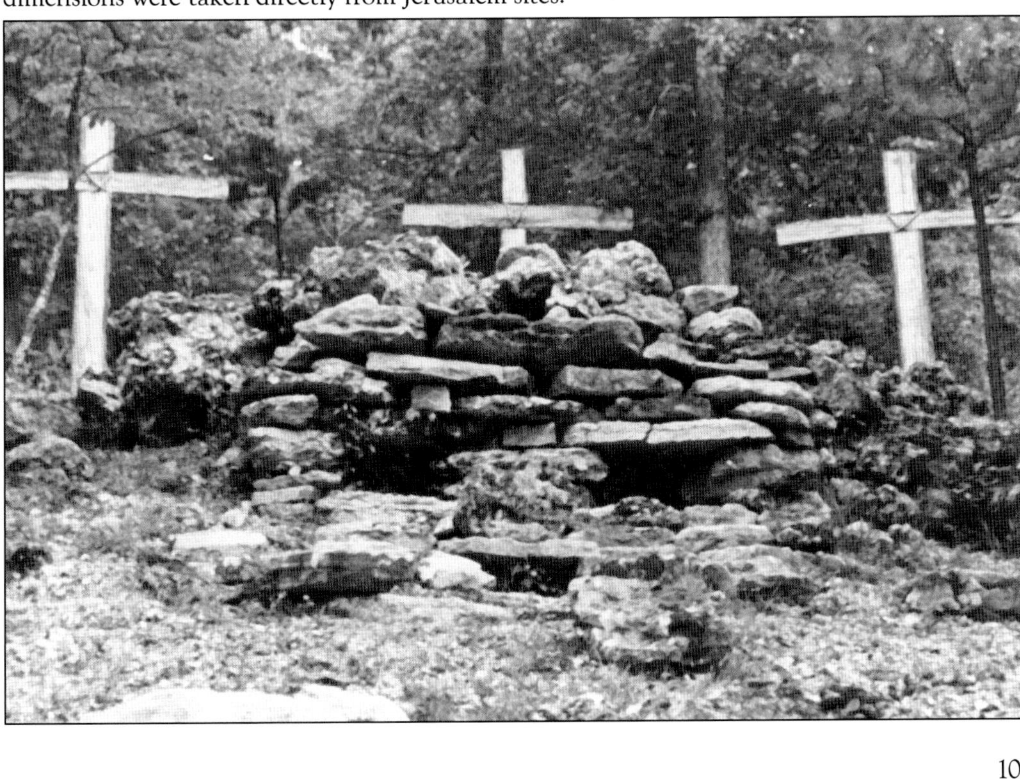

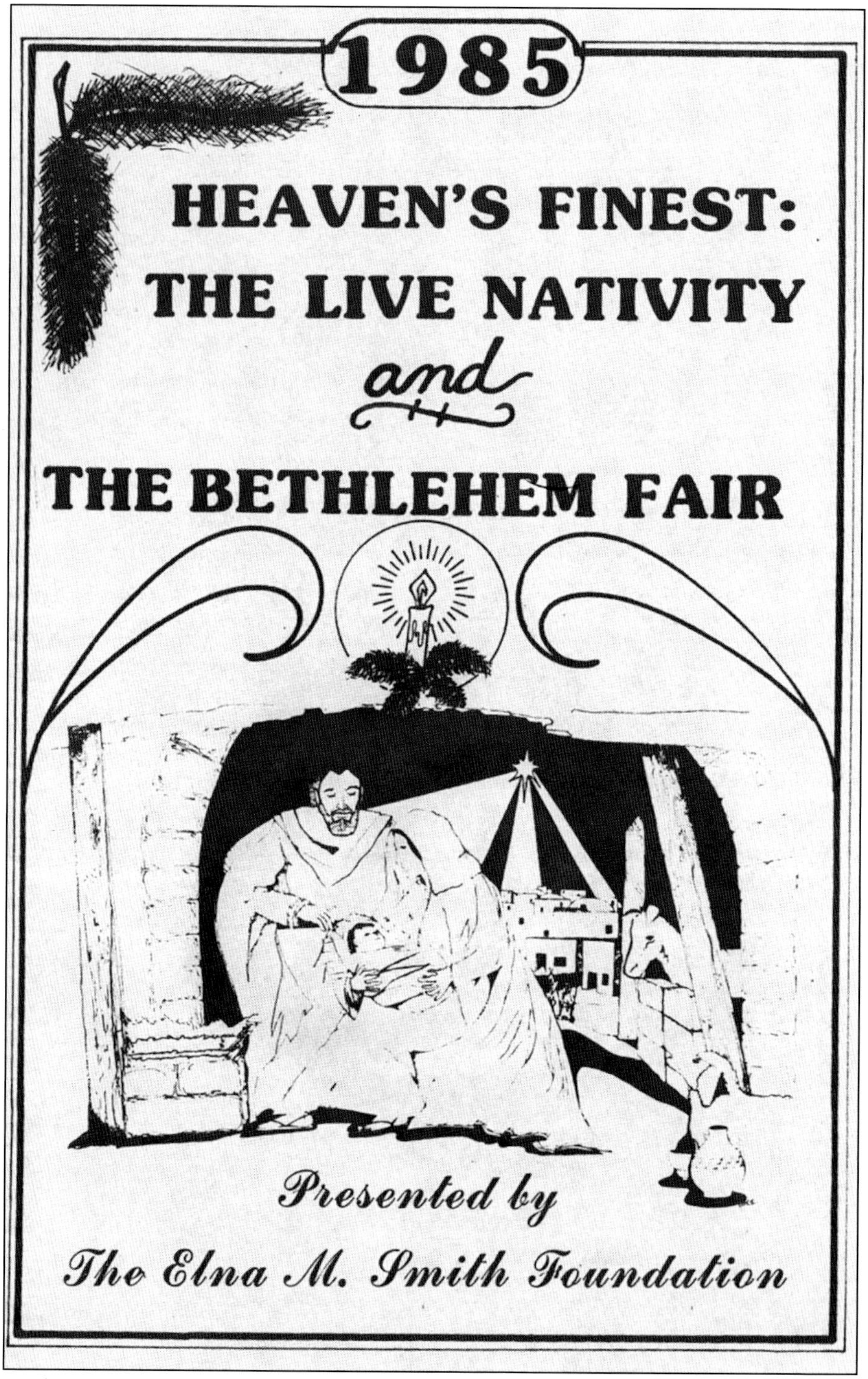

In the mid-1980s, the Elna M. Smith Foundation began an annual Christmas program. Much like its original projects, these performances evolved over time. The Nativity was originally staged behind the New Holy Land entrance and then it moved to the Passion play set. Today the Christmas program, entitled *Beyond Dickens*, is again held in the New Holy Land.

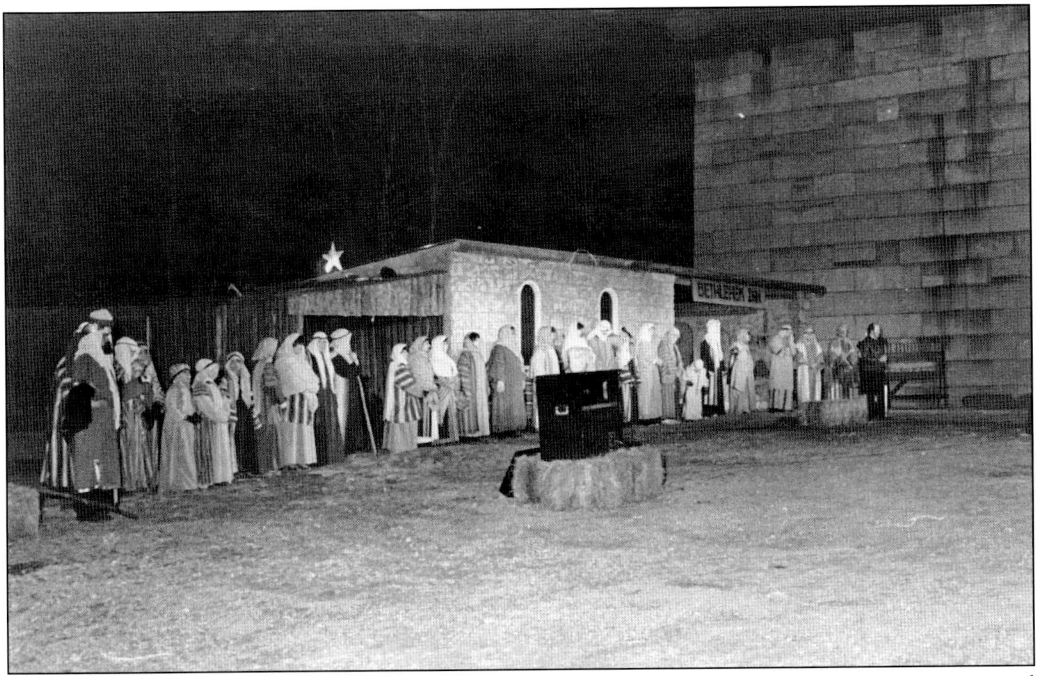

The first live Nativity was a much smaller production then the Passion play. The cast was comprised of volunteers and performed on a makeshift set behind the New Holy Land wall. Microphones, speakers, and wires could not be hidden, and audiences sat on either makeshift bleachers or the cold ground.

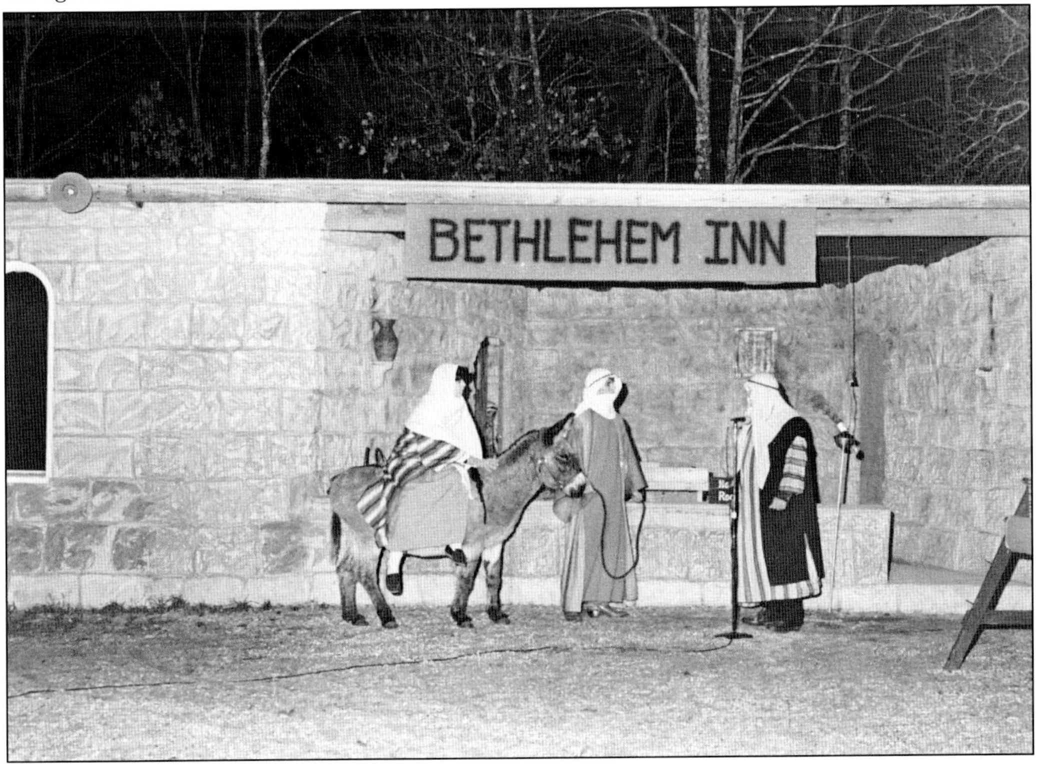

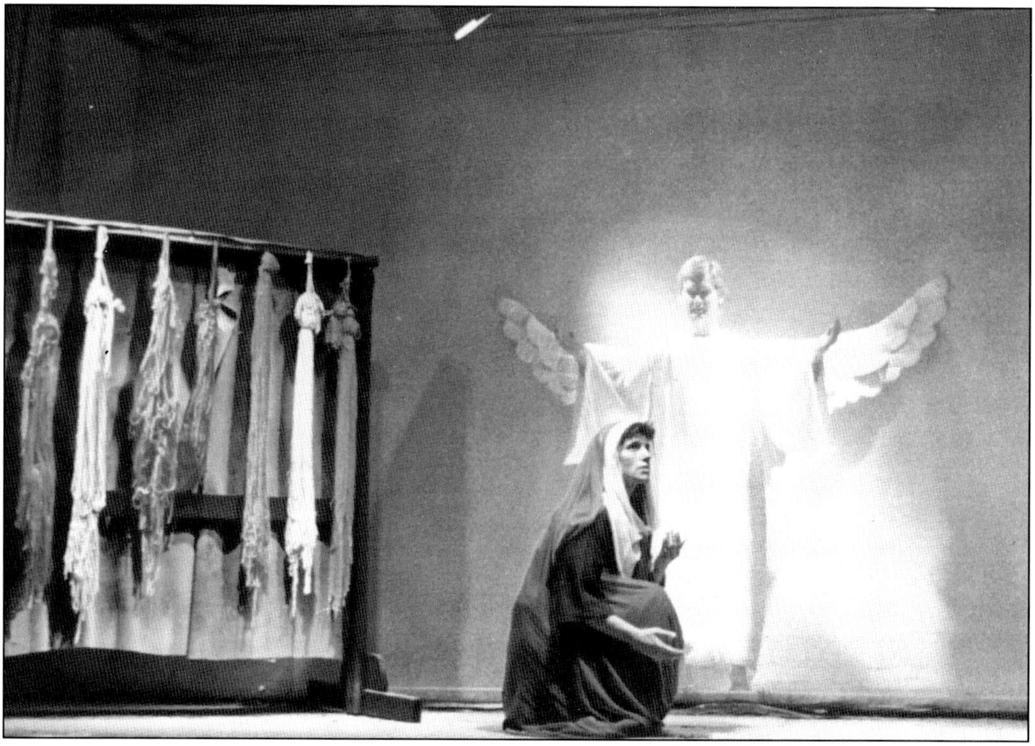

In 1989, the Nativity was moved to the set of *The Great Passion Play*. This allowed the production to utilize the play's many special effects, including the appearance of an angel and the presence of several large animals.

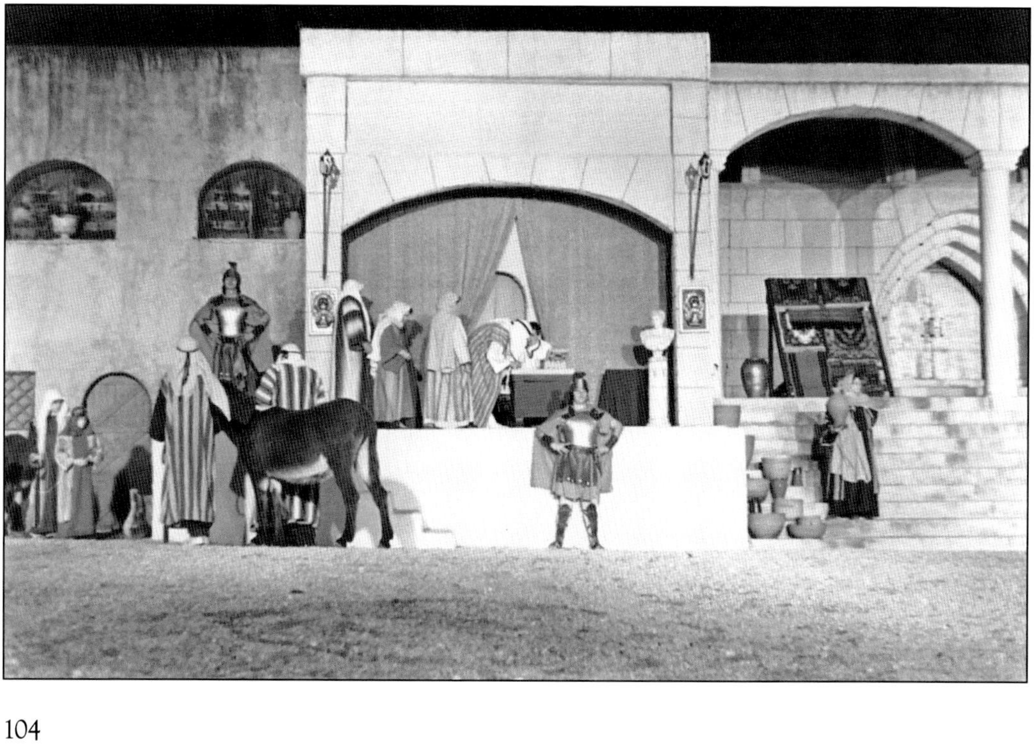

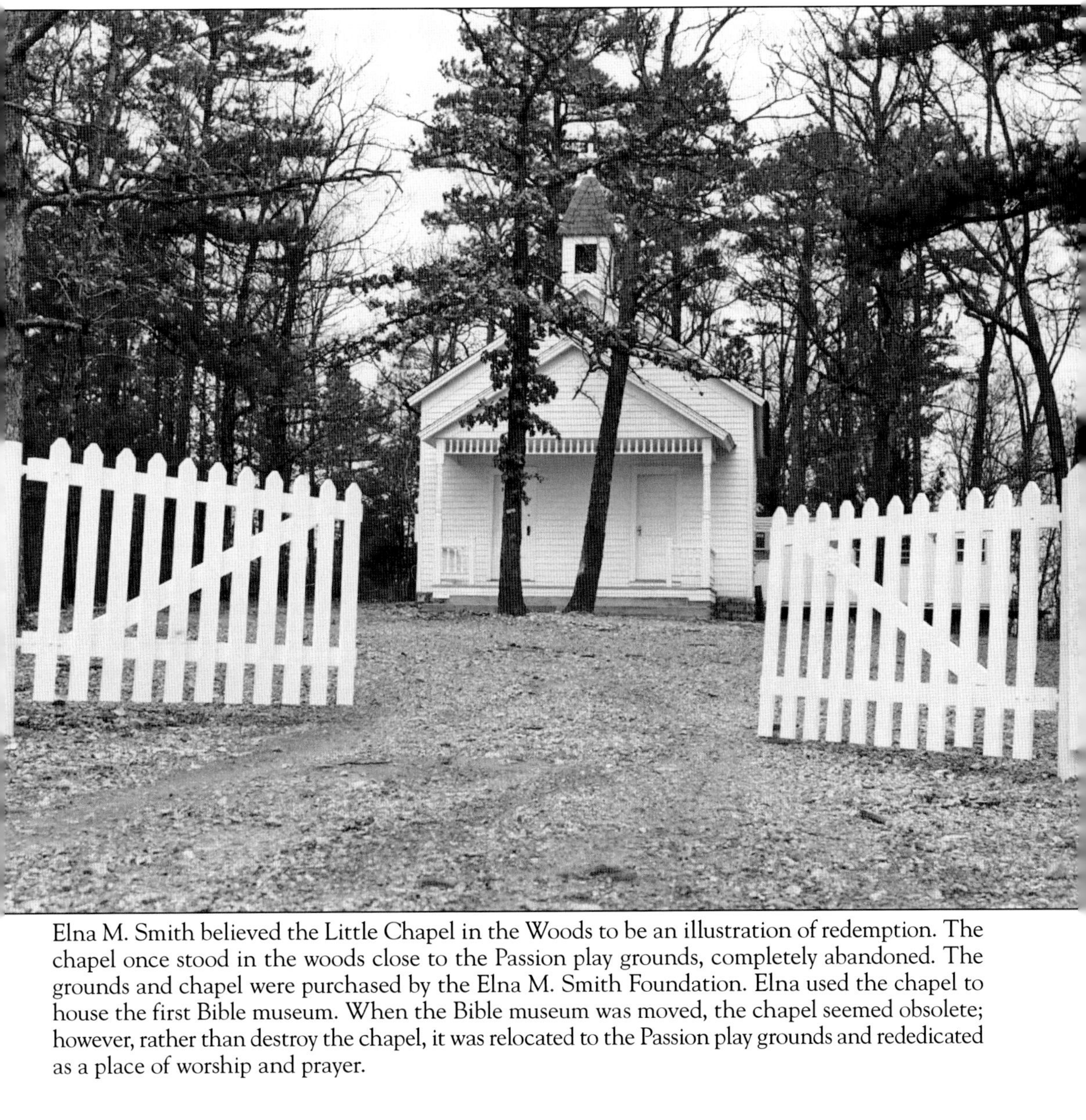

Elna M. Smith believed the Little Chapel in the Woods to be an illustration of redemption. The chapel once stood in the woods close to the Passion play grounds, completely abandoned. The grounds and chapel were purchased by the Elna M. Smith Foundation. Elna used the chapel to house the first Bible museum. When the Bible museum was moved, the chapel seemed obsolete; however, rather than destroy the chapel, it was relocated to the Passion play grounds and rededicated as a place of worship and prayer.

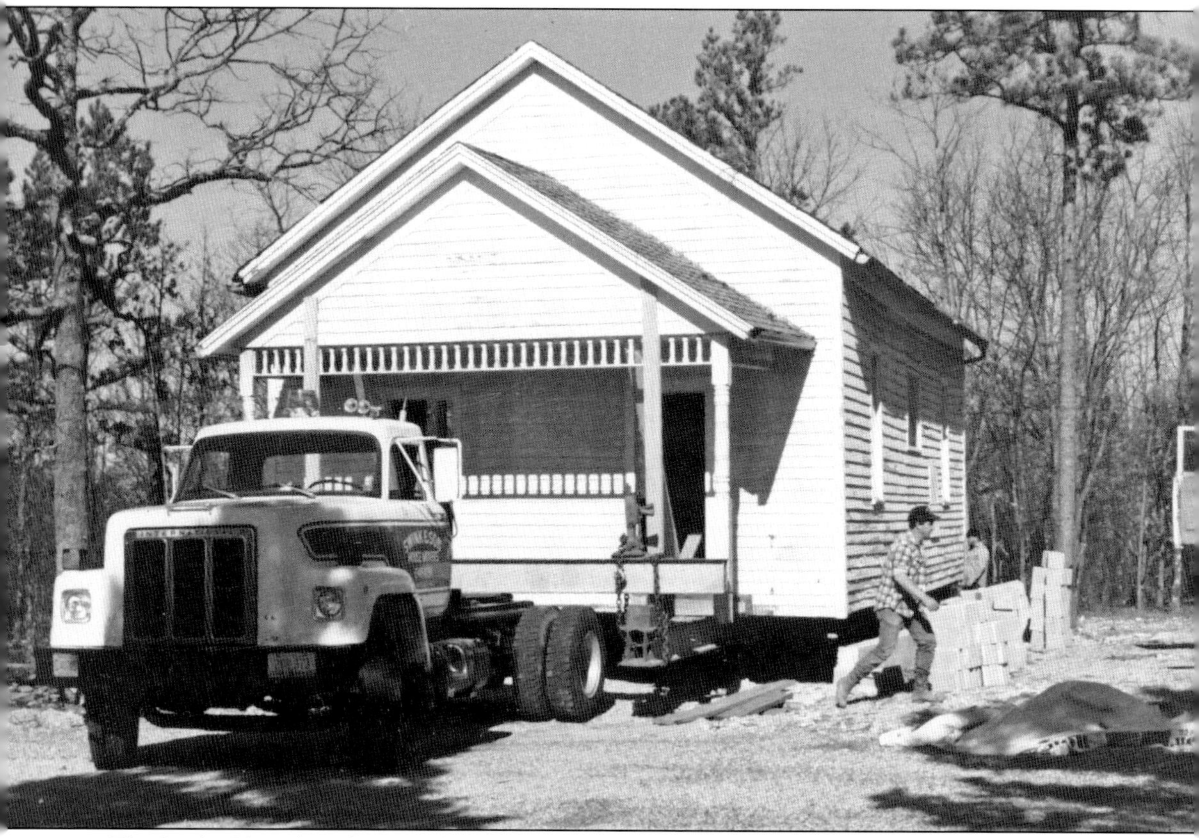

The Little Chapel in the Woods originally sat four miles from the Passion play grounds. It was nestled in the woods close to Highway 62 and was slowly falling into disrepair.

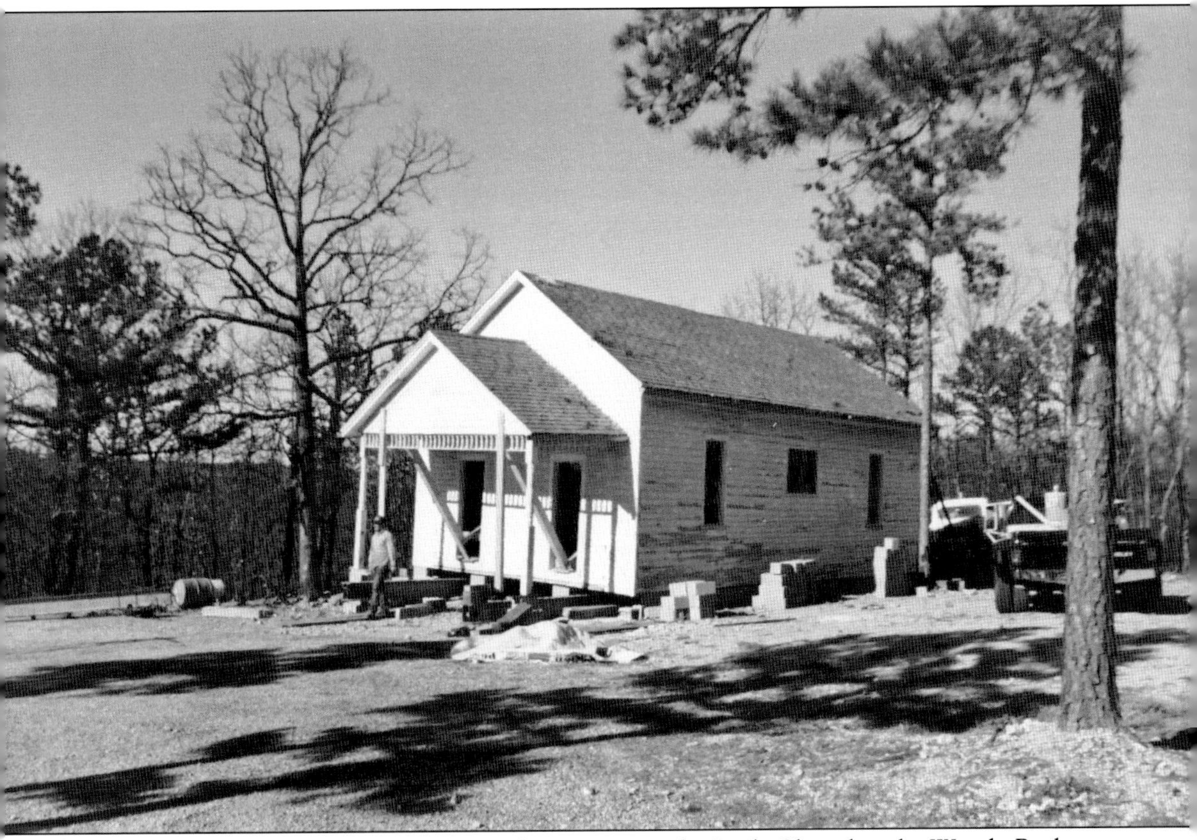

In the early 1980s, a decision had to be made concerning the Little Chapel in the Woods. Rather than destroy it, it was decided to move it.

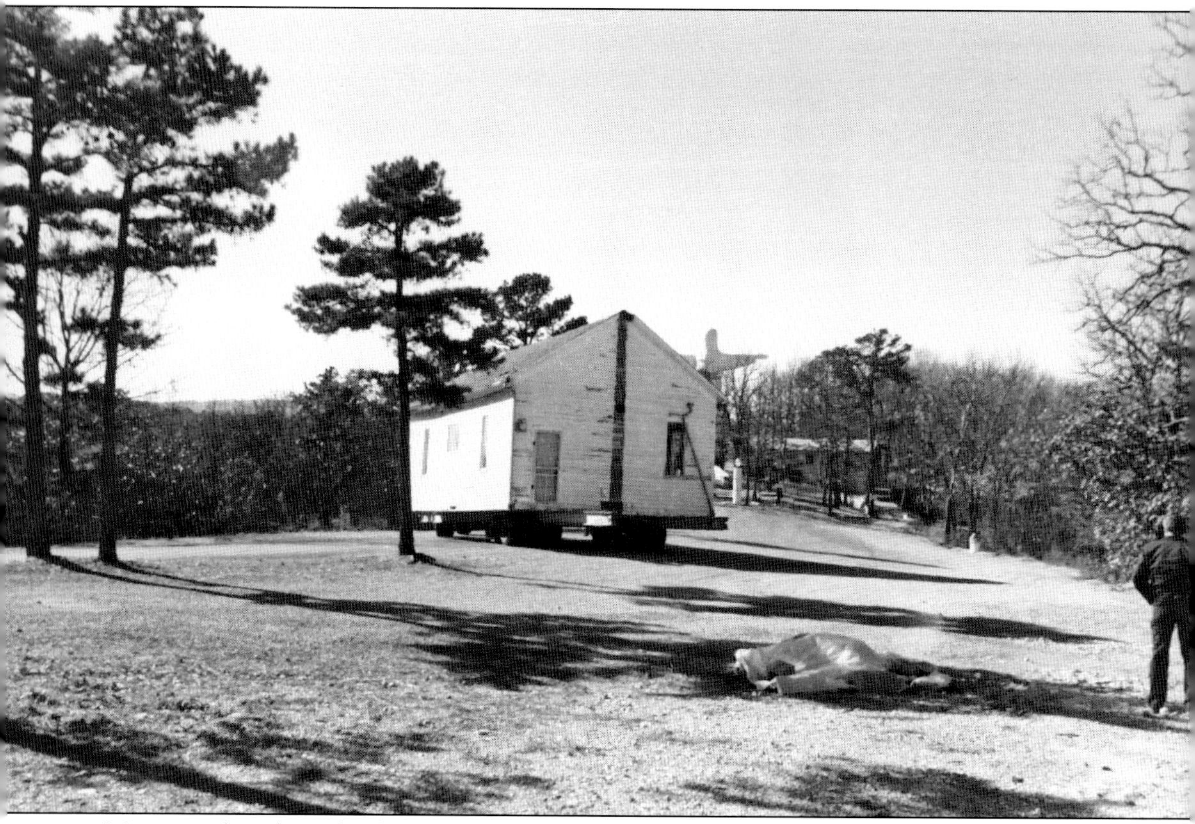

Moving a chapel on wheels was a sight to behold. It was cumbersome and slow work. For a matter of hours, it blocked traffic on the highway in both directions.

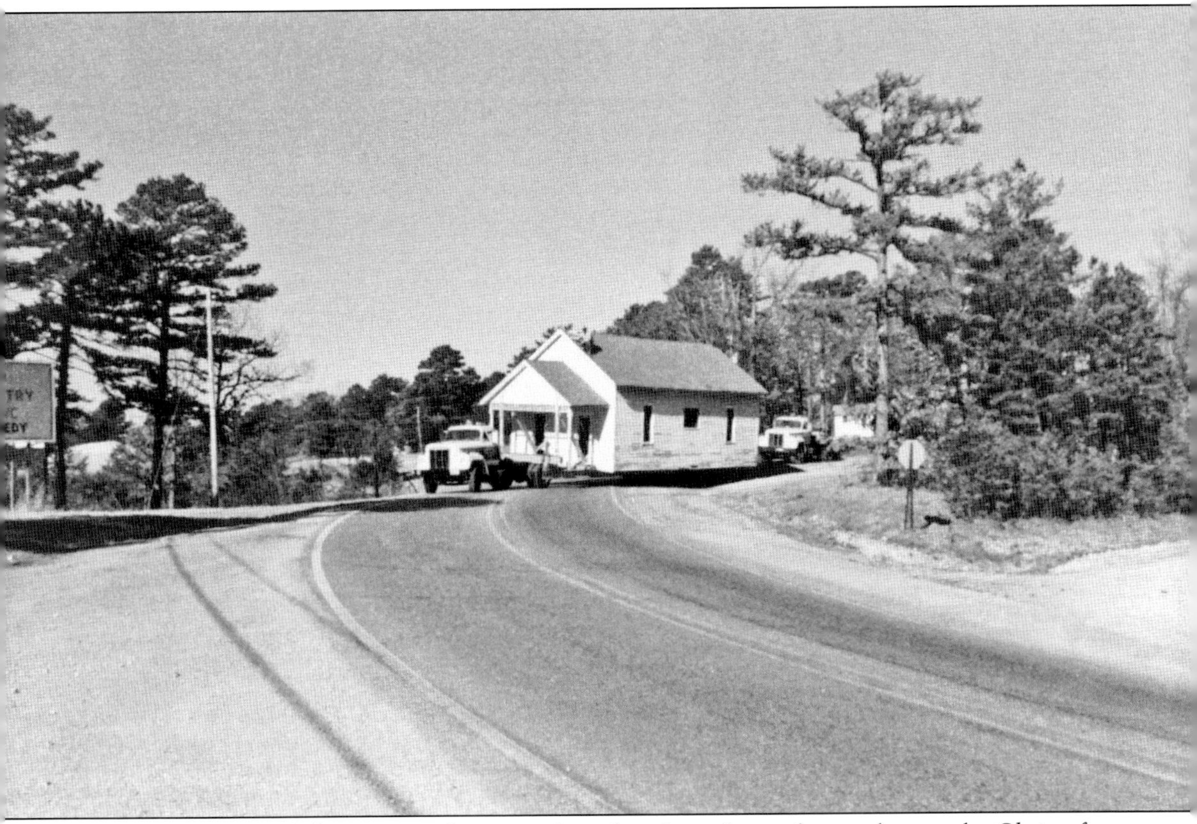

As the chapel reached the Passion play grounds, it found a welcome home close to the *Christ of the Ozarks* statue. Today it is a place of worship, prayer, and reflection.

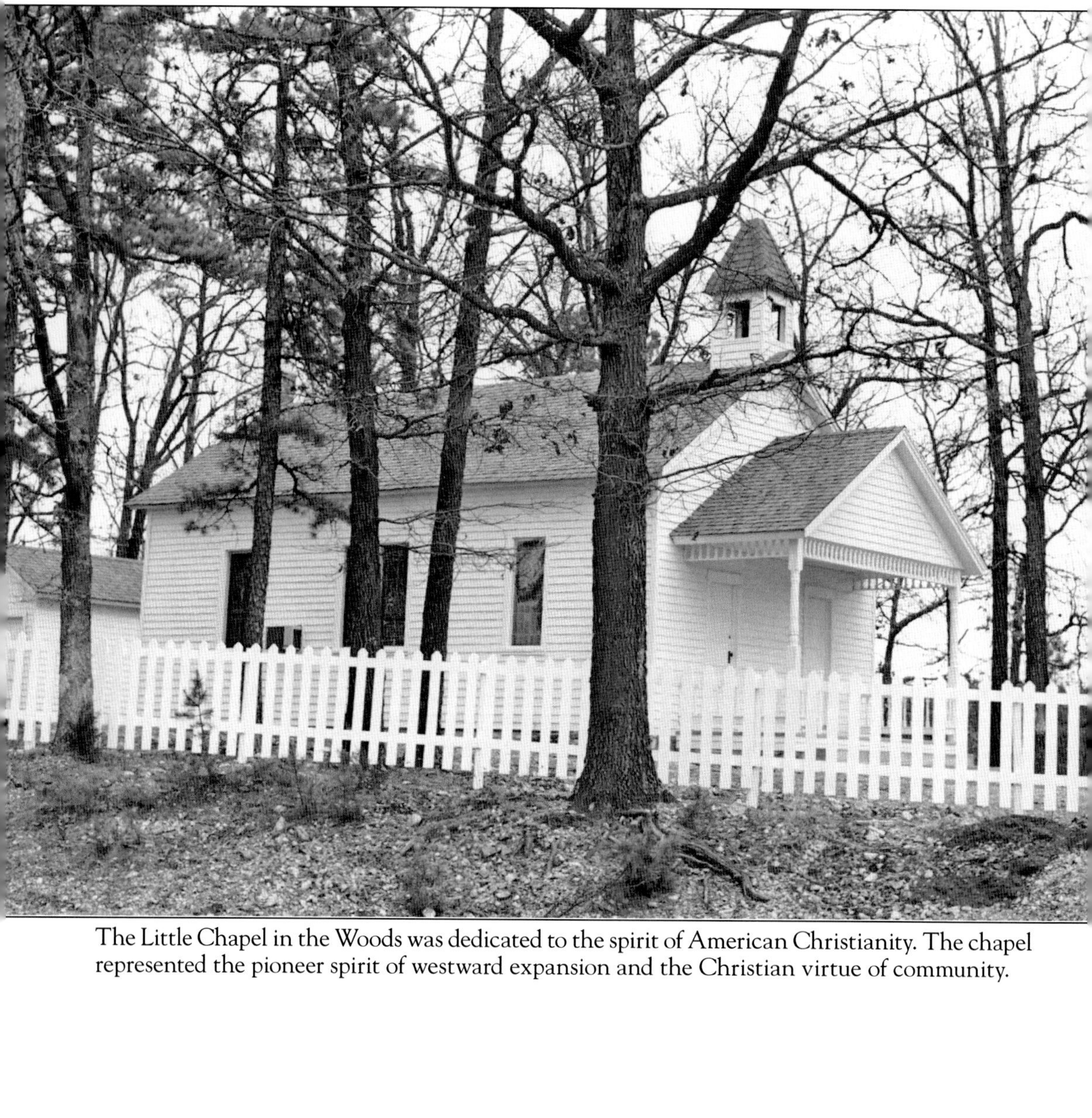

The Little Chapel in the Woods was dedicated to the spirit of American Christianity. The chapel represented the pioneer spirit of westward expansion and the Christian virtue of community.

Five

Behind the Scenes

The Great Passion Play is a large production. But the employees of the foundation are a family. This idea was fostered from the beginning. In fact, the original cast did not get a paycheck. Their earnings were donated to their local churches. In other words, they participated because they believed in the projects and their inherent worth.

Over time, the cast changed and evolved. Some members have been there for 40 years. Others have participated in the Passion play since the year of their birth, and still others commute from hours away just to be in the cast. These employees perform in all roles and contribute at all levels. The current director and chief sound technician were both part of the original cast. Some others have added their voices to the soundtrack, and some characters have played the same role for decades. It is an elite fraternity that comes with its own special pleasures.

Within this community are the tricks of the trade. When the audience looks at the set, they see a street in Jerusalem. When the cast looks at the set, they see hidden passageways, curtains that aide in the special effects, alcoves that hide technicians, props that look authentic but are either plastic or fiberglass, cue lights, and much more. This perspective takes away some of the mystery, but it adds to the drama of the production.

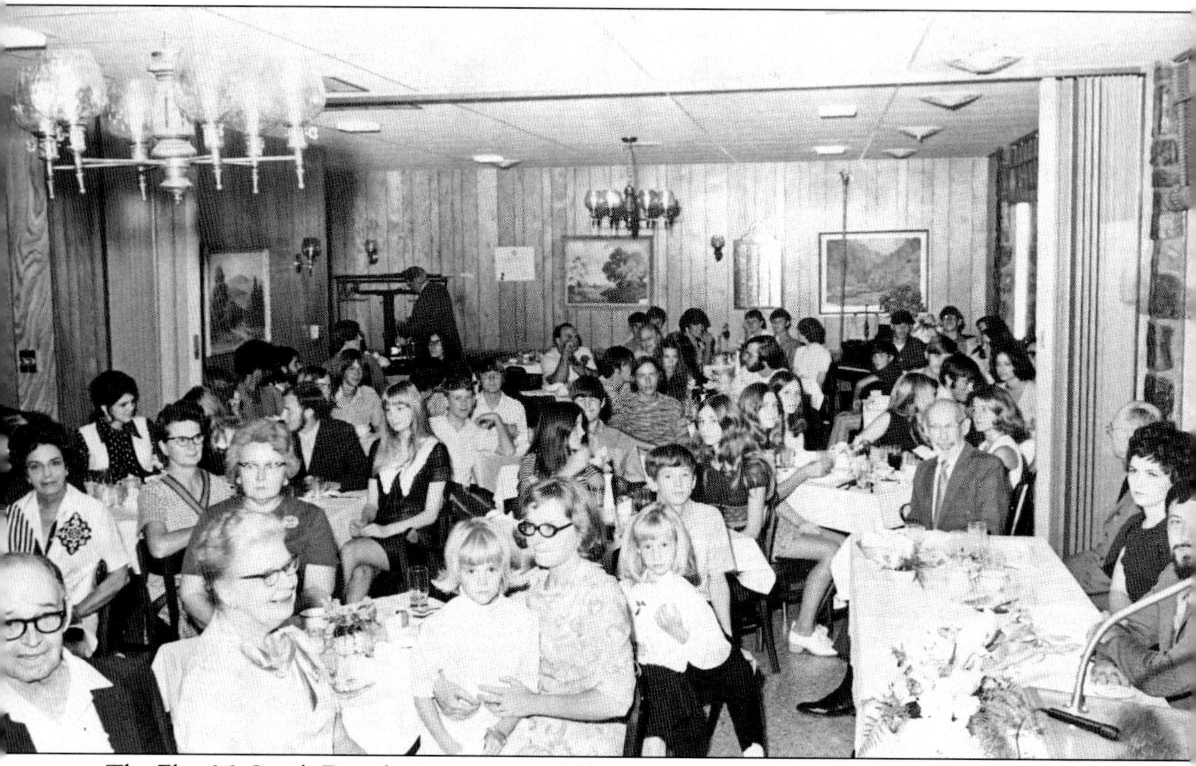

The Elna M. Smith Foundation was incredibly proud of its accomplishments in 1968. To honor the local cast members, the foundation sponsored an end-of-the-year banquet, pictured above. Such banquets were held annually until recent years.

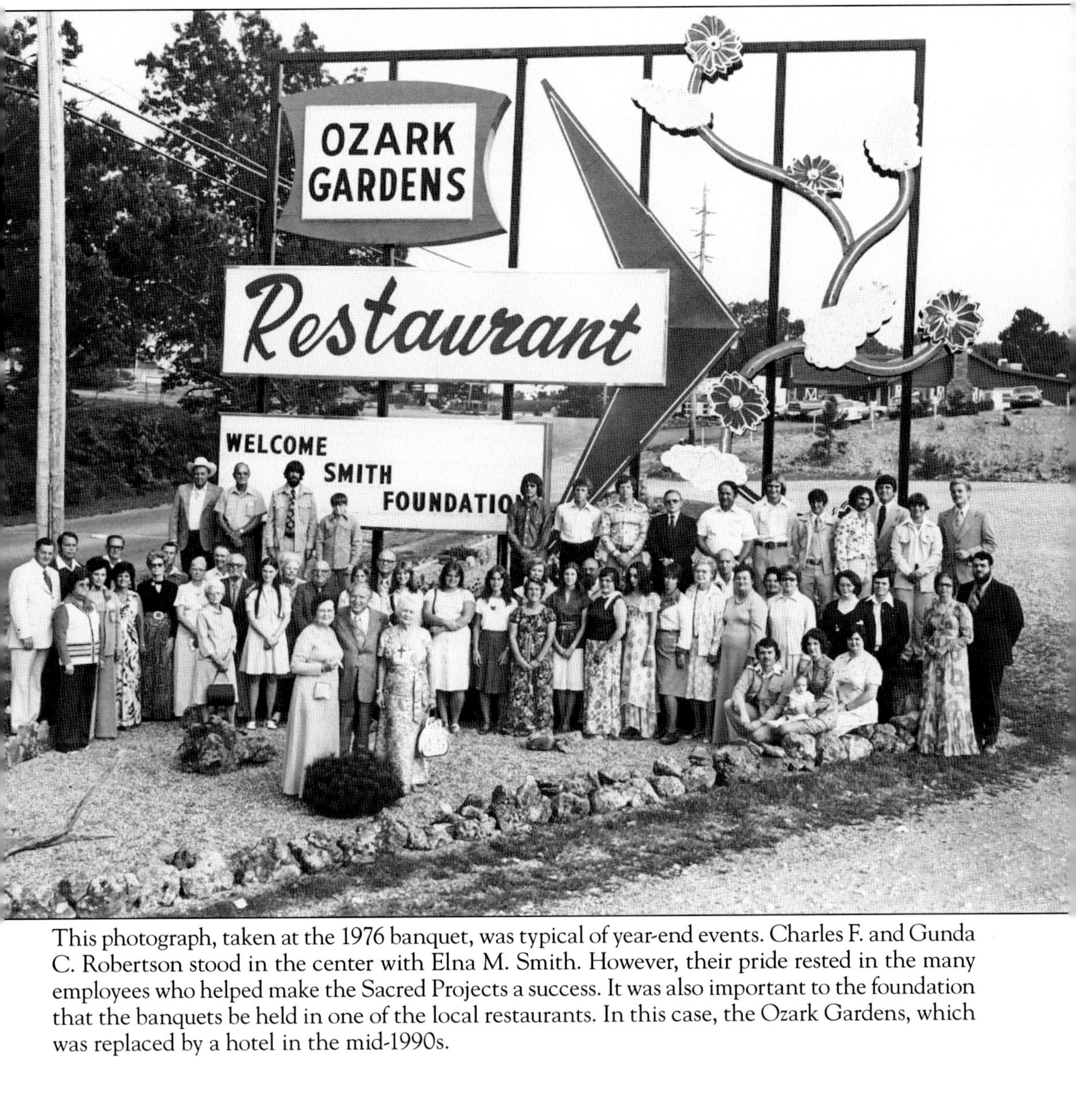

This photograph, taken at the 1976 banquet, was typical of year-end events. Charles F. and Gunda C. Robertson stood in the center with Elna M. Smith. However, their pride rested in the many employees who helped make the Sacred Projects a success. It was also important to the foundation that the banquets be held in one of the local restaurants. In this case, the Ozark Gardens, which was replaced by a hotel in the mid-1990s.

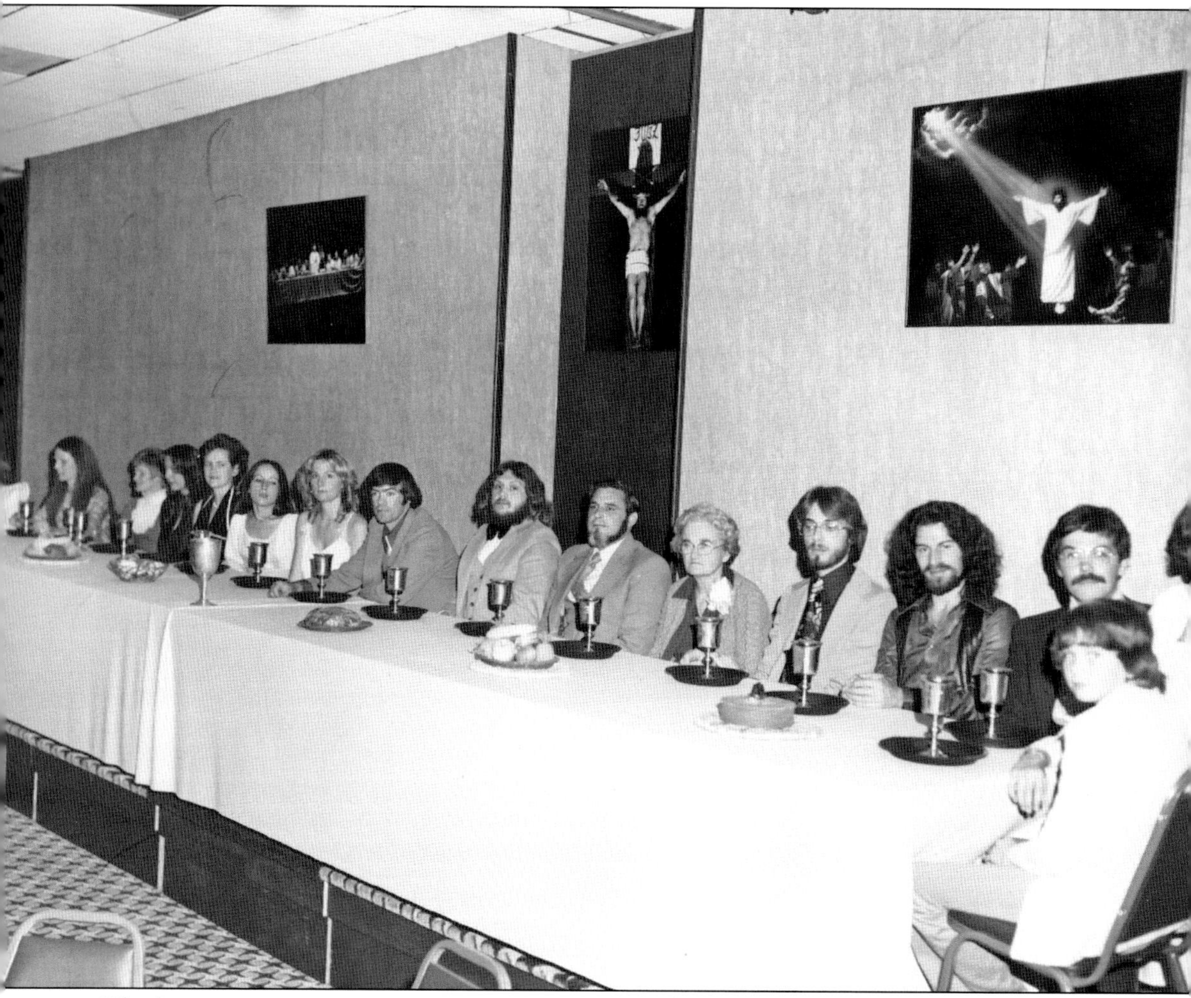

The banquets were opportunities to recognize significant achievements among employees. In this photograph, employees who worked for the Elna M. Smith Foundation for 10 years were honored with silver cups.

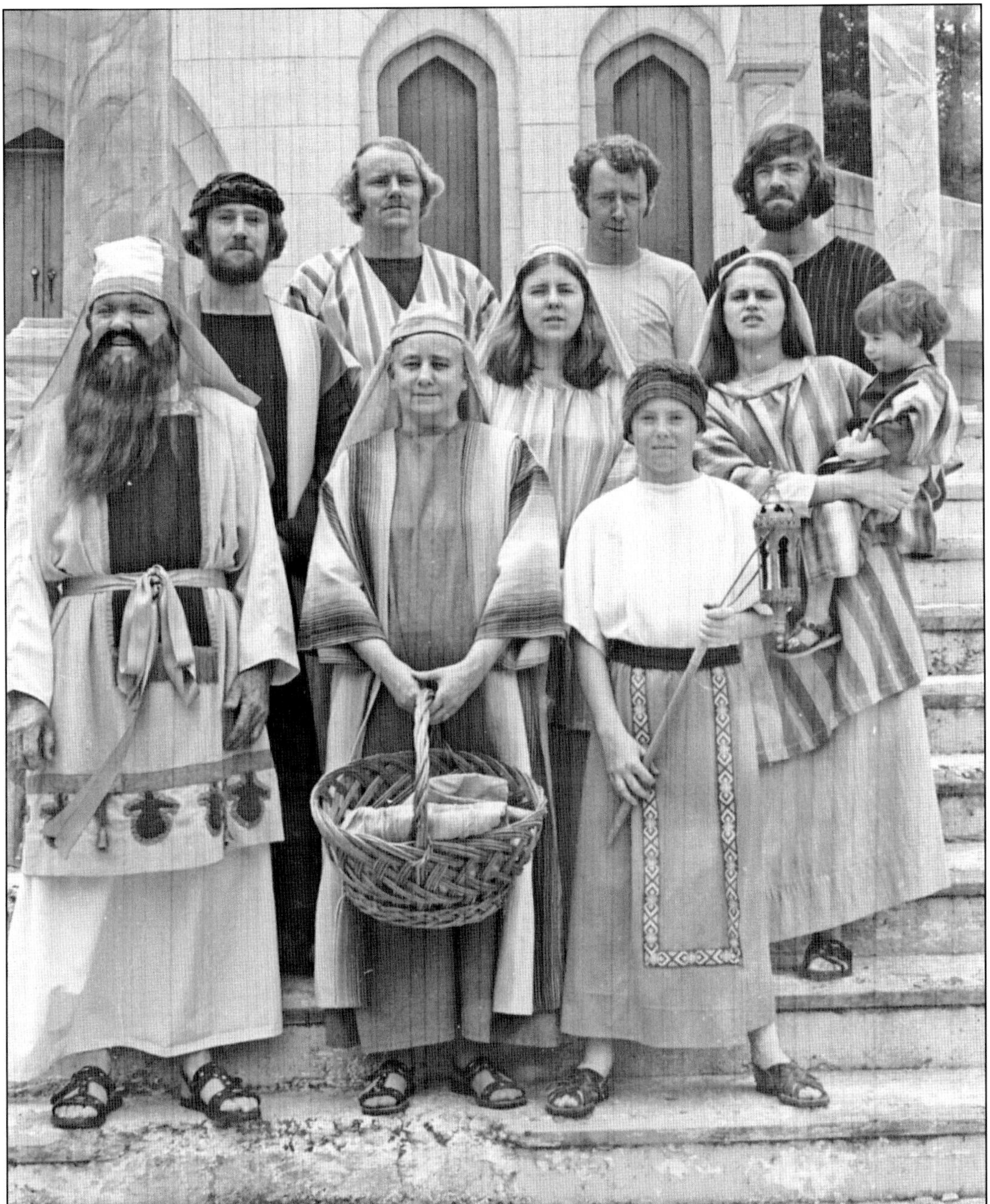

The Elna M. Smith Foundation encouraged family participation from its inception. Many of these families had long tenures at the Passion play, including the Clark family, which was part of the original cast. Such families still play a central role in the production of the play. For example, Benny Clark is the current director of production, and Floyd Clark is the chief sound technician. Pictured from left to right are (first row) father Bud Clark, mother Anna Lee Clark, and son James Clark; (second row) son Robert Clark, son David Clark, daughter-in-law Loveina Clark, son Floyd Clark, daughter-in-law Linda Clark holding grandson Joseph Clark, and son Benny Clark.

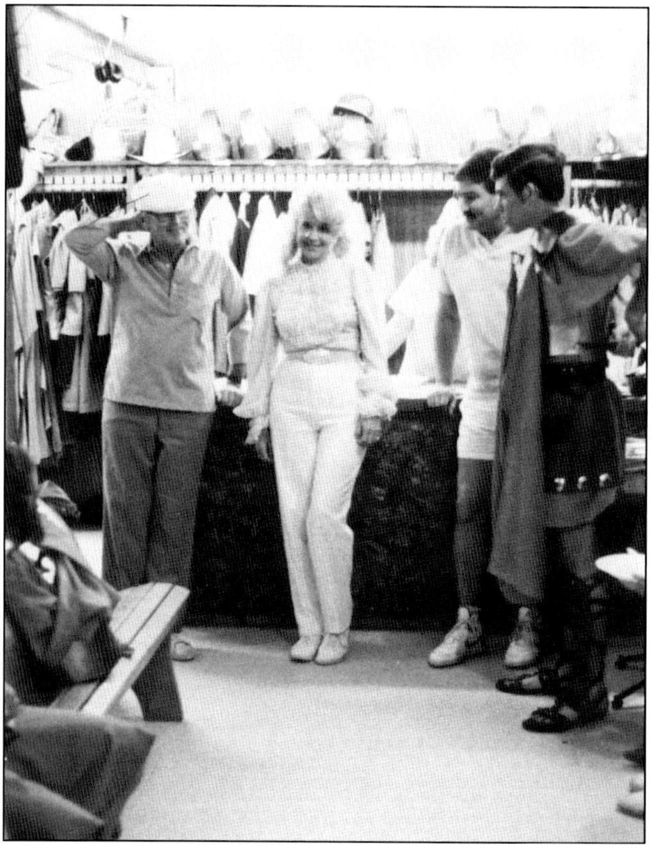

Over the years, many prominent individuals have visited performances of *The Great Passion Play*, including Hollywood celebrities and African royalty. In the early 1990s, Donna Douglas, best known for her role as Daisy Mae in *The Beverly Hillbillies*, visited the cast and was given a personal tour backstage by director Don Berrigan.

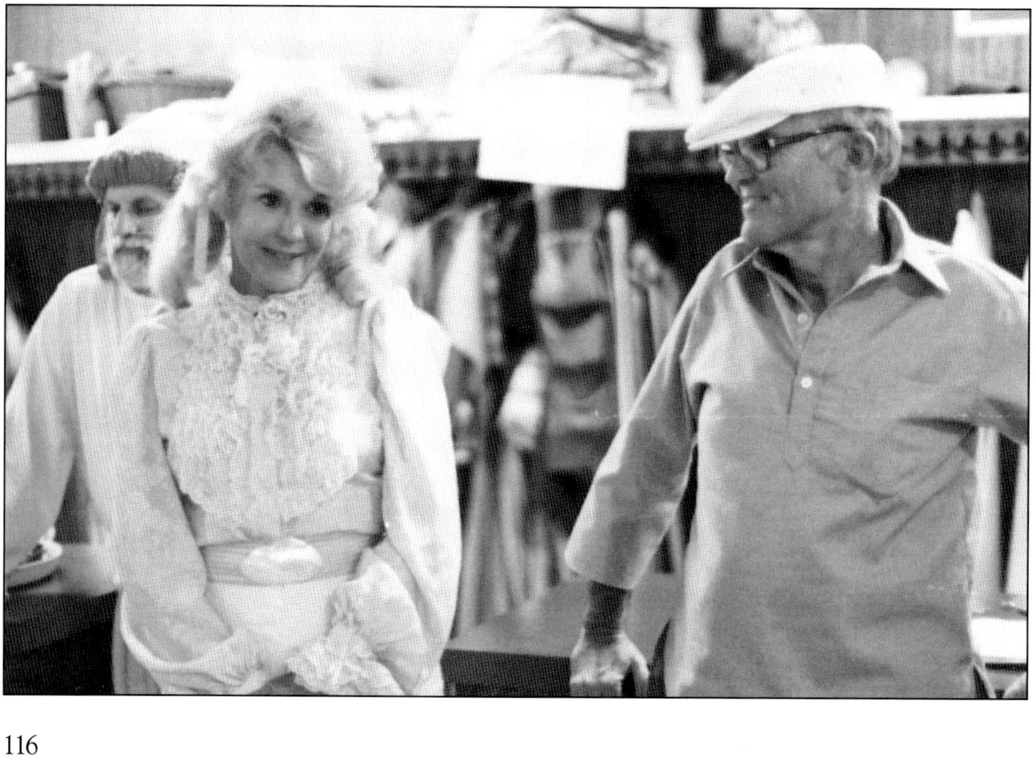

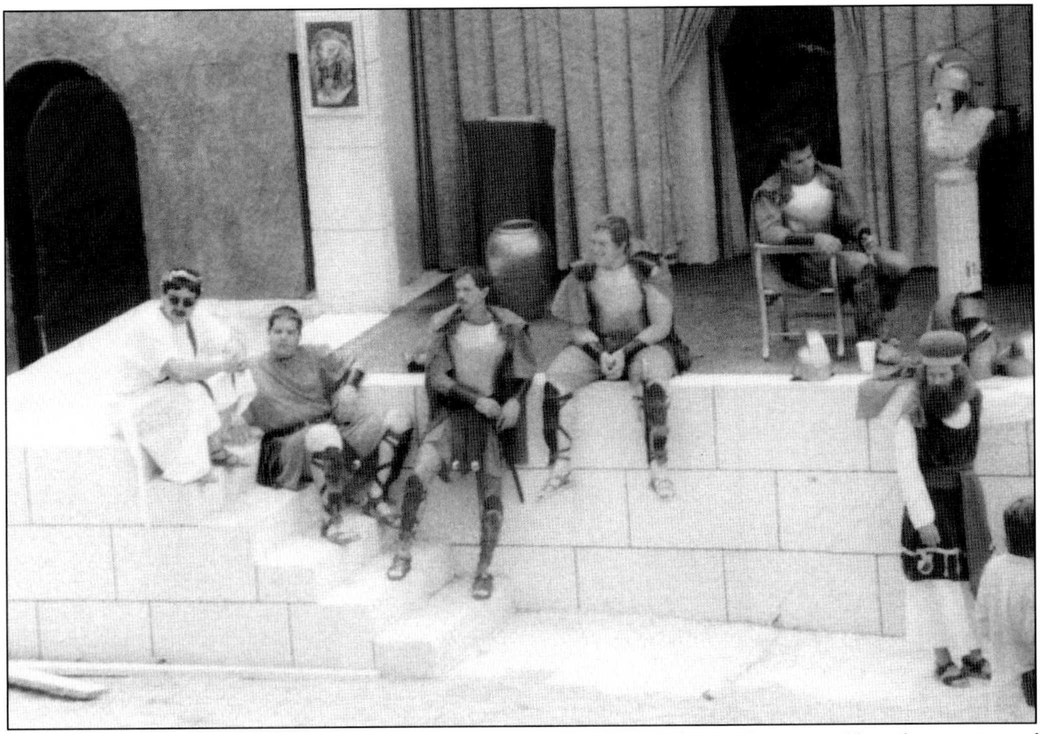

In 1991, *The Great Passion Play* became a movie set. Fire By Night productions filmed a portion of Michael W. Smith's video *Secret Ambition*. The production crew used cast members for key roles in the film. The production also required all available laborers, who helped move the equipment to strategic locations, as shown below.

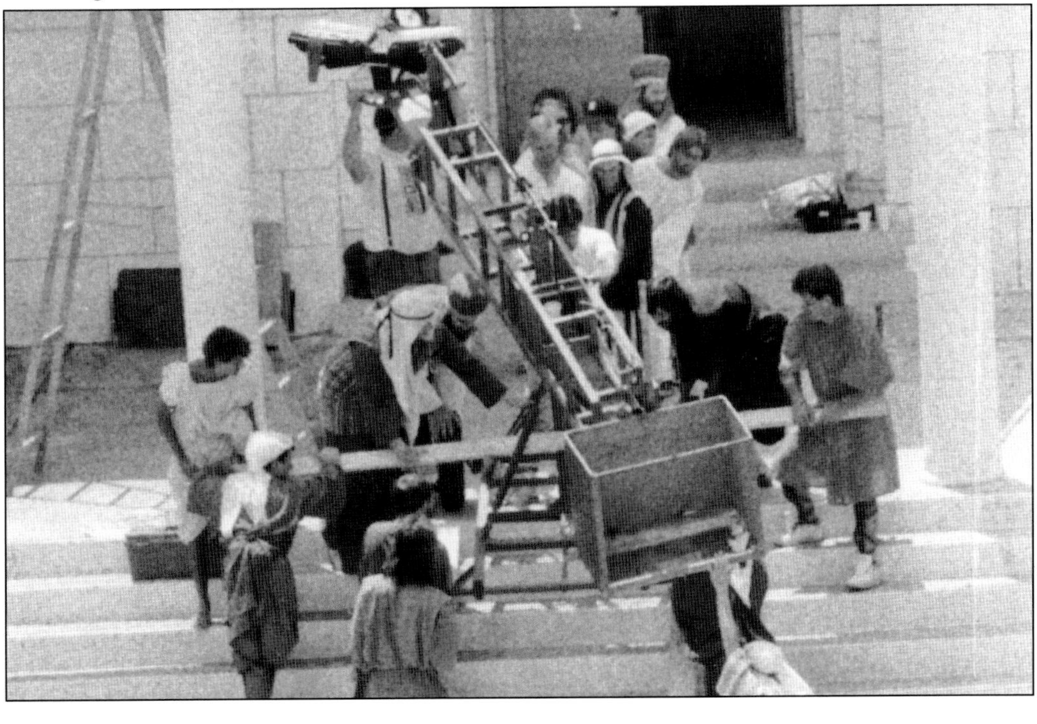

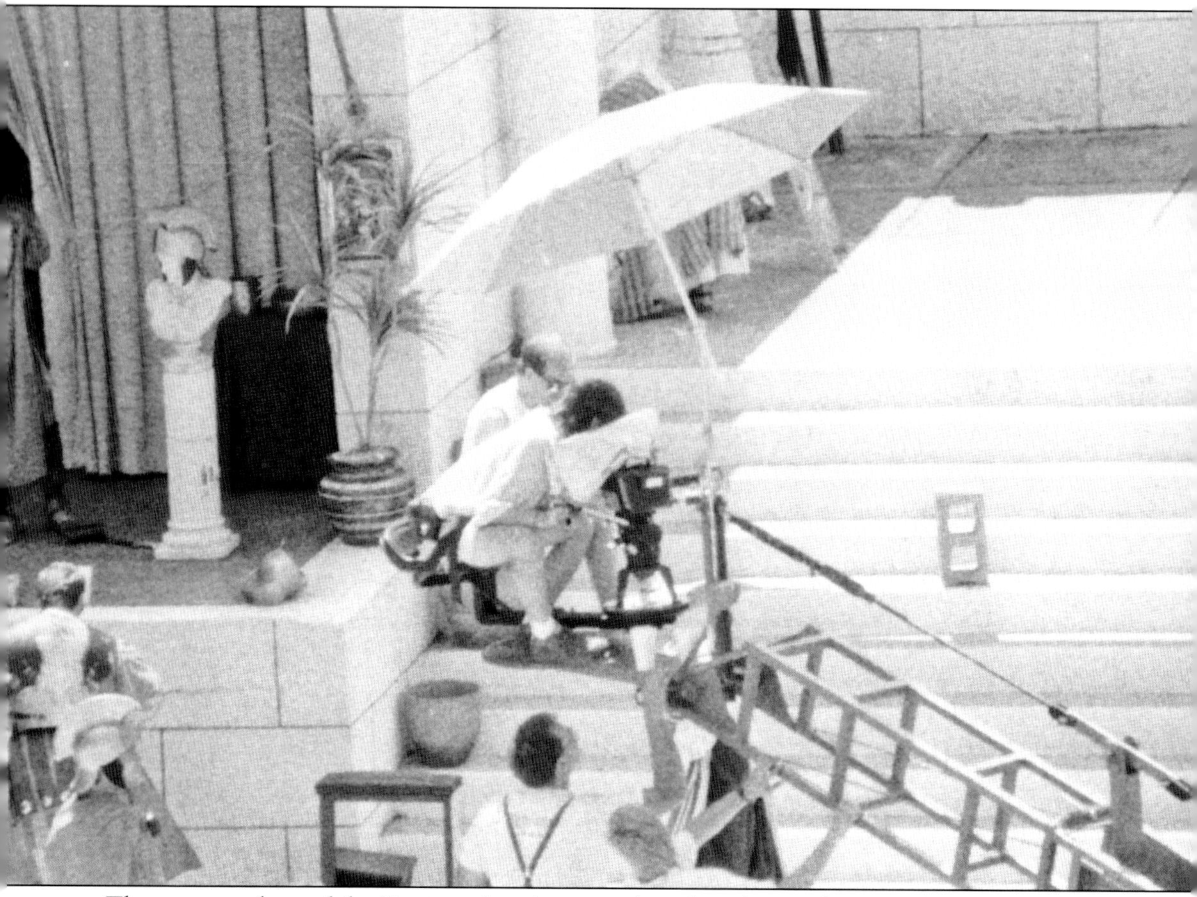

The cast members of the Passion play also contributed to the production of *Secret Ambition* by offering their logistical support. Carrying the photography equipment up the temple steps was arduous and dangerous, but it was accomplished.

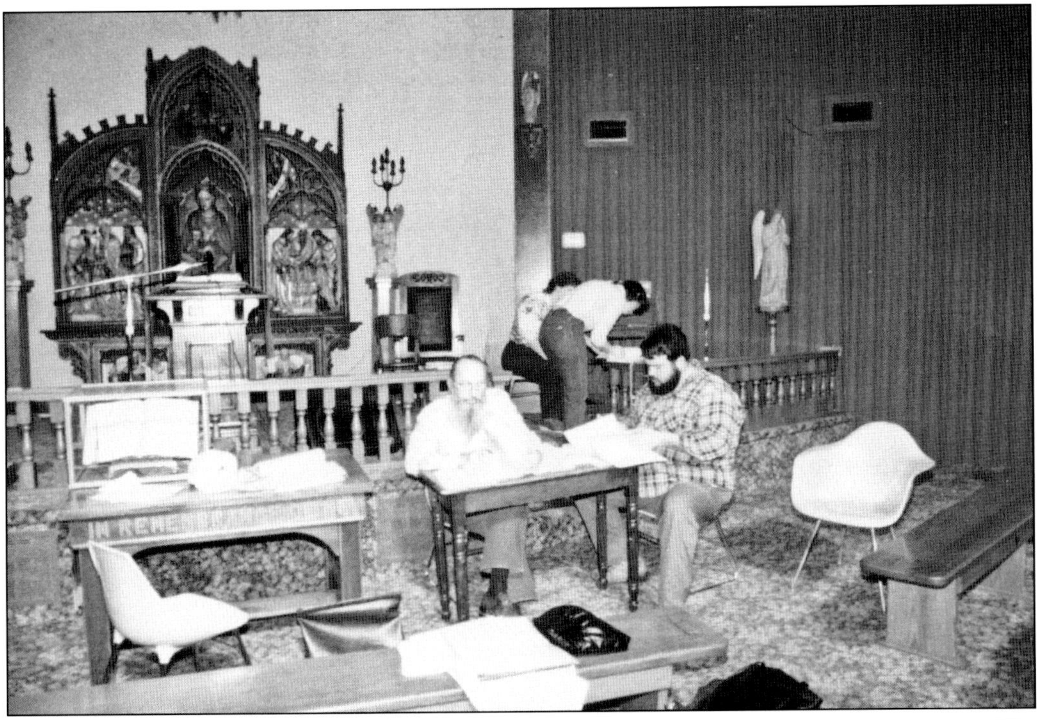

Local talent was the cornerstone of *The Great Passion Play*. In the 1980s, cast members provided voices for a new soundtrack. Pictured from left to right above are Bill Rotramel and Tim Garrison. Rotramel served for many years as a room manager and cast member. Garrison, also pictured below, played the part of King Herod for more than 20 years.

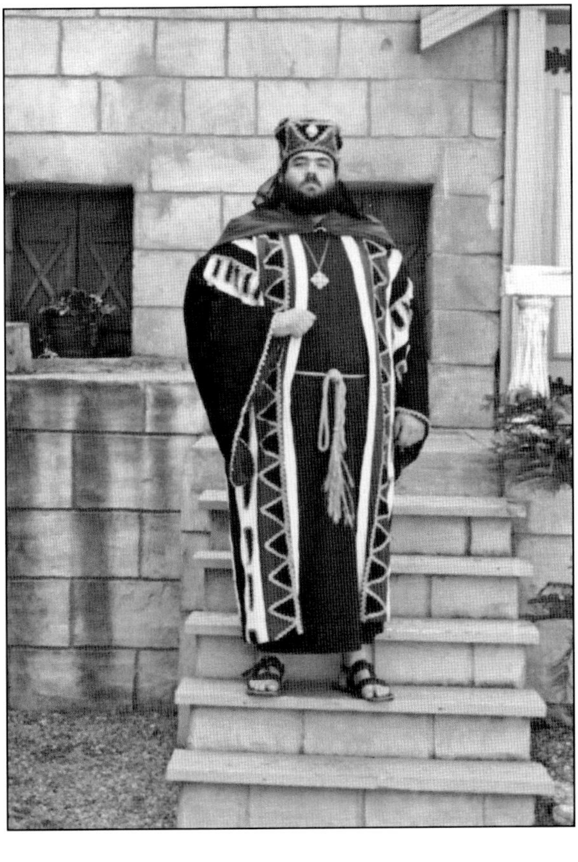

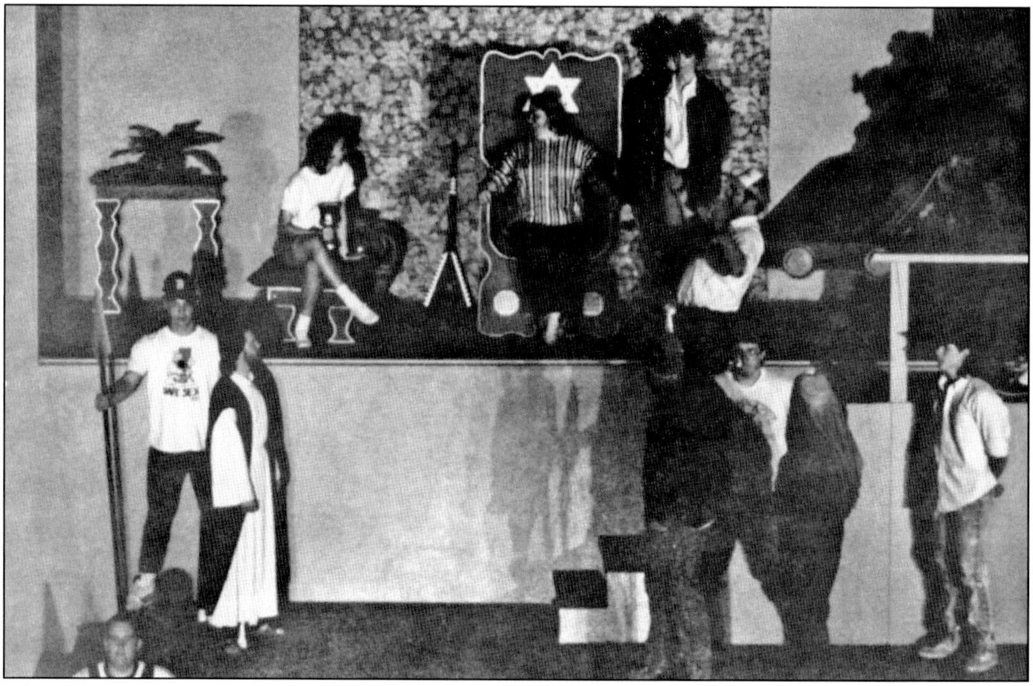

The Passion play runs five days a week for more than five months of the year. As a result, returning cast members have perfected their parts. Rehearsals at the beginning of each season have generally taken on a relaxed atmosphere. These photographs taken at a rehearsal in 1990 reveal the casual nature of the cast. On display are comfortable clothing, glasses, watches, ripped jeans, basketball jerseys, and the like. All of these are, of course, forbidden during performances. Although, from time to time, an occasional watch is spotted on set, and cast members may have forgotten to take off their glasses!

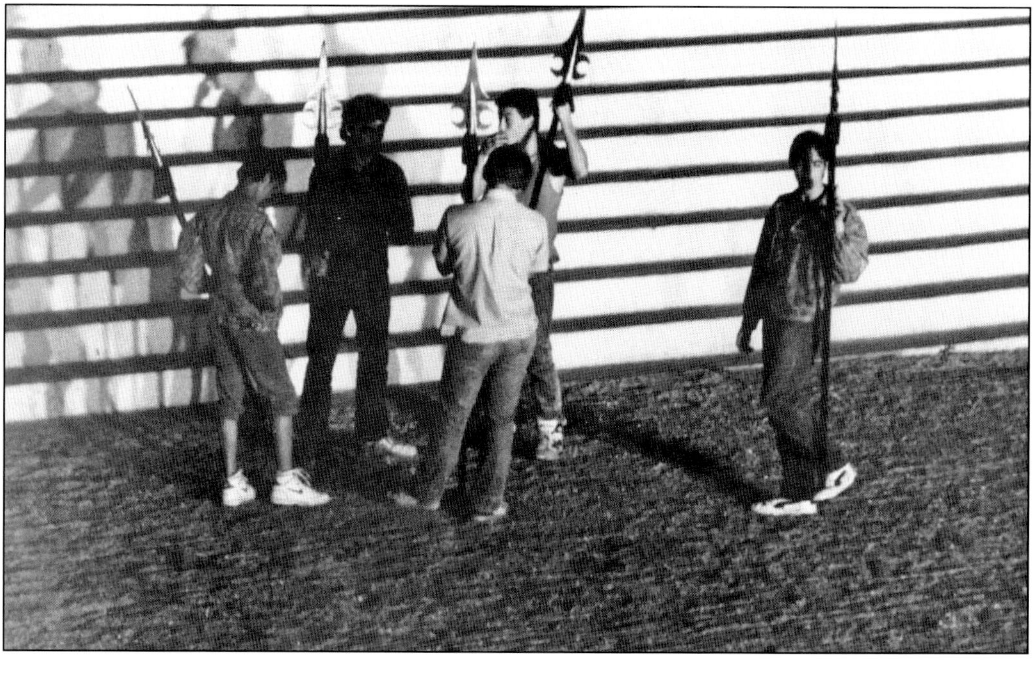

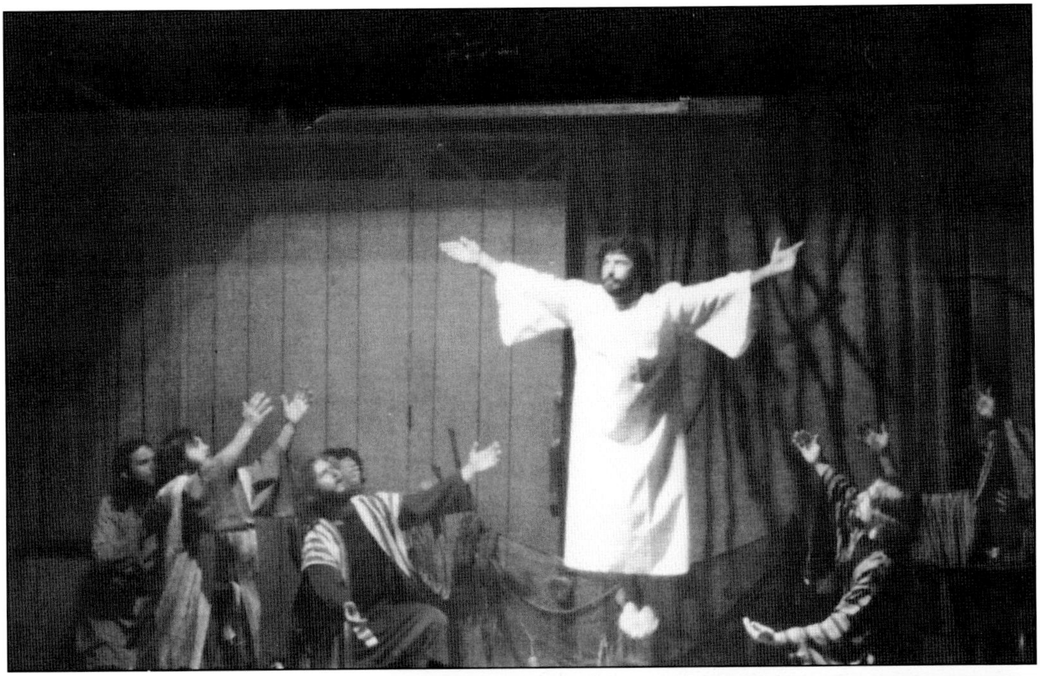

Today the ascension is done with a set of wires. The original ascension was held in a building behind a veiled screen. Such a screen allows for lighting that can hide certain features, especially equipment. These screens are also used to help Jesus appear and disappear. Lighting can expose the transparency of the screen, or it can create the illusion of a solid wall.

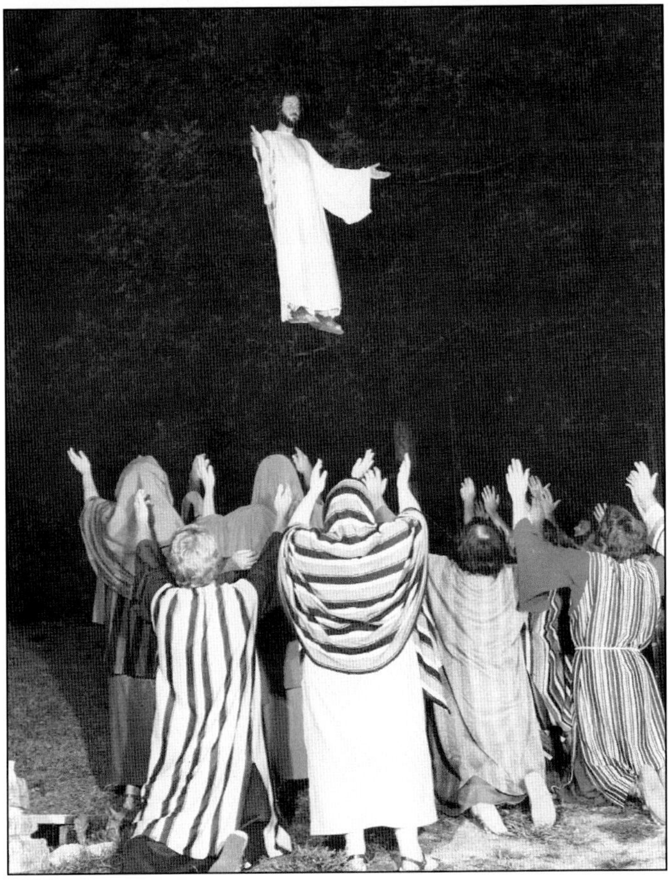

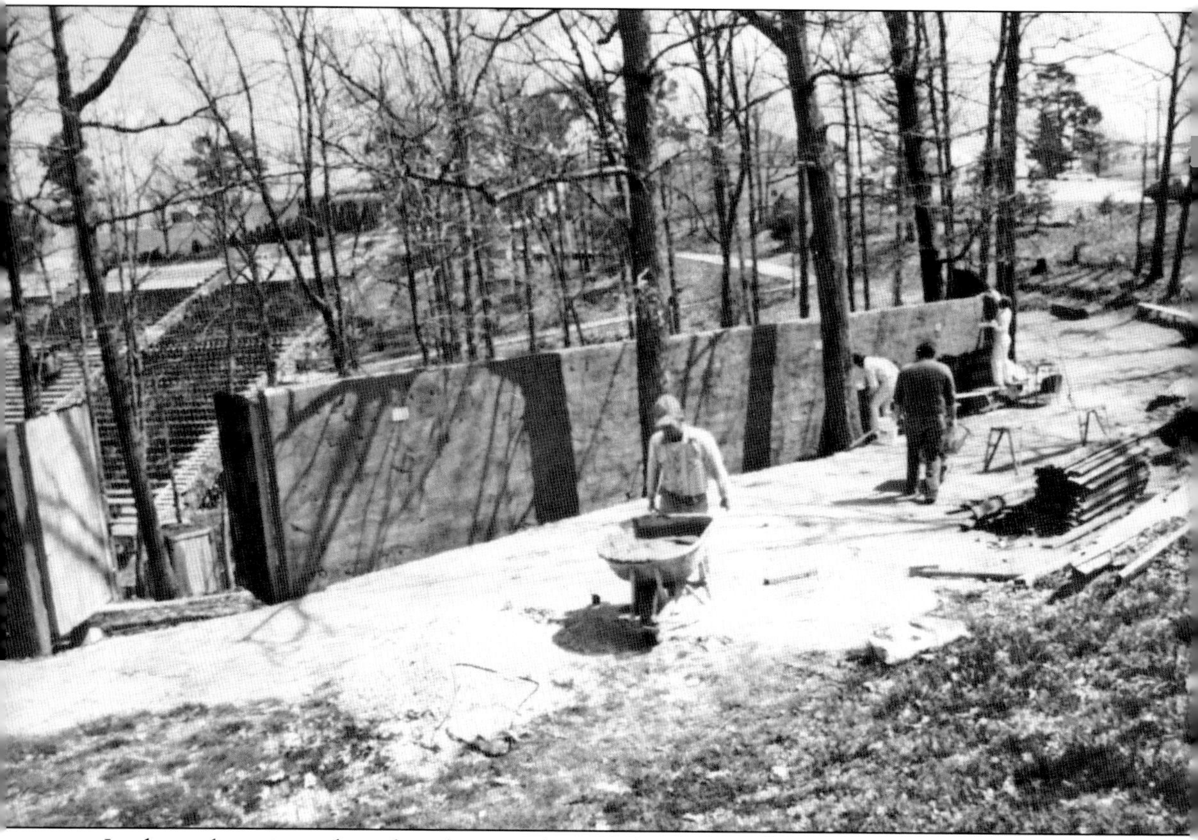

In the early spring, when this photograph was taken, there is not much that can be disguised. Construction crews were building a wall that is designed to hide cast members as they wait to enter the set. However, the strategy used for such walls is to hide them among trees and bushes. When plants are in full bloom, they hide any number of speakers, hidden doors, lighting towers, and special pathways.

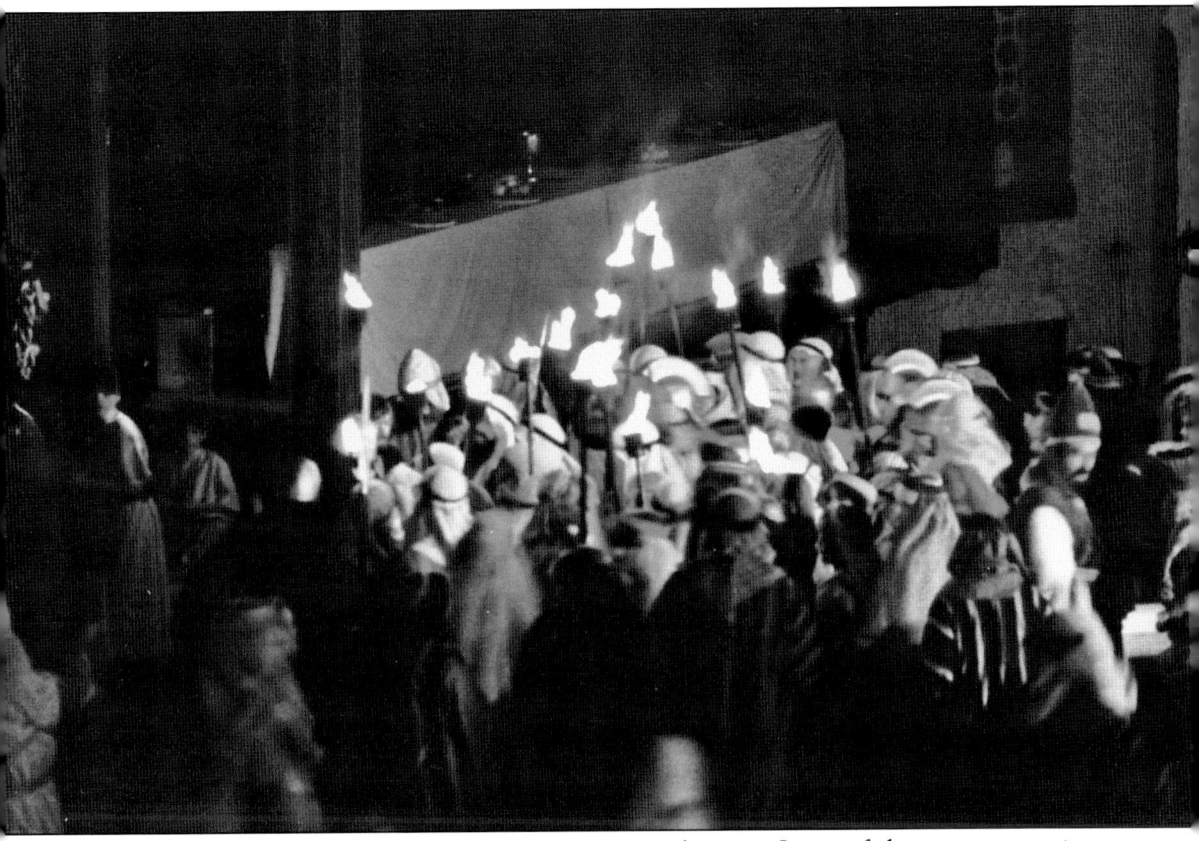

The Great Passion Play uses numerous props in its production. Some of these props require creative application. In this scene, an angry mob is roused in the middle of the night. In place of torches, a special prop is used to simulate the effect. A tin can filled with cotton and kerosene is placed on a pole. The kerosene burns within the can and minimizes the danger of fire in such a large crowd.

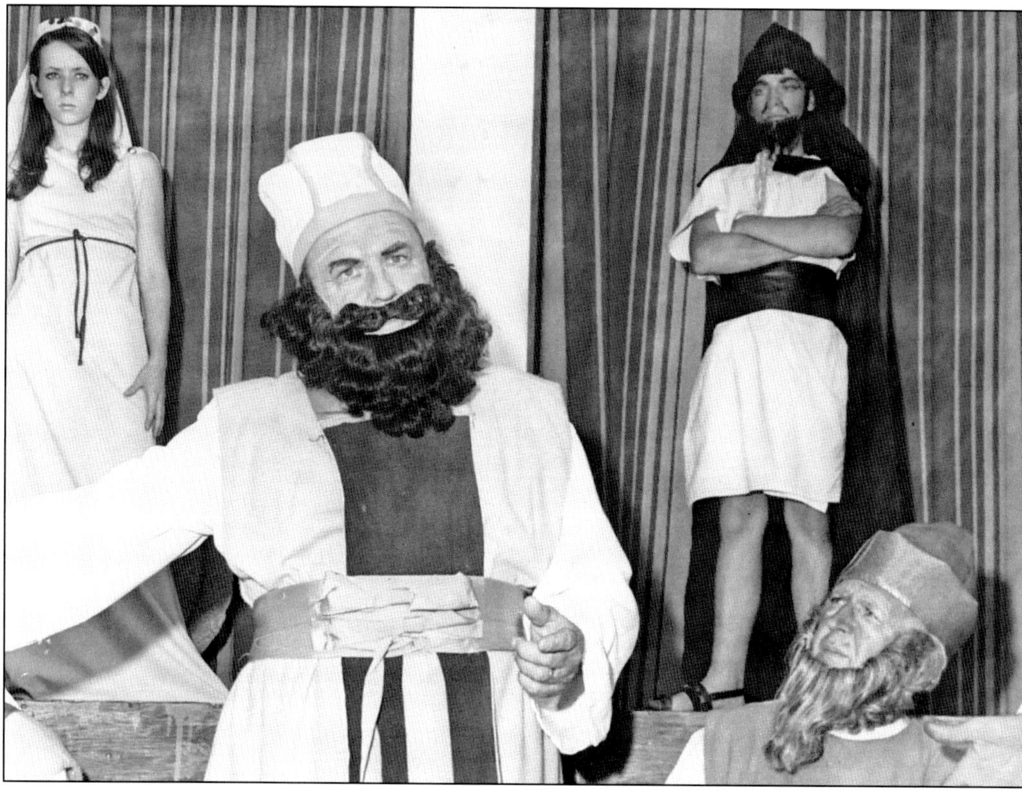

BEARDS

Supplies for cleaning
1. Toothbrush
2. Small bowl of cleaning fluid
3. Paper towels (folded or 2 or 3 layers thick for absorbency).

Cleaning Process -- ABSOLUTELY MUST BE CLEANED AFTER EACH USE.
1. Lay beard on paper toweling.
2. Dip toothbrush into cleaning fluid. (ABSOLUTELY DO NOT PUT BEARD INTO CLEANING FLUID.)
3. Brush mesh side of beard from fold out. (The way the hair grows). BRUSH IN ONE DIRECTION ONLY -- NOT BACK AND FORTH.
4. Continue this process until all spirit gum is removed.
5. Comb beard very carefully and pin on block to dry.

Note -- After several cleanings the beard may become dry and dull. Rub a very little VO-5 into palm of hand and apply very lightly to the beard. BE EXTREMELY CAREFUL NOT TO GET ANY ON THE MESH AS THE BEARD WILL NOT STICK.

To remover beard and mustache
Pull gently from outer sides to the middle and then from the bottom up. DO NOT TEAR OFF FAST.

WIGS

Care of wigs
1. Wigs must be put on block immediately upon removal from wearing. Wigs must NOT be allowed to lay around but <u>must</u> be kept on blocks whenever not in use.
2. Shape and straighten wig carefully/when finished wearing.
3. If possible wigs should be sahmpooed and reset half way through the season but only by a professional as mesh will shrink from water, etc. They must be thoroughly cleaned and restored at the end of each season.

Cleaning of wigs
1. Dip wigs into cleaning fluid for few seconds. (DO NOT LEAVE IN CLEANING ~~XXX~~ FLUID FOR A LONG PERIOD OF TIME.)
2. Remove from fluid and shake all fluid out of wig.
3. Put on block.
4. Shap and comb hair carefully. (Do not pull hair __ Hold hair on top when combing. Be especially careful with front and top of wig.

Note - If wig becomes dry and dull from dleanigg apple a small amout of VO-5 to palm of hand ands and apply lightly to wig.

Another essential prop is the fake beard. Many of these beards were handcrafted specifically for the Passion play. They were intentionally exaggerated to maximize their effect on such a large stage. The first director, Robert Hyde, was especially proud of these props, and special care was expected.

Do You Remember...

...The day that Norm Moyer, while he was playing Judas, knocked himself out after the Last Supper? He hit the wall in the tunnel by Gate 10. Joe Senneca put on his costume to finish the play with blood on the costume.

...The Garden Scene the night the copperhead was on the edge of the wall where David Bland, playing Jesus, always went to pray? The Disciples saw the snake and told David as he was going toward the snake with his arms in the air. He immediately put himself in full reverse, backing away from the snake. The scene went on as if nothing was wrong.

...The night when Phillip Gould and Joe Senneca were Emmaus Disciples and met a skunk waiting on the sidewalk up by the wall. When they came around the skunk went down the hill. They commented that, with their luck, the skunk would be waiting for them by the bridge. Guess what? The skunk was there. They waited for the last second and, fortunately for them, the skunk went down the hill just before the lights came up.

...Wayne and Barbara Jagow's young granddaughter exclaimed happily as David Bland walking in the wardrobe room in costume, "It's Jesus!" Immediately Joe Smith followed, and she said with amazement, "It's MORE Jesus!"

...The night Carl Hill accomplished the best Judas bag throw of all – he hooked it on a stray Christmas bulb nail on the temple wall.

The cast has a sense of humor. This circular was passed around at the annual banquet in 1990. Mishaps are a matter of routine, but the show always goes on!

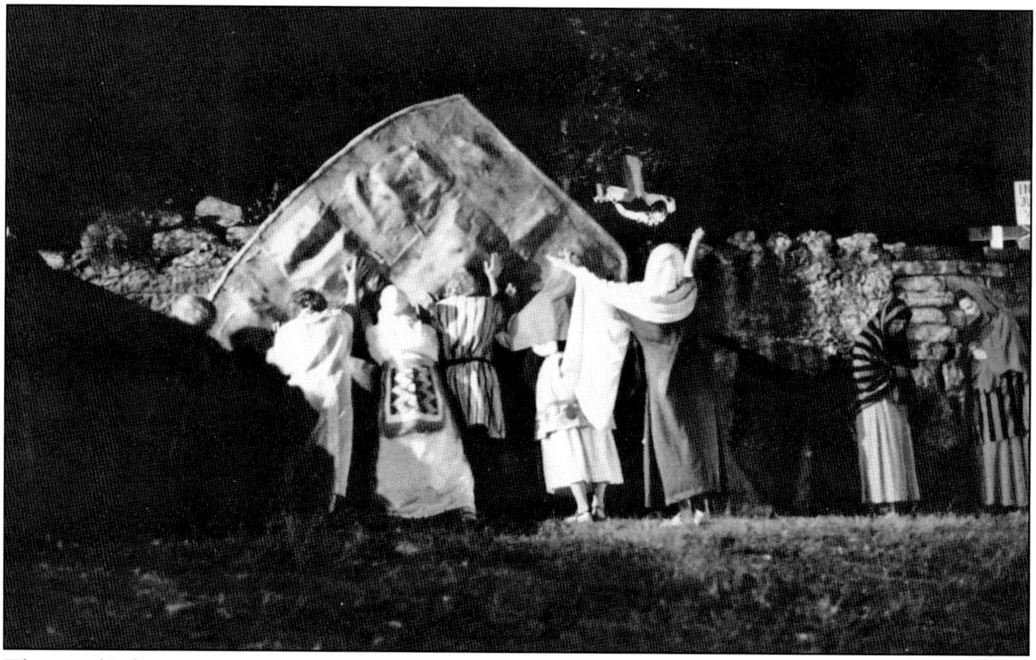

The tomb's large stone is actually plastic, and a technician inside the tomb does all the work. While people on set help roll the stone, a bar guides the stone into place.

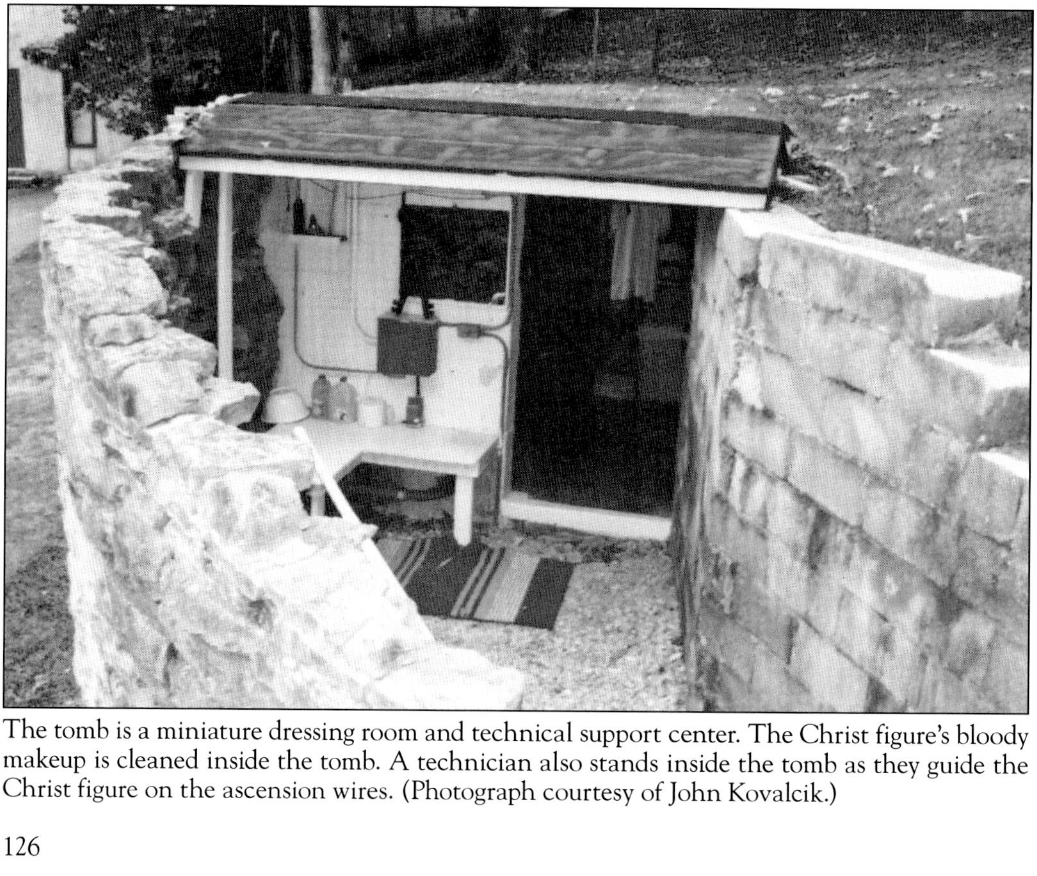

The tomb is a miniature dressing room and technical support center. The Christ figure's bloody makeup is cleaned inside the tomb. A technician also stands inside the tomb as they guide the Christ figure on the ascension wires. (Photograph courtesy of John Kovalcik.)

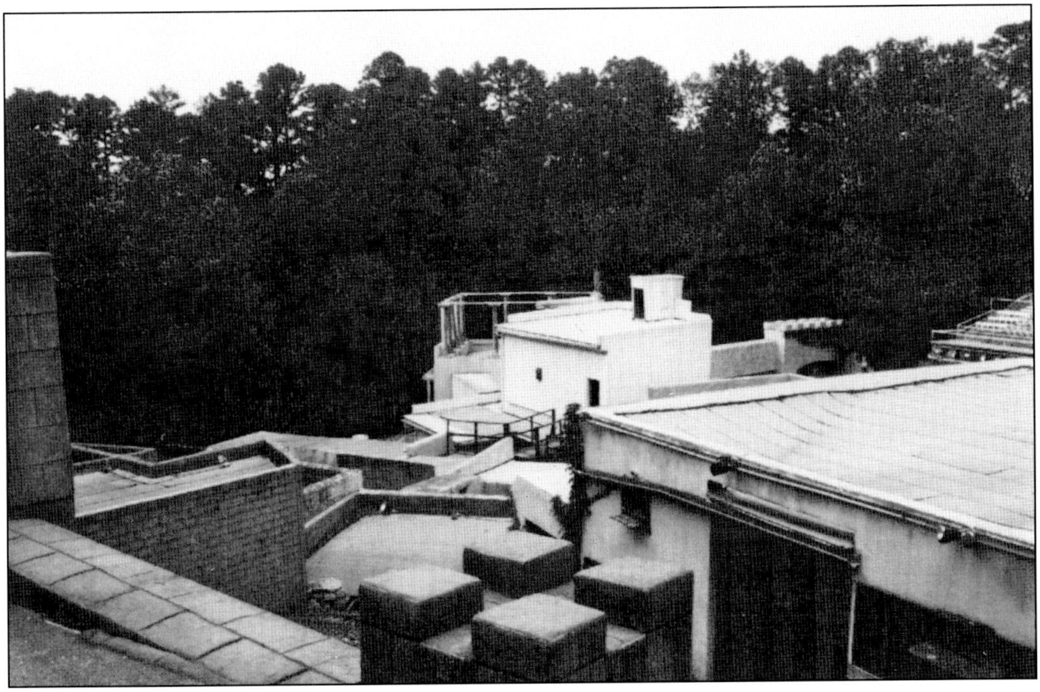

The set was designed to create the illusion of a Jerusalem street. The staging, however, is linked by an intricate set of passageways, stairs, ladders, hidden doors, and paths. Cast members appear and disappear, creating the illusion that they traveled long distances. (Photographs courtesy of John Kovalcik.)

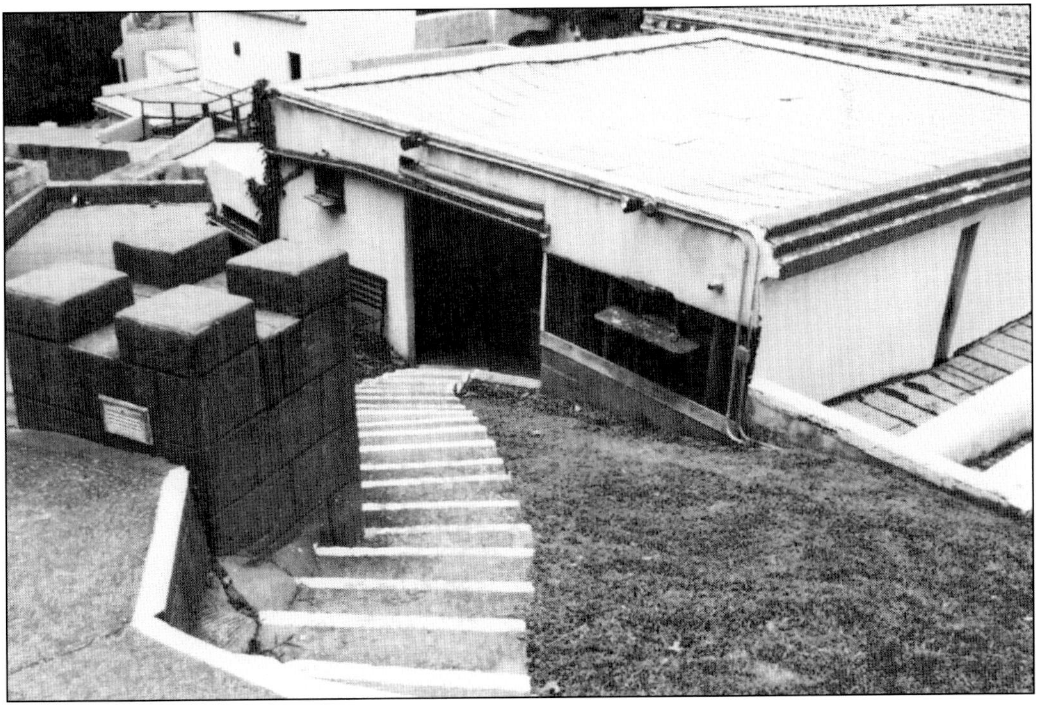

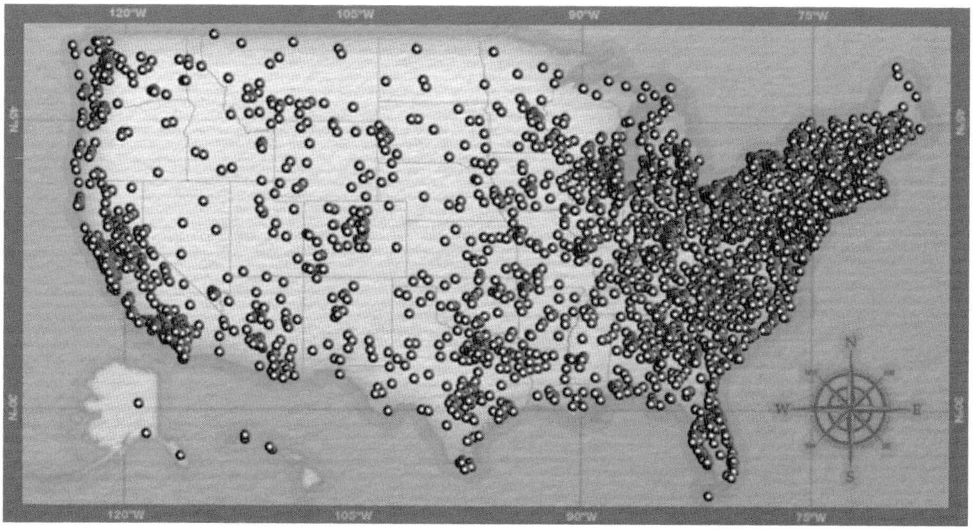